Mike,

Thanks for all
your help and advice
over the years.

Doug

Encountering God

Be Transformed by His Word
Reflections of God's Word for Each Day of the Year

Marsha Glynn

WESTBOW
PRESS®
A DIVISION OF THOMAS NELSON
& ZONDERVAN

WestBow Press books may be ordered through booksellers or by contacting:

WestBow Press
A Division of Thomas Nelson & Zondervan
1663 Liberty Drive
Bloomington, IN 47403
www.westbowpress.com
1 (866) 928-1240

ISBN: 978-1-9736-0381-8 (sc)
ISBN: 978-1-9736-0380-1 (hc)
ISBN: 978-1-9736-0382-5 (e)

Library of Congress Control Number: 2017914159

Print information available on the last page.

WestBow Press rev. date: 12/22/2017

Preface

Encounter God today. Enhance your relationship with him by reading, pondering, and applying lessons from the Bible. *Encountering God* guides you to form a stronger living relationship with our Lord and Savior. The book, designed to focus on verses from scripture, causes you to reflect, meditate, and apply God's word daily. You may want to have a Bible close at hand to read the full revelation God gives in the scripture passages.

Ponder the verses and how they impact your journey with Christ. Invite God to communicate with you through scripture. Listen, learn, and practice his truths. Then enjoy the balm of God's presence and his peace as you build a strong relationship with him. Trust in his mercy, seek his refuge and peace, and live in his love. Let God's spiritual truths awaken and enrich your life. Grow in holiness each day as you encounter God and be changed from the inside out. You will find reading *Encountering God* a life-changing experience.

Acknowledgments

I dedicate *Encountering God* to my sister, Nancy Gardiner, whose understanding and knowledge encouraged me to seek answers to the mysteries of life through reading the Bible and studying scripture. I also want to thank Very Rev. Michael J. O'Connor. His profound knowledge of the Bible and joyful preaching bring God's word and renewed hope to a troubled world. He has provided spiritual guidance, understanding, kindness, but most of all has helped me build a closer relationship with God and encounter him every day.

Through the darkest hours of my life, my sister comforted, cried, listened, and reminded me to take one step at a time to get through the funeral of my beloved teenage son. More than the routines of daily life, she prayed with me when I felt God had abandoned me. She never gave up on me and finally turned me toward the light of God.

Several weeks after the funeral, alone and hopeless, I could not work or care for my other son or husband. Normal daily tasks such as eating, dressing, and bathing were beyond my capability. I found myself avoiding others. My life, dark and with little hope, was in shambles. My heart was shattered.

With jumbled and unclear thoughts, my mind kept returning to the week before the funeral and to those who helped me survive. I remember my sister telling me to open the Bible to the middle and start reading. She said I would find answers for my troubled broken heart.

I searched for the family Bible on a bookshelf in the guest bedroom. The leather-bound Bible looked new. Opening to the center, I read, "The Lord protects the simple; I was helpless, but God saved me" (Ps. 116:6). Were those words written for me?

Every day I read a few more verses. The tears ebbed and I had glimmers of hope. I found myself forming a relationship with God.

He was someone I could talk with at any time. I felt God's healing hands of mercy as he spoke to me through scripture. Then I started to write my thoughts about the passages, whatever I believed he placed on my heart.

Reading and writing my reflections brought me closer to God. I found answers and renewed strength. After months, I realized the death of my young son was not the end. He had journeyed on without me to eternal life with God.

I returned to church after convincing myself God would welcome me. Week after week, I hear and reflect on my pastor's words. Father Michael helps me encounter God every day through prayer, praise, and the Eucharist. He reminds us to welcome people, no matter their race, nationality, or position in life, and to see others as spiritual traveling companions not as adversaries. I listen and learn how to love and serve others. His messages touch my heart and open my mind to all of God's possibilities.

I continue to read the Bible every day and draw closer to God through prayer. While in his presence as he communicates to me through scripture, I encounter him and feel his love. I am changed from the inside out. My heart mends each day because I know God's peace.

I pray you encounter God every day. May Almighty God, the master of all things, bless you as you build a lasting relationship, grow closer to him, and find love and peace in his presence. Let his light shine upon you so you are filled with new life and his everlasting love.

January 1

*My son, keep my words, and treasure my
commands. Keep my commands and live, my
teaching as the apple of your eye; bind them on
your fingers, write them on the tablet of your hearts.*
— Proverbs 7:1-3

As we begin a new year, make a resolution to read the Bible every
day. Ponder the meaning of God's words. He does not expect us
to be perfect, but he asks us to keep his commandments and abide
by his truths. Begin in faith. God knows each of us by name. He
considers us his children. Come to him with a teachable spirit. He
gives us instruction and answers in scripture. Start each day with
prayer and words of thanks to our LORD and Savior.

Throughout the year we experience challenging obstacles and
make important decisions. At times we succumb to the temptations
of Satan, but God remains faithful to us. He loves us beyond our
human understanding. God asks us to repent when we sin. He
sends mercy and love.

Focus on God and keep him central in our lives. He sends hope
and the promise to never abandon those who love him. Live in his
presence and grow in wisdom, knowledge, and understanding of
his truths. God supports, strengthens, and directs us as we journey
through time. He has made a resolution to love and bless his
children. He is patient like a loving parent dedicated to teaching
and forming us in his image.

1 John 5:20-21; Psalm 34:23
Point to Ponder: Keep God's commandments and prosper.

Pray: Lord, empower me to draw closer to you and accept the
challenges and the possibilities of the New Year.

January 2

*Cast all your worries upon him
because he cares for you.*

— 1 Peter 5:7

Turn to God in every circumstance. Seek him through prayer and let the encounter shape our hearts and minds; let it shape our actions and expectations. In order to draw closer to the Lord, sit quietly with him. Open the Bible and read scripture. Meditate on the passages and ponder how the words affect you personally.

Count on God to be your anchor. He holds us fast to his mercy and presence, and he never abandons us in troubled times. Pray for his assistance, direction, and comfort. In Christ, we have everything we need to live righteous lives. Strive to have Christ-like mannerisms. Cast your worries to God.

He gives us what we need and eases our burdens. Every time we come to him, he provides the nourishment of his grace so we may grow. He sees us pray and hears our pleas. God brings joy to our hearts. He has all authority in heaven and on earth. Cling to God in child-like trust because he cares. Pray every day for his guiding light.

Mathew 28:18-20; Psalm 100:5
Point to Ponder: Trust in God because he cares. He knows your strengths and weaknesses.

Pray: God, burn in my heart. Be with me through my trials and during my joyous times. I trust you to protect me and lead me to take one more step forward today.

January 3

*Cast your care upon the L*ORD*, who*
will give you support. God will never
allow the righteous to stumble.

— Psalm 55:23

God's help and strength are abundantly available. He lives in us even when darkness, trials, and troubles seem to overpower all good. The Lord does not see only our hidden faults; he sees our virtues too. He hears our uplifting words and humble acts of kindness. God hears every prayer.

Believe and stand firm in faith. God never abandons us. Face troublesome situations with an open heart and a teachable spirit. Listen for God's voice. We may hear him speak in our thoughts, in scripture passages, or in the simple yearning of our hearts. Sometimes he shouts to us through our pain, or whispers a message while we relax, or talks to us through song lyrics.

Every offering through prayer affirms our love for him. When we pray, he responds. We are never lost but instead a prayer away from his steadfast love and support. His divine Word strengthens our resolve, lifts up our spirits, and helps us stand firm. Make each day holy and praise him. Live a righteous life as you cast your cares to the Lord and seek him at every turn.

Psalm 22:1-12; John 5:14-21
Point to Ponder: Pray for God's strength and support.

Pray: Lord, hear my prayers throughout the day. Open my ears to recognize your voice, place trust in my heart, and fill my mind with wisdom and understanding.

January 4

Many are the sorrows of the wicked, but love
*surrounds those who trust in the L*ORD.

— Psalm 32:10

God's unfailing love surrounds those who trust him. Renew this
bond every day through prayer and praise. Trust God to know
our strengths and weaknesses. He sees our flaws but also our
persistence to live by his word.

Sometimes we feel powerless to change things? We feel
inadequate, unworthy, and forgotten. If burdened and lost, seek
God through prayer. Do not try to hide. He sees our needs and sins
clearly. Whisper his name, "Jesus, I need you." Be open to God and
ask for guidance. He waits for the right time to intercede.

We find hope in his unfailing love. Being close to God has a
soothing affect. Keep your eyes fixed on his light and pray often.
Disregard negative voices and reframe thoughts. Do not let fear
overpower your faith and keep you away from God. Our hearts
change as we place our trust in him. He transforms us. Our actions
and attitudes testify to the joyful, grace-filled life that only he
sends. God's unfailing love protects us. Trust him to be there at all
times.

Proverbs 8:21; Romans 12:12
Point to Ponder: Surround yourself with God's love.

Pray: God, give me the grace to turn to you and seek your
guidance. Forgive my poor choices. Let the light of hope guide me.

January 5

You have sent me many bitter afflictions,
but once more revive me.

– Psalm 71:20

When tragedy strikes without warning and a friend or loved one
dies, we feel real pain. It seems doubly heart-wrenching when a
child dies. No words or actions take away the pain and sadness. We
feel an unfathomable void in our hearts.

Draw on faith and the Lord's steadfast love in times of sorrow.
Read the scriptures, meditate on the passages, and let them find a
way into your heart. Open the Bible to Psalm 34:19. "The LORD is
close to the brokenhearted, saves those whose spirit is crushed."
God promises to mend our broken hearts, to give relief and full
deliverance to those who have lost hope. Though difficult at the
time, offer the pain to God for his purposes. Our suffering draws
us closer to God. Look to him continually for help, comfort, and
answers.

God has our names written on his palms (Is. 49:16). We are
his children. He comforts us and is our refuge. God makes straight
our paths as we journey with him. The grief may remain for many
days, months, or years, but his love revives us as we walk with him
day by day. Stay in his presence and find peace.

James 1:1-4; 2 Corinthians 1:1-5
Point to Ponder: God revives you.

Pray: Lord, you know when I lose hope and my faith crumbles.
Strengthen me. Pour out more of your Spirit so I live closer to you.

January 6

*Beloved, if God so loved us, we must love
one another. No one has ever seen God. Yet,
if we love one another, God remains in us,
and his love is brought to perfection in us.*

— 1 John 4:11-12

As we grow in faith and love, strive to be more Christ-like. God has given each of us his divine love and wants us to share it. The Lord blesses us with grace to forgive, wisdom in a stressful situation, love that rises from within, and protection from Satan's temptations.

As we rush through the day, we make choices that play a vital role in the unfolding of God's plan. We choose to smile, greet others, listen, or give of our time. God knows every act of love and kindness we demonstrate.

When we meet people who do not know God, we tend to shy away from them or say little about our faith and spiritual lives. We may experience feelings of anxiety, mistrust, and alarm when we encounter people who do not practice the same beliefs, customs, or traditions. People who live on the peripheries of society, the marginalized, and the poorest of the poor may cause feelings of fear. Pray for these people. Demonstrate through words and actions how God's love strengthens and gives all people direction. Practice the same unconditional love God gives to us.

What incredible love God has for all of us!

Psalm 46:2-4; Luke 21:27-28
Point to Ponder: God remains in you and loves you unconditionally.

Pray: Lord, thank you for your steadfast love. Shape me so love flows out of me to others.

January 7

... You shall love your neighbor as yourself.
                                        – Matthew 22:39

Why do we find difficulty loving our neighbor? We all know people who get on our nerves. They may talk too much or demand the last word in every conversation. They want to be right at all costs. These people are hard to love but it is not impossible. Love is a choice and not just an emotion. Challenge yourself to love more, and let God's love shine through. Be aware of all God's children even when their views and habits are different.

Pause long enough to do a little self-evaluation. Relax in God's presence. Pray, listen, and let his voice penetrate your heart. Do not hesitate to reach out and assist others. God desires us to see our neighbors and friends as brothers and sisters. He wants us to build awareness of their needs. Matthew 25:40 says, "Amen, I say to you, whatever you did for one of these least brothers of mine, you did for me."

Through simple acts such as saying a warm hello, listening, and comforting those in need, we are doing more than showing kindness. We become vessels for Christ and project love. The more we give, the more God empowers us. He blesses us with a deep sense of security and compassion in his love when we serve others.

The Lord's love shines through us. Love guides and encourages us to reach out to people. Enjoy love; revel in it, and give it away.

1 John 4:19-21; Proverbs 21:2
Point to Ponder: Love your neighbor. Be gentle with an open heart.

Pray: Help me see my neighbor as a friend, Lord. Create in me a loving attitude.

7

January 8

*The L*ORD *is close to the brokenhearted,*
saves those whose spirit is crushed.

— Psalm 34:19

Many people have experienced the death of a loved one and feel emotional hurt and pain. The sorrow runs so deep, many find prayer difficult. The shock sometimes forces the light in our souls to grow dim. Our faith is tested especially when the death is unexpected and tragic. It is not uncommon for trials to tempt us to doubt God's love. Remember to resort to the small glimmer of faith that remains in our hearts. Yield to God and count on his faithfulness to reach out and carry our burdens when the load is too heavy.

Christ knows all our needs and sets blessings into motion long before we ask. Trust him to be with us every moment, watching over us, and sending strength. He heals us emotionally and binds up our wounds even with limited faith. Reach out to him and simply say, "Help me, Jesus. Increase my faith." We soon find sadness balanced with calmness, confusion by direction, anxiety by peace, and fear by trust. Praying in his name calms the soul.

Remember he opens wide the gates of heaven so our loved ones are born to eternal life. Death is not the end. God's healing light continues to shine on those left behind. His mercy and love heal the poor in spirit and those shattered by grief. Trust God to carry us when our burdens are many, and we have little strength to move forward. Pray for his healing power and find rest in his comforting arms.

Psalm 40:2-4; Luke 11:9-10
Point to Ponder: The Lord restores your faith and heals the brokenhearted.

Pray: Heal my soul, God. Let your light shine upon me and give me peace.

January 9

Let us reach out our hearts toward God in heaven.
　　　　　　　　　　　　　　　　– Lamentations 3:41

How do we live a righteous life honoring God? We start by praying and building our trust and love for him. Prayer renews us to act righteously and brings God into our presence. We draw closer to him when we pray.

God has made a place in heaven for each of us. Do not let past suffering contaminate our view of heaven. Christ hears our heartfelt prayers. He protects the faithful and holds precious those who call his name. We have only to reach out to him and live his truths. Our prayers, often intimate, refreshing, and powerful, honor God.

Our relationship with God is saturated in grace and is a gift to cherish. He knows our hearts. Focus on him whether in grief or rejoicing, fear or thanksgiving, and in sadness or great joy. Prayer keeps us close to God. He is a whisper away. Whenever we call out to God, he responds. Communion with him renewed Jesus's strength, soothed and refreshed his spirit, and filled his heart with love. It does the same for us. What a friend we have in him!

2 Corinthians 4:16-18; Psalm 97:10-12
Point to Ponder: Pray for God's mercy and love.

Pray: Lord, prepare a place for me in heaven where love abounds. Teach me how to follow your ways.

January 10

*May the Lord give might to his people; may
the Lord bless his people with peace.*

— Psalm 29:11

The more we focus on God and encounter him through scripture, prayer, and worship, the more we have access to his unending love. Our lives change when we accept Christ and embrace his teachings.

Make ready our hearts for the Lord. When we praise and glorify God, we feel a sense of peace and contentment. He leads us from the womb to the tomb when we open our hearts and souls to him.

Answered prayers draw us closer to God. We learn to follow his ways. God gives us the gift of an advocate, the Holy Spirit, to guide and protect us. When we yield ourselves to the Spirit, we learn about love, joy, peace, patience, kindness, generosity, faithfulness, gentleness, and self-control (Gal. 5:22). These qualities are the fruit of the Spirit. Seek to acquire these traits for they lead us to live righteously.

Today, deepen our friendship with God by trying our best to follow him and the Holy Spirit's promptings. Let God work through us so we show others Christ-like behaviors. Seek the Spirit's power to dwell within our temples, and teach us how to live in a manner pleasing to God. Build a relationship with him. Help others see his mercy and love through our actions and words. Grow in peace.

Psalm 145:8-9; Psalm 25:4
Point to Ponder: The Lord blesses his people with peace.

Pray: God, help me make righteous choices. Guide me to do your will and find heavenly peace.

January 11

*This is the day the L*ORD* has made;*
let us rejoice in it and be glad.

– Psalm 118:24

Today is unique. Each moment can never be repeated, so have a sense of urgency to start fresh. Begin each day with prayer. Give thanks to the Lord because he has given us time to use our gifts. Pray for calm and his grace to meet every challenge and opportunity.

God is everywhere. Feel his presence throughout the day as the moments flee by. Sense him in the beauty of sunrise, or the warm touch of a child, or in the sweet melody of "I love you," or in the smell of flowers. God presents situations and then invites us to join him. Walk closely with the Lord throughout the day, and watch as he brings his promises to fruition.

Be grateful for this day full of surprises, opportunities, and blessings. Everything we possess – our intellect, health, and state of being – come from God. Turn to the Lord often and whisper short prayers of thanks for times of challenge and days filled with hope and joy. Grow ever closer to God. He keeps a careful watch on those who love him. Rejoice in this day!

Psalm 126:3; John 16:33
Point to Ponder: Rejoice and be glad for each new day.

Pray: God, bless me so I grow closer to you and serve you joyfully.

January 12

The LORD is our light and our salvation; whom
do I fear? The LORD is my life's refuge; of whom
am I afraid? When evil doers come to me to
devour my flesh, these my enemies and foes
themselves stumble and fall ... Though war
be waged against me, even then do I trust.

— Psalm 27:1-3

Find peace by opening our hearts and minds to the Lord. When trouble abounds and darkness prevails, seek God. He knows our needs even when words cannot express our desires. Read scripture and encounter him in the pages of the Bible. As long as we focus on God, we are safe.

Find safety in his never-ending love. Jesus wants only good for us. He walks with us. Fear is not the answer. He is our hope and the promise of comfort.

Our understanding of God's ways comes to us gradually. Reframe from moving away from him when he does not answer prayers immediately. Instead, remain steadfast. He answers at exactly the right time. No act of faith or trust goes unnoticed.

Stay close to the Lord, follow his teachings, and wait as he blesses us with his grace. Trust God because he is our refuge and our strength.

Philippians 4:6-7; Isaiah 29:24
Point to Ponder: Spend time with Christ.

Pray: God, guide me. I trust you to show me the way you have prepared.

January 13

Come to me all you who are labored and
burdened and I will give you rest.

— Matthew 11:28

God works in our lives. He gives us hope and reassurance, releases us from guilt, and makes us eager to know him better. Look for signs of his presence. Through prayer and studying the Bible, we draw closer to him. He transforms us to be more Christ-like. In the presence of God, whether through signs, during prayer, or while reading scripture, our thoughts, actions, and words show others what we believe about him.

God tests us. Be careful not to become bitter if God answers our prayers differently than what we expect or leads us into unfamiliar areas. Instead, trust him to lead us to salvation and away from sin. His plan for our well-being never takes a negative turn.

When we hit a rough spot, we tend to feel abandoned and distant from God. In fact, he is faithful and invites us to draw closer to him. Let his voice penetrate our hearts.

Be patient and wait. Silence the noise and harassment in our lives. God's most meaningful touch comes when we sit alone and seek his direction. Pray and ask God to open our eyes, ears, and heart so we perceive and receive all his blessings. Remember prayer is two-way communication. Listen and be alert to God's messages. Be prepared to respond in faith. Our burdens feel lighter when we release them to the Lord. He provides rest.

Psalm 67:2; Romans: 12:2-8
Point to Ponder: God answers your prayers according to your needs.

Pray: Lord, thank you for remaining faithful. Open my ears to hear you, my eyes to see your glory, and my heart to be pure to receive your teachings.

13

January 14

The L<small>ORD</small> is my strength and our shield, in whom
my heart trusted and found help. So my heart
rejoices; with my song I praise my God.

— Psalm 28:7

Have you ever been asked, "Who are you?" We tend to respond depending on what others want to hear. For example, we may answer: a mother assisting her son with homework, a grandmother playing with her grandsons, the principal of a school, a wife, sister, or a myriad of other titles. These answers and descriptions label us temporarily but only scratch the surface.

Our worth is not based on our surname, position, beauty, activities, or wealth. We, beloved children of God, matter greatly to him. In our hearts we should respond, "I am a child of God." Knowing God and having a relationship with him that includes love, praise, joy, and peace far outweighs any worldly standard or title. When our awareness of God's presence falters and dims, life experiences feel lonely and fragmented. If we do not have God at our core, we never experience the blessings he sends.

Take time today to think about the question, "Who am I?" If you silently make excuses for why you are not experiencing an abundant and fulfilling life, ask God to give you the strength and grace to turn away from the world's way of finding satisfaction. Settle for nothing less than God's best for your life. Be his ambassador through holiness and devotion. Enjoy an abundant life filled with his blessings. Rejoice! You are a child of God.

John 10:15:4; Philippians 4:12-13
Point to Ponder: Be proud to be a child of God.

Pray: Thank you, God, for loving me and giving me an abundant life.

January 15

My son, if your heart be wise, my own heart
also will rejoice; and my inmost being will
exult, when your lips speak what is right.

— Proverbs 23:15-16

God gave man the freedom to choose. Many choices are clear such as choosing love over hate or truth over lies. Others are not as concrete. Unfortunately, sometimes our choices do not align with what God would do. Satan lurks, ready to enter our souls and sway us to turn our backs on God. The evil one leads us down a dark path away from God.

With sins comes hardship. In a sinful state, man tends to hide from God, rather than seek him. Sinful acts make us feel unworthy of God's mercy. Our poor choices have a negative impact on us and those around us. Sin weighs down our anxious souls. Darkness prevails.

Start today to rid ourselves of selfish, sinful ways. Reduce the anxieties, fears, and obstacles that keep us from serving God. Pursue justice, kindness, and forgiveness. Let our actions and words reflect God's will and not earthly choices.

Learn obedience even when it hurts. God plans trials so we learn to depend on him. He teaches us to stay spiritually sharp by keeping our hearts open to him. God did not spare his own son from hardships and pain. When troubles abound, we grow closer to the Lord.

Persist in prayer. Choose God's way. His love blesses us with radiant peace.

Genesis 3:8-10; Psalm 105:4
Point to Ponder: Please God by speaking and acting in a Christ-like manner.

Pray: Lead me, God. Help me to make choices according to your plan. Teach me to speak words that honor you.

January 16

May the Lord of peace himself give you peace at all times and in every way. The Lord be with all of you.
— 2 Thessalonians 3:16

God wants us to soften our hearts and reframe from judging. We see faults in others but do not recognize the gaping holes in our own souls. Recognizing our neediness is half the battle. We then have to act and trust God to guide us to mend our ways.

He provides all we need and guides us when we seek him. Fear of change causes us to be worried and restless. When this occurs, stay in touch with Christ through constant prayer. Learn more about the Lord by reading scripture. This requires us to turn off television and cell phones, find a quiet place, and read. Look for messages about God's mercy and love. Be still and let the passages ring true and seep into our hearts.

In addition, always focus on God's goodness. Listen to hymns and sing along praising him. Attend church or join a Bible study group where God is the focus. Pray constantly.

Then wait expectantly for God and be ready to receive him. Obey his call and begin to feel a deeper trust in his plan. Ask him to increase our faithfulness. Do not hold back from asking big things from God. Nothing is impossible for him.

God changes us and softens our hearts as his peace shines upon us. Seek his peace and never-ending love every day.

Psalm 37:23-24; 2 Corinthians 4:6
Point to Ponder: The Lord sends peace.

Pray: God, soften my heart. Let me face change head-on. Let your grace shine in my heart and give me peace.

January 17

Consider it all joy, my brothers, when you
encounter various trials, for you know that the
testing of your faith produces perseverance, and
let perseverance be perfect, so that you may
be perfect and complete, lacking in nothing.

— James 1:2-4

Understanding God and his mysterious ways does not happen quickly. His ways become clearer overtime as God gives us the gift of himself. Most of us have witnessed his mercy, unending love, and patience. Persevere through all situations. Practice his truths and commandments.

Our wisdom increases with time. Our lives are the sum of the responses we have made toward God. We see clearer through active listening, watchful actions, and silent praise and thankfulness. Seek God in confidence and do not shy away from him. Strive to use the gifts he gives and share them with others. This honors God.

He rewards the faithful. Each time we trust God at a higher level, he reveals more of himself. Seek his presence through joyous times and in our darkest hours. He understands our humanity because when God gave us his son, Jesus, he entered fully into our human condition, and was subject to all the human experiences we face, except sin.

Blessings come wrapped in trials as well as in moments of pure bliss. Persevere in seeking to know God more intimately. Build a relationship with him based on faithfulness and love.

Romans 12:9-11; 1 Corinthians 15:57-58
Point to Ponder: Strong faith allows you to persevere and seek God at all times.

Pray: God, grant that I persevere through trials with steadfast faith. You are my refuge and strength.

January 18

*I tell you, on the day of judgment people will
render an account for every careless word they
speak. By your words you will be acquitted,
and by your words you will be condemned.*

— Matthew 12:36-37

God condemns profane and vile usage of heinous words. We
hear profanity but strive to never anger God by repeating the
utterances. What about foul speech spoken in haste? These words,
spoken carelessly without concern for their impact on others, cut
and offend. God is fully aware of the devastating nature of this
language; he hears and sees all things.

Words come from our mouths and give a glimpse of our hearts.
The book of Proverbs suggests we speak less at the risk of saying
something harmful. We are in less danger of saying something
hurtful or offensive if we keep our lips sealed. Listening is more
difficult than responding impulsively. Be patient while listening,
and alert to the way remarks affect others. Pray each day to speak
only uplifting comments to bring grace.

Think before we speak. Be careful our humorous comments
do not border on sarcasm because it cuts deep and destroys others.
Prepare the way for an accounting to God. Heed his warning and
eliminate careless, harmful utterances, and sarcastic remarks.
Listen more to the quiet voice within. Listening and reflecting are
keys to spiritual growth and bring us closer to God.

Proverbs 17:28; Ephesians 4:29
Point to Ponder: Words matter. Listen more.

Pray: God, help me be a positive influence. Let me make comments
that are uplifting and kind.

January 19

*Trust in the LORD with all your heart, on your own
intelligence rely not; in all your ways be mindful
of him, and he will make straight your paths.*
– Proverbs 3:5-6

For many people time passes quickly. One day blends into another.
People become so busy with routines, appointments, meetings, and
work, they seldom pause to pray or experience God's interventions.

God has a plan for us each day. He even plans for those who
do not believe or have a relationship with him. Believers find
it difficult to imagine a day without at least one sign of God's
love. Not bound by time and space to grace us with his love and
his miracles, he sends them every day. Take time to be mindful
of God.

Daily routines are necessary for a healthy body. God wants us
to share his vision and passion with others through our words and
actions. He works through us. We become his hands and feet on
earth. Begin looking at others through God's eyes. He provides
grace and strength as we approach different individuals and
situations. Embrace God's creative plan. He enables us to bring his
loving presence to others. God controls the details of our lives.

We, as children of God, have one thing in common. We have
no power of our own. Times may change, but God never does. He
never gives up on us. Trust him to show us the way.

2 Corinthians 5:7; Psalm 16:7-8
Point to Ponder: Place yourself at the mercy of God.

Pray: Help me see you more clearly, God. Teach me to trust in your
ways.

January 20

My soul, be at rest in God alone, from whom
comes my hope. God alone is my rock and my
salvation, my secure height; I shall not fall.

— Psalm 62:6-7

Some people live without reading the Bible, praying, or listening to God's word. Many do not know him. Praising and worshiping God provides the foundation of a life filled with his grace. Scripture is life itself not a series of messages about do's and don'ts.

God wants us to reach out and build a relationship with him. How do we start? Take small steps to draw closer to him. Talk with God. Be alert to his response. Read the Bible. Rest in his presence and meditate on his word. Question how to apply God's teachings. Whisper simple prayers, "Jesus, help me understand." As we stay in close contact with him, he sends hope and peacefulness beyond what has been experienced previously.

God, our greatest friend, rejoices as we draw closer to him. He refreshes our souls. Obey God's word and pray continuously. These are sure ways to draw closer to him and experience what he has in store for our lives.

Psalm 118:1-2; Zephaniah 3:17
Point to Ponder: God sends blessings of hope.

Pray: Lord, open your arms so I grow closer to you. Love me and fill me with hope. Hold fast to me.

January 21

What eye has not seen, and ear has not heard,
and what has not entered the human heart, what
God has prepared for those who love him.

— 1 Corinthians 2:9

What will heaven hold for us? Scripture tells us God will wipe tears away; there will be no more death, no more mourning or crying and no more pain (Rev. 21:4). Heaven is too vast a concept to fully comprehend but God has put eternity in our hearts. Eternity extends beyond death. God has placed a longing in our hearts to understand and seek wisdom about life with him in heaven.

We focus on God's teachings to help us understand. We learn in scripture to be imitators of God in all things (Eph. 5:1). God works in us every time we learn a new insight into his truths. He brings us to a place of fellowship. Trust that God honors our responses to him by teaching us more and giving us the grace we need to draw others to him. Be inspired by God. Encounter him daily through prayer. Be attentive to the call of discipleship. Follow him all the way to heaven.

Salvation is a process and a journey. Obey God so he uses us mightily and we grow in spiritual strength. Praise his holy name. God makes perfect eternal life. Heaven waits for those who follow him every step on the journey of life.

Ecclesiastes 3:9-15; Proverbs 11:18
Point to Ponder: Walk with Christ all the way to heaven.

Pray: God, teach me so I grow in knowledge. Bless me with eternal life.

January 22

*For this reason I kneel before the Father, from
whom every family in heaven and on earth is
named, that he may grant you in accord with
the riches of his glory to be strengthened with
power through his Spirit in the inner self ...*
— Ephesians 3:14-19

The Holy Spirit guides and teaches us. We learn to develop our
faith and understand the riches of our inheritance through the
Spirit. God gave us the gift of the Holy Spirit after the death of his
Son, Jesus.

The Spirit whispers God's truths. He guides, protects, and
prompts us to have Christ as our central focal point. Do not quench
the Spirit. He calls us by name and rescues us from darkness and
the chaos of sin. He guides us by speaking words of purpose and
hope, and he directs our thoughts so we think more clearly. The
Holy Spirit has divine power to strengthen our resolve, lift us up,
and assist us to stand firm. Trust him who resides within our souls
to lead us to abundant life. No one can remove this gift. Learn to
hear the promptings, and ponder how God teaches us through the
Holy Spirit.

Romans 15:13; 1Thessalonians 5:19-21
Point to Ponder: The Holy Spirit is powerful.

Pray: God, let my heart overflow with hope by the power of the
Holy Spirit.

January 23

Trust in the LORD forever! For the
LORD is an eternal Rock.

— Isaiah 26:4

Form the habit of prayer and get to know God better by spending time with him. Start each day with a joyful song of prayer giving thanks for life and time to draw closer to him. During the day, feel God's presence. Pray for those who are hurting over family issues, fighting an illness, or stressing over problems at work. Ask God for direction. Whisper a prayer of thanks when we see God's work at hand.

When prayer occurs naturally, we call it prayer without ceasing. Lift up prayers throughout the day to the Lord. Fervent prayer entails a conversation with God when our hearts remain in tune with his heart. We raise our hearts and minds to him. We begin to understand the heart of God only when he shares his heart with us.

If we pause, find a quiet place, and listen, God may speak to us. Not necessarily with his voice, but through the words in scripture and through our hearts. When we make time alone with God, we see more clearly and develop a better understanding of his will. We become aware of his continual presence when our thoughts and prayers focus on him. God directs our paths to a place of peace and victory, and he may empower us in ways we never imagined. Pray and praise him every day.

2 Timothy 1:3; Proverbs 8:17-19
Point to Ponder: Be persistent in prayer. God hears and responds.

Pray: God, my rock and my salvation, hear my prayers. Keep me in your presence so my heart intertwines with your heart.

January 24

Your word is a lamp for our feet,
a light for our path.

— Psalm 119:105

How do we become familiar with God's word as written in the Bible? We take time out of our busy schedules, and find a quiet place to pray and read scripture each day. The readings do not have to be long passages. God speaks to us in the depths of our souls through the written word. As we read the Bible, do we sense he has something to say directly to us? Or have we been reading without being transformed in any way?

Make time with the Lord a priority. When we attend church and listen to the pastor's message, do we ever feel the Gospel seems aimed directly at us? Remember that the Holy Spirit teaches us through scripture. Try to discern God's word so our lives align with his plan. Do the readings focus on forgiveness or serving others? God knows our hearts. Have we reached out to others in need or to those who are hurting? Always make the connection of God's words and the messages he sends. Take scripture seriously, knowing he judges our hearts and intentions.

God's truths in the Bible are powerful. We grow closer to him through reading and applying his messages. When Christ resides in our souls, we appear different to others. Welcome his embrace and love.

Joshua 1:8-9; Mathew 4:4
Point to Ponder: Inspirational wisdom comes to those who read and study the Bible.

Pray: God, help me quiet my mind. I want to learn through reading the Bible.

January 25

So be imitators of God, as beloved children,
and live in love, as Christ loved us and
handed himself over for us as a sacrificial
offering to God for a fragrant aroma.

– Ephesians 5:1-2

We imitate God through our actions and with the words we speak. Be careful with comments to others. The Bible stresses words spoken are a barometer to how we feel in our hearts. When we speak words that uplift and encourage others, our hearts feel real joy. When we are thankful for our relationship with God and tell others about his goodness and mercy, we demonstrate pure hearts. When we counsel our neighbors and share scripture to lessen their burdens, we send messages of hope and love.

If, on the other hand, we make harsh and critical remarks and regret our words once spoken, our hearts do not reflect God's heart. Do we make jealous comments and react bitterly when we are not the focal point? Do we gossip and place doubt in another person's mind? Do we grumble and complain about the small stuff? If so, stop.

A heart like God's heart reflects encouragement to others. If we have not used kind words, seek God. Ask him for the grace to change our ways. Be a spokesman for God. When we seek him, God strengthens us. Seek to imitate his loving ways. We never finish encountering God; he has more to teach us. Open our hearts to him.

Mathew 15:18; 1 Peter 4:11
Point to Ponder: Be deeply converted to God's ways.

Pray: God, help me imitate your goodness and mercy through the words I speak and the actions I take.

January 26

Let everything that has breath
give praise to the Lord.

— Psalm 150:6

Start each day by handing ourselves over to God in prayer. Before getting out of bed, give thanks for another day. He has given us a new day to draw closer to him. He molds our hearts and makes us ready to receive him and serve others. Let our lives become a praise song to God.

During the day, praise God frequently. Stand firm when trials occur. He places difficulties in our lives so he can teach us how to respond. He guides and protects us. Rely on God's strength, love, and control even when things appear hopeless. Be steadfast in prayer and faithfulness. Give worries and fears to God. He makes our troubles seem less cumbersome.

We may have thoughts and ideas about situations but we need to hold those plans tentatively. God's plan for us may be different. Turn to God in faith and clear our minds of clutter. Allow him to come to the forefront and occupy our consciousness so we see his plans as best. Trust him to show us the way. Be patient and listen for his message. Have faith in God.

At night, before you rest, again thank God for his presence in your life. Praise him for teaching you how to live according to his plan. Be grateful for his faithfulness. He remains infinitely powerful, tenderly loving, and wise beyond understanding.

Psalm 150:6; Proverbs 3:1-2
Point to Ponder: Follow God's will to make the ordinary parts of your life extraordinary.

Pray: Thank you, God, for directing and teaching me your ways. Help me follow your will.

January 27

*We have come to know and to believe in the
love God has for us. God is love, and whoever
remains in love, remains in God and God in him.*

— 1 John 4:16

We cannot be close to God without being affected by his love. God loves us not because we deserve his love, but because love abounds in his core. God wants to share a glimpse of his love when he joins two individuals in marriage. The love between a husband and wife and the sacrament of marriage are intended to last forever. But marriage can be difficult and filled with conflict. Marriage is not about the wedding but all the days after. Couples encounter tests.

Some people lose sight of God in their marriages. Sin creeps in. We are quick to point the finger of accusation. Sinful ways and poor choices enter and destroy the union. Hearts harden with painful hurt. When marriage vows are broken, trust eludes the couple.

Turn to God. Seek his mercy and guidance. God wants us to be kind to one another and treat our spouses with respect and dignity, gentleness and care. It is about doing small things with great love day after day.

Surviving trials in marriage requires God to be present. This takes discernment, faith, and courage. God helps all who seek him. Standing before God and professing love for another person is a vow not to be taken lightly. The greatest gifts you give to your marriage partner are purity, fidelity, and the promise of unconditional love.

1 Corinthians 13:13; Genesis 2:24
Point to Ponder: Marriage is sacred. Keep love alive.

Pray: Teach me how to love unconditionally.

January 28

I, then, a prisoner of the LORD, urge you to
live in a manner worthy of the call you have
received, with all humility and gentleness,
with patience, bearing with one another
through love, ... one God and Father of all,
who is over all and through all and in all.

– Ephesians 4:1-6

We have an infinite treasure when we know God and believe in his sovereignty. His blessings never end. Everyone who believes finds God and receives the gift of his presence. Seek God wholeheartedly because he desires to show us his: unconditional love, unfailing justice, constant mercy, and gentle compassion.

Pray continually, asking God to show us his way. Let down our guards and lift up our hearts and souls to him. God places many choices before us. We choose to grumble about the results of our decisions or accept the outcomes and have God walk with us. We can face any issue with his guidance and protection.

Although difficult, seek to live in the now and give worries to him. Let God lead the way. Only when we allow him to renew our inner self, do we find the treasures promised to all who believe. Thank God for all the blessings and the difficulties we encounter. We grow closer to him in our times of trouble. Seek him and watch how he transforms our trials into blessings. We have the treasure of his love.

1 Corinthians 10:13; Proverbs 19:20
Point to Ponder: Love changes your perspective on any circumstance.

Pray: God, draw me closer. Hear my prayers as I seek your presence in my life.

January 29

Be sober and vigilant. Your opponent the devil is prowling around like a roaring lion looking for someone to devour. Resist him, steadfast in faith, knowing that your fellow believers throughout the world undergo the same sufferings.

— 1 Peter 5:8-9

Satan seeks to rob us of every good thing God has given us. The evil one promotes sinful ways. He creeps into our lives when we let down our guard and lose focus. Blinded by Satan's power, we are lulled into thinking small sinful acts against others do not count. Then the sin increases and we die inside reduced to lives of drudgery and shame and self-condemning thoughts. He poisons happiness by injecting discontent. We live in darkness. Changes in personality may occur. Attitudes become more negative. Problems in relationships at home or at work are more frequent and linger longer. Answers do not come as they once did from God.

So how do we stop Satan and sinful ways? Return to God. Sit in a quiet place and talk with him. He knows our sins before we repent. Be persistent with prayer. God has the power to heal our souls and wash away our sins. He releases us from Satan's hold immediately, no matter how entangled we have become.

Abide wholeheartedly in God's word. Stay close to him. He frees us to experience the abundant life he intends for all his children.

Psalm 51:11-16; Ephesians 6:10-11
Point to Ponder: Always keep God as your focal point. Resist Satan.

Pray: God, lead me in your ways. Let me draw my strength from you.

For by grace you have been saved through
faith, and this is not from you; it is the gift of
God; it is not from works, so no one can boast.
For we are his handiwork, created in Christ
Jesus for the good works that God has prepared
in advance, that we should live in them.

— Ephesians 2:8-10

Pay attention to feelings. We may feel joy, happiness, sadness, envy, anger, or resentment or a combination that challenges our human way of thinking at any time. The Lord empowers us to feel all kinds of emotions.

Busy days filled with a myriad of emotions and activities become excuses to cut back on prayer time we desperately need with God. Without prayer, we lose the ability to hear God's inspiration and guidance. We carry our emotions in our hearts. Negative emotions change the way we interact with others and often impact how we perceive ourselves.

God guides us even during times of challenge, when we fail to turn to him. He reminds us of our utter dependence on him. The Lord helps us deal with our emotions and calms our spirits. Things do not always go according to our plans. God makes the final decision. Be thankful he leads the way. Rejoice in his work and allow thankfulness to flow freely from our hearts in response to his glorious blessings.

Hebrew 13:5-6; Psalm 73:23-26
Point to Ponder: Live according to God's plan.

Pray: Remain in my heart and my soul, God. Thank you for the gifts of grace and faith. Teach me to live in your presence.

January 31

In his mind a man plans his course,
but the LORD directs his steps.

— Proverbs 16:9

People have a natural tendency to plan for events and activities. Sometimes our plans do not go as we expect. If we are surprised by the outcomes and by God, what do we do?

Be flexible. Keep our eyes and minds wide open. Be sensitive to what God does in our lives. Do not become discouraged when plans change, or prayers go unanswered, or they are answered differently than what we anticipated. God directs our steps. He sends what we need to cope. The final plan rests with him. He wants us to set goals and be open to all he has to teach us through our experiences. He protects and guides us each day.

Do not worry about the future because it is not promised to anyone. Remember we cannot relive the past. Focus on one day at a time. View the challenges we encounter as setting the scene for God's intervention. Seek his will and his plan. God has unlimited resources to provide what we need.

Reach out to Christ and pray continually. Build a personal relationship with him. This is essential as we learn to listen for his message. Give God thanks and praise, because good comes to the faithful. Trust God to direct our steps all the way to eternal life with him.

Proverbs 16:9; Psalm 33:11-12
Point to Ponder: God's will and his plans are best.

Pray: God, guide me and teach me. Show me how to be strong and faithful to you in all situations.

February 1

Lord, open my lips; my mouth
will proclaim your praise.

— Psalm 51:17

Do you believe God, who gifted us with the Holy Spirit, works mightily through us? He places us precisely where we have a purpose and need to be. Take time to think about this truth. How does God plan to use us?

As we go about our day, we demonstrate our love for God through our words and actions. When our work runs smoothly and things flow in a positive manner, we glorify God and give him thanks. When someone whispers, "Thank you, Jesus," or "Praise the Lord," she is not being disrespectful but rather focusing on God's goodness.

Seek to become more Christ-like. The Holy Spirit resides in the deepest depths of our being. He knows our hearts. Be alert to the Spirit's promptings and act. The Spirit may nudge us: to teach a child, or assist a needy person, or reach out to the homeless, or take an elderly person to church. Show God through simple acts of kindness that we want to do his will. God sends all we need.

When we proclaim God's goodness and mercy and take advantage of opportunities, we feel peace and contentment. We witness things happening in our lives that only God can explain by his powerful presence. Value the blessings God sends. Find joy and peace in his presence.

1 Peter 4:11; Colossians 3:16-17
Point to Ponder: Praise God with words and actions.

Pray: Lord, help me build others up so they feel your love.

February 2

Peace I leave with you; my peace I give to you.
Not as the world gives do I give it to you. Do
not let your hearts be troubled or afraid.

— John 14:27

When we are filled with fear, some situations seem to paralyze us:
a job interview, a diagnosis of cancer, loss of employment, or the
death of a loved one. Any one of these life events may shake our
souls.

Fear takes over, accompanied by confusion and anxiety. These
feelings do not come from God. Most fears evolve because of
doubts and worries about the unknown. We sometimes do not
know what lies ahead, and so we avoid difficult situations that
make us anxious and apprehensive. We may take a cowardly stand
and hide from situations or make ourselves sick. Our imaginations
magnify problems. We fear the worst.

When this happens, pause and turn to God in prayer. He knows
the frailty of our hearts. Open the Bible, read, and ponder a few
verses. Draw closer to God. Our neediness links us to him. God's
love for mankind far outweighs fear. He is almighty and endures
to give strength and protection. He wants to be the constant in our
lives that provides stability and direction when fearful situations
arise.

As God reveals his plans and opens our eyes, he gives us
courage and power to face our fears. Christ enables us to regain
self-control. Rely on him. Seek God in every situation. He shows
us the way forward and walks with us out of fear and into his light.

2 Timothy 1:7; Psalm 56:3-5
Point to Ponder: Do not be afraid. God walks with us.

Pray: Take away my fears, Lord. Let me rest in your peace.

February 3

I will instruct you and show you the way you should walk, give you counsel and watch over you.

— Psalm 32:8

Why do we worry about situations? During stressful times when a child wakes with fever, or unpaid bills pile up, or a parent suffers a stroke, and images of terror flash across the news, we feel troubled, tired, and pulled off balance. Worry is inevitable.

Some people envision life as a journey. They choose to enjoy the scenery. God leads them. Others rebel or mope around and have a sour attitude about worldly happenings, family issues, or financial trials. But, a negative attitude, anxiety, and worry do not change our speed or route. We still face the journey of life.

When we seek to imitate God, we avoid habits of worry and negativity. He does not take all our worries away, but Christ carries the load. Seek his guidance. Be humble and pray often. Serve the Lord with internal spiritual thoughts and external actions. Depend on him to lead the way and make our burdens lighter.

When we reflect on our attitudes and level of trust in God, and we realize he determines our paths and steps, we can give worries to him. The more we turn over to God, the more we see him handling the things impossible for us to do anything about. Power flows from God. He has everything in control.

Galatians 1:10; 1 Peter 5:6
Point to Ponder: God guides and instructs you.

Pray: God, be my steadfast companion and give me courage and strength to face all situations.

February 4

*Man may make plans in his heart but what
the tongue utters is from the L*ORD.

— Proverbs 16:1

God does not want us to just read the Bible to learn about him and his good works and to gain knowledge and wisdom. He wants us to experience and demonstrate his truths and tell others. By taking scripture passages and applying them to life situations, we become disciples of Christ.

Whenever we teach or counsel, make certain our words and actions come from the Lord and not our own thinking. Receive his messages with sensitive, obedient, and trusting hearts. Then share his teachings with others.

Pray for a deeper union with God. He reaches out to us and speaks when we listen and are receptive to his voice. He communicates through scripture, in the quiet voice of a parent or friend, or in the recesses of our minds prompted by the Holy Spirit.

Pray for the right words to speak to those who suffer. We do not have to have the perfect techniques or an irrefutable set of arguments ready. In fact, a simple approach works best. Stay close to the Lord, be who we are, and let God's words flow from us. He works through us. God gives us what we need to lead others to him.

Proverbs 25:11; Deuteronomy 6:4-9
Point to Ponder: A word spoken at the right time endures.

Pray: God, guide me with my words. I want to proclaim your goodness, mercy, and love.

 February 5

For God so loved the world that he gave his
only Son, so that everyone who believes in him
might not perish but might have eternal life.

— John 3:16

No human comprehends God's everlasting love. We know how much he loves us from scripture. We are all imperfect. God loves us anyway with all our imperfections. He never gives up on us.

Some people reject the Lord and his teachings. They spend no time in his presence and do not pray. Many turn to material riches to find happiness and love. They seldom turn to God to ask him to realign their thoughts and actions. Only through times of great difficulty, or in times of severe weakness and vulnerability, do they return to God and seek his assistance.

Those who worship and love God are transformed by him. He empowers his believers through his love and gives them grace to keep following him. With Christ-like love our attitudes change. We forgive others more quickly, and if someone hurts, we take time to care about their sorrows. We give of ourselves and care about others.

Even when we sin, God still loves us with an everlasting love and waits for us to return to him. We are precious to him and the delight of his heart. Remember that Jesus gave his life for us. We are purchased with his blood. Seek to be more like him and love as he loves.

Romans 5:8; Jeremiah 31:3
Point to Ponder: Trust God. Encounter him daily.

Pray: God, help me to love more deeply. Be my rock and salvation.

February 6

*Therefore, gird up the loins of your
mind, live soberly, and set your hopes
completely on the grace to be brought to
you at the revelation of Jesus Christ.*

— 1 Peter 1:13

Some of us do not have God in our lives every day. We go about our busy schedules and build earthly riches. In our production-oriented world, we focus on the next promotion, a higher paying job, or the next event that signals us out as successful by human standards. We rush about, forget to read scripture, pray seldom, and fail to sit quietly and allow God to refresh us. We have little time to think about God's words or his life-changing ways.

We become poor in spirit because we do not have God as our focal point. We forget our strength and success come from him. We allow sin to creep in, sometimes ignoring God and separating ourselves from him. He seems far away.

God never changes. His love for us is constant. He sees us as the pinnacle of his creation, perfect in his eyes. In our busyness we change, and our spiritual lives falter.

Only when our world changes and we feel weighed down with nowhere to turn and trapped by circumstances we cannot change, do we humble ourselves under God's mighty hand. We lift our eyes to heaven and ask God to give us strength. He never tires of us but waits for us to return to him. Ask for forgiveness. He knows our hearts and hears our pleas. Seek his amazing grace. Watch as things change.

James 4:6; Hebrew 4:16
Point to Ponder: Set your hope on God's grace.

Pray: Lord, I cannot live without your strength and grace. Keep me close. Protect and guide me.

February 7

When he is dealing with the arrogant, he is
stern, but to the humble he shows kindness.

— Proverbs 3:34

God places people in our lives for a reason. He does not do this haphazardly. He knows our needs and talents as well as our strengths and weaknesses. God sends us the resources to help ourselves and others. Sometimes we are lazy and do not respond. This is part of the human condition.

Reflect on his blessings. Has God blessed us with material riches? If so, be prepared to share with someone less fortunate who cannot afford food or the basics of life. Has God granted us a strong healthy family? Do we serve others with a glad heart? Has God's peace comforted us in times of great loss? Might we sit with someone who has lost a loved one and communicate God's message and his steadfast love? Do not be hesitant when invited by God to assist others.

God purposely builds things into our lives so that he can work through us. Do not complain when God calls. Go joyfully as he directs our paths. He sees and remembers every act of kindness. When we freely give of ourselves, God blesses us in all our work. Watch for his powerful hand. Be humble and kind to all of God's children. Practice loving as God does, unconditionally. Reach out in kindness and love to serve the Lord.

Galatians 6:2; Deuteronomy 15:10
Point to Ponder: Serve others with a glad heart.

Pray: God, humble me so I serve others with kindness.

February 8

For I am convinced that neither death, nor life, nor
angels, nor principalities, nor present things, nor
future things, nor powers, nor height, nor depth,
nor any other creature will be able to separate us
from the love of God in Christ Jesus our Lord.

                                 – Romans 8:38-39

No matter how far we remove ourselves from Christ's presence, he watches over us continually and knows our circumstances. His love never ends.

When we face adversities and challenges, we question whether God cares about our struggles. He never promised we would not face hardships, persecution, poverty, sickness, or danger. He did promise he would not abandon us (Heb. 13:5).

At times, when things look bleak, we need to tell ourselves, that nothing is able to separate us from the love of Christ. No matter how terrible or frightening the experience, he is with us. If we start to doubt God could love us and allow us to face adversity, think of Jesus and his suffering. God sacrificed his only Son, Jesus Christ, to die a painful death on a cross so we could be saved.

Trust him to always be ready to enter into our suffering and reach out his comforting hands. Do not question his love based on our circumstances. Instead, evaluate our circumstances from the perspective of God's love. Give all our worries and fears to the Lord. Reach out to him through prayer. Rest in his presence and let his light guide us.

Psalm 86:5-6; John 15:16-17
Point to Ponder: God's love is always available.

Pray: God, never allow me to be separated from your love. Teach me to love as you love.

February 9

For "everyone who calls on the name
of the Lord will be saved."

— Romans 10:13

Step out in faith and walk with God. He watches over us even when we are unaware of his presence. Sometimes our journey leads us into temptation. We dwell in a dark valley and flounder trying to find our way out. In our despair, dismay, and loss of direction, we seek God.

He waits for our return to teach us and show us his ways. He has all the resources to help us make the right choices. God has limitless power and strength. He sends us the courage and strength we need to take small steps to find our way out of darkness and sin.

Call out to God. Never give up on him or lose faith in his goodness and mercy. He meets us in our workplace, in our home, driving on the highway, and at our place of worship. God is everywhere. He has all the resources we need to untangle the bonds which hold us back from his comforting arms.

When God speaks, what we do next demonstrates what we believe. Do we hesitate and challenge him saying we lack ability? Do we argue with God and start making excuses? Do we avoid difficult situations? Or do we trust God, rest in his presence, and let him direct our steps?

God calls us to make changes and use our talents to build his kingdom. Be open to God's voice and his plans. Listen, pray, and believe. Then, be willing to take a chance and see what blessings follow.

Jeremiah 33:3; Psalm 91:15
Point to Ponder: God gives you what you need to do his will.

Pray: Lord, fill my heart with faith and hope.

 February 10

He who guards his mouth and tongue
keeps himself from trouble.

– Proverbs 21:23

Be alert. Stop and think before we say or do something hurtful. Words spoken may cause others to be uplifted or pierce the heart with hurt.

As we go through our day, we may encounter stress and worry. This has a wearing effect on us mentally and physically and may cause negativity. In times of stress, we sometimes blurt out offensive, injurious comments we wish we could take back. We try to forget harsh words, but they keep playing in our minds. Many people try to numb the pain with food, drink, television, or the Internet.

When this happens, pause and seek God. Hear the promptings to humble ourselves, and apologize to those we may have hurt. If we learn to hold our tongues and be still, God gives us the right words to speak at the appropriate time. Trust him and listen for his direction before speaking.

Instead of negative and hurtful ways, make a fresh commitment to be thoughtful and make comments pleasing to God. Ask him to curb our harsh words, hold our tongues, and grace us with peace of mind. Scripture cautions believers to be quick to hear, slow to speak, and slow to wrath, because the wrath of a man does not accomplish the righteousness of God (Jas. 1:19-20). Be Christ-like and demonstrate kindness and express uplifting words on our journey to eternity.

Psalm 34:14; James 1:19
Point to Ponder: Listen more. Think before you speak.

Pray: Lord, teach and guide me in what I say so that my words encourage others.

February 11

*In the beginning, God created the
heavens and the earth.*

– Genesis 1:1

Yes, heaven is real and belongs to God. We ponder what heaven
looks like. Each person sees heaven differently. We learn through
reading scripture that heaven is spectacular and beyond all human
imagination (Rev. 21:4).

So what do we have to do to get to heaven? Stay close to God.
Become a slave to righteousness and follow God's word and the
Ten Commandments. Allow him to free us from sin so we stand
firm and find strength to fight temptations. In every area of our
lives, honor God.

He gives us an advocate, the Holy Spirit, to be our guide and
to protect us. The Spirit fills our hearts with love and gives us a
glimpse of heaven where there are no more tears, no more death or
mourning, and no pain. The Spirit is evidence that God is at work
in our lives as we journey on earth.

Be bound to righteousness: pray without ceasing, read
scripture, practice God's teachings, and praise and worship him.
Through the Holy Spirit, strive to systematically implement the
truths of God's word every day. If we honor God and follow his
teachings, we shall all meet in heaven.

John 5:24; Romans 2:6-8
Point to Ponder: Heaven waits for those who follow God's
teachings and commands.

Pray: God, I want to keep my eyes on heaven so I have eternal life.
I commit myself to you.

February 12

You alone are the God who did wonders;
among the peoples you revealed your might.

— Psalm 77:15

When Jesus lived, he performed miracles which could not be explained by natural law. He accomplished these wonders in public in the presence of a multitude of credible witnesses. His miracles always had instantaneous effects.

Biblical scholars point out miracles came in many different forms. There were supernatural acts of creation such as creating the universe (Gn. 2:1-2). Miracles that involved acts of nature, a ferocious storm on the Sea of Galilee (Mt. 8:23-27), Jesus's ability to walk on water (Jn. 6:16-21) and healing the blind (Jn. 9:1-7), and the lame (Acts 3:1-10). There were signs demonstrating divine power over death. Lazarus, dead for four days, came back to life (Jn. 11:43-44). And most important is the resurrection of Christ (1 Cor. 15:12-19). Jesus performed divine authority over certain material things. He turned water into wine (Jn. 2:1-11) and multiplied loaves of bread and fish to feed thousands of people (Jn. 6:1-14).

The miracles performed by Jesus established the validity of his claim of being the Son of God. The disciples saw his wonders and believed. Christ's powers are endless. His miracles demonstrated he was a "man approved of God" (Acts 2:22). Live in his light. Witness the power of Christ daily. Praise God and expect miracles.

Ephesians 2:4-6; John 3:17-18
Point to Ponder: Believe in miracles from God.

Pray: Jesus, I want to grow in holiness each day. Build a strong spiritual foundation in me.

February 13

*Ask and it will be given to you; seek and you
will find; knock and the door will be opened
unto you. For everyone who asks, receives;
and the one who seeks, finds; and the one
who knocks, the door will be opened.*

— Matthew 7:7-8

God hears our prayers. Be persistent and stay in communion with him. Throughout the day, whisper short prayers. Believe God has all the resources to meet our needs. He looks beyond our actions and thoughts, and he sees directly to our hearts. God chooses to respond to our prayers in his time, not our time. He is not bound by twenty-four-hour days.

When troubles abound, especially when we feel weak or weary, strive to stay focused on God. Frustration sets in if we try to figure things out on our own. We want a quick fix. Satan weasels in when we let our guard down. Do not be fooled by the evil one. Cry out to God. Whisper his name, reverently, lovingly, and prayerfully in order to draw closer to him. Turn to God with all things and in all circumstances.

God listens before he answers prayers. He wants us to persist in our prayers and seek him. The answer he sends may not be what we expect. Understand that God knows each of us by name (Ps. 91:14). Never doubt or lose faith in him. He sends what we need.

Begin living a life reflecting absolute trust in God. Rest peacefully, secure in the knowledge that God loves us and wants only good in our lives.

Psalm 138:3; James 5:13-15
Point to Ponder: God answers all prayers.

Pray: God, strengthen my faith. Hear me when I pray. Watch over me so I follow your plan.

February 14

Until now you have not asked anything
in my name; ask and you will receive,
so that your joy may be complete.

— John 16:24

In society today, we are not used to receiving things without making a purchase. The Bible talks about receiving, not bartering or buying things we need. God is not for sale; we cannot purchase him. His gifts of love, peace, mercy, grace, gentleness, kindness, patience, and forgiveness do not cost money. When our spiritual eyes and hearts are pure, we receive God's blessings. He is incredibly generous to those who love and follow his ways.

Christ teaches his followers through scripture. The Beatitudes tell us what God expects: be humble, repent our sins, be willing to change, be unassuming, seek righteousness, show mercy, be pure through faith, be a peacemaker, accept persecution when others insult our beliefs about Christ, and rejoice that heaven awaits those who love and trust the Lord (Mt. 5:1-10).

Look for an intricate connection between receiving and trusting God's message. Pray for God's mercy and forgiveness. When we encounter God, our hearts rejoice. Strengthened by faith, we receive his blessings abundantly.

He never stops looking for ways to bless us. Be true to God, praise him, and reflect his grace to the people around us. Receive his love and joy with a glad heart.

Matthew 5:1-10; Psalm 24:5
Point to Ponder: God sends blessings to share with others.

Pray: Lord, strengthen my faith in your love for me.

 **February 15**

But to you who hear I say, love your enemies,
do good to those who hate you, bless those who
curse you, pray for those who mistreat you.
— Luke 6:27-28

Even the smartest minds have trouble understanding how to love our enemies. We live in a society where man looks out for himself and takes care of his own needs and wants first. Having the ability to love and forgive our enemies is counter to our sense of reasoning.

God wants us to love everyone and treat people with dignity. When we meet another Christian, we come face-to-face with Christ. The person may talk and dress differently. They may have a different skin color and unique mannerisms. But all people are made in God's image (Gn. 1:26-27).

Do not live as if we have no responsibility for our fellow Christian brothers and sisters. God holds us accountable for how we treat each other. We have a responsibility to care for one another, and put to death our natural inclination to be self-centered. Ask God to soften our hearts. Allow him to transform us as the light of his presence filters through. Demonstrate greater kindness and patience and forgive others who trespass against us. Though it is difficult for many, God helps those who want to let go of personal biases and follow his ways. Pray for those who are hurtful and unaccepting of their fellowman. Be persistent and strive to love unconditionally as God loves.

Matthew 5:44; Mark 12:31
Point to Ponder: Love more deeply and unconditionally.

Pray: God, I want to grow in your likeness and pass on your love.

February 16

Your every act should be done with love.
— 1 Corinthians 16:14

Proclaim love for: life, family, country, fellow Christians, and most important God. We often rush from place to place, chasing after fleeting pleasures, accumulating material wealth, and forgetting the importance of standing firm and proclaiming our love for God. We find ourselves too busy to worship and give thanks. When this occurs, slow down and take time to pray. Make a commitment to return to God. Draw closer through prayer and praise.

God gave us his only Son, Jesus, so we could be freed from sin and have eternal life. When Jesus walked among men, he recognized his Father's love was no ordinary love. He drew strength from his Father's love. Jesus prayed that God would place this same love in his disciples (2 Cor. 13:11). We find strength in Christ's love.

Love assumes the best about others so that when someone offends us, our first thought should be the offense was unintentional. Seek to forgive. If someone speaks harshly and uses cruel and ugly words, be patient and do not snap back with a cutting or sarcastic remark. Instead, turn the other cheek, ponder what may be happening in the other person's life, and practice unconditional love. Never lose hope in the ones you love. Though difficult, continue to love them through troubled times. Focus on God and pray, "Show me how to love. Help me." He shows us the way forward as he constantly teaches us. Rejoice in his love.

1 John 4:7; Luke 6:31
Point to Ponder: Share love. Begin with a smile and kind words.

Pray: God, teach me to love more deeply. Be with me always.

February 17

Be merciful, just as [also] your Father is merciful.
— Luke 6:36

God never conceals his expectations from us. Sometimes we choose to ignore or fail to hear his promptings. God protects and prompts us to follow his plan. He wants us to love our enemies and be merciful (Lk. 6:35). This is difficult for most of us.

When we focus on God, we remember his teachings and how to act righteously. He wants us to be honest, forgive others, and not retaliate when wronged. Instead, show mercy. We feel God's mighty hand working in our lives when we forgive. At other times, when faced with challenges, seek God more often. Sometimes he feels distant. Fight the temptation to turn away from him when conflict evolves. Handle things with his help and in his time. Be patient but persistent, and hold onto God. Call out to him in prayer. He never tires of helping us.

God desires that we walk humbly with him. He does not expect perfection. Service to him should not be difficult. Strive to walk with God every day for he gives us grace and safe harbor. Cultivate his teachings into our daily activities. Pray often and give thanks for his goodness and mercy. Demonstrate his love so others see our joy.

Put God first in our hearts and minds. There are no limits to his mercy and love. God blesses his children. Through him all things are possible.

Proverbs 22:4; Micah 6:8
Point to Ponder: Be merciful as God is merciful.

Pray: Show me how to be more merciful and compassionate. I want to model your ways.

February 18

Wash yourselves clean! Put away your misdeeds
from before my eyes; cease doing evil; learn to do
good. Make justice your aim: redress the wronged,
hear the orphan's plea, defend the widow.

— Isaiah 1:16-17

Christ knows our hearts and sees all we do. He may dispense gentle discipline if we do not abide by his way or defy his call to change. God knows our weaknesses and needs.

Change happens gradually. When we find ourselves focusing on the negative, the Holy Spirit prompts us to reframe the situation to have a more positive outcome. For example, our eyes and faces send an instant message to people we meet. If we have the tendency to frown and be critical, practice saying positive comments and smile. This may cause others to be uplifted. Allow God to work through us.

God has authority in heaven and on earth. Trust his plan. When we ask, he sends strength and empowers us to be more righteous in our actions. Pray to work through issues and stand firm drawing on God's strength. Leave the rest to him.

He blesses us with his peace that transcends from our heavenly Father. He lifts us up, empowers us to do good works, and teaches us how to show kindness and love to our brothers and sisters. Praise him now and forever.

Matthew 23:11-12; Galatians 6:9-10
Point to Ponder: God transforms you to do good works.

Pray: Lord, teach me your ways so that I can help others. Build up strength within me to share love.

 **February 19**

Be strong and take heart, all you
*who hope in the L*ORD.

— Psalm 31:25

Be patient, and God's promises will come to fruition. When God speaks, he stands by his word. He never deceives us. He transforms us to have trusting hearts full of hope.

Sometimes we become impatient and tire of waiting for the Lord to answer our prayers. When we go through tough times with no relief in sight, we lose hope. Our human ways tend to grasp power and strength through others as our patience wanes. Waves of adversity wash over us. We seek relief at all costs and want instant change and results.

Though our circumstances may be painful and difficult, they are not worthless. God sees and knows the details of every situation we experience. He feels our pain. We forget about his sovereignty over our lives and all our experiences.

When things do not go as planned and we focus on problems and concentrate on the reasons why something cannot be done, we become pessimists. Optimists, on the other hand, do not ignore the difficulties; they know they are there. Optimists know God is in control and always present. This gives them hope and encouragement to press on.

Seek to acquire an optimistic attitude. Strive to have hope in all situations. Make ourselves available to God's grace, and be assured all things are possible with him leading us. He sends us the resources we need. Count on God. His timing is always best.

Romans 15:4; Psalm 39:8-9
Point to Ponder: Be patient and wait for God.

Pray: Lord, my security rests in you alone. Send me hope and strength to press on.

February 20

He who shuts his ear to the cry of the poor
will himself also call and not be heard.

— Proverbs 21:13

We are blessed by God every day and called to be intentional about our Christianity. God invites us to come to him with open hearts, willing to help others. As we watch our fellow man, some settle for a shallow lackadaisical relationship with the Lord. Others draw closer to God through prayer, reading and studying the Bible, and worshiping him. He blesses us according to our response. If God sees we have generous hearts that freely give to others, than he responds to us in a like manner.

Invest in a relationship with God and spend ample time reading the Bible and practicing the truths of scripture. God enriches our lives. When we share our riches (both materially and spiritually) with the poor, he sends all the resources we need. God guides and blesses us with good things. Remain in prayer with the Lord. He sees all we do as he works through us.

Our Christian maturity is deeply affected by what we do to serve God. Choose to give generously and cast a wide net to rich and poor alike. What we reap changes when we welcome God in our hearts and become more Christ-like. We find ourselves modeling kindness, compassion, and love. Help the poor and needy encounter God. Extend a gentle, generous hand to all and find true meaning and satisfaction in life. God gives us strength to press forward. We have control over our efforts.

Psalm 12:8; Acts 20:35
Point to Ponder: Be gentle, compassionate, generous, and loving to everyone.

Pray: Let me see all people as children of God. Lord, send me strength to help others.

February 21

We know that all things work for good for those who love God, who are called according to his purpose.

— Romans 8:28

From our limited perspective, our lives may be confusing with puzzling twists and turns. God has a master plan filled with love and goodness, not chaos, hurt, and evil. We do not see his plan clearly. At any given time, we see only a small piece of a massively big picture. Many people find a life filled with peace and righteousness hard to envision. A wise man remembers all things work for good for those who love God. Goodness always triumphs over evil.

At times, when life becomes difficult and we suffer, our faith is challenged. We pray for relief. When God does not answer our prayers in our time and makes us wait, we become impatient and question if God hears our prayers. We wonder if God has forgotten us or if we have offended him or made him angry.

During difficult and confusing times, God teaches us patience and reminds us to wait and pray. He wants us to build our faith in him. We grow closer to God when we pray. The small voice within tells us to trust him. Remember he brings good out of everything we encounter.

No one separates us from God's love. He gives us strength to move forward. God is faithful. Trust him to walk with us all the way to eternity.

1 Corinthians 15:33; Psalm 51:3
Point to Ponder: God brings good from all situations for those who love him.

Pray: Lord, I believe in your goodness. Thank you for loving me. I want to build my faith in you.

February 22

My God will fully supply whatever you need, in
accord with his glorious riches in Christ Jesus. To
our God and Father, glory forever and ever. Amen.
— Philippians 4:19-20

God stands ready to meet our every need but we must do our part.
As Matthew writes in scripture, "Ask and it will be given to you;
seek and you will find; knock and the door will be opened to you
(Mt. 7:7). But recognizing our neediness is only half the battle. We
must believe God is almighty and powerful.

When we feel we have done everything within our human
power, be still and pray for God's intervention. Sometimes he
pours abundant energy into us as we spend time with him. At
other times, he gives us enough strength and hope to keep moving
forward one day at a time. God may choose to give us sufficient
resources for the moment. This may be his way of keeping us close
and leaning on him. Listen for his messages in church, through a
friend or parent's voice, in the melody of a song, or in the quiet of
the night. Have faith and trust in our heavenly Father.

God meets all our needs. He helps with: finances, health issues,
family conflicts, grief, and loneliness. He has abundant resources.
No one has ever exhausted God's supply of blessings and gifts.
Believe and have persistent prayer for them.

Psalm 103:1-5; Mathew 7:11
Point to Ponder: God sends abundant blessings. Glorify him.

Pray: Lord, direct my steps every day. Lead me forward step-by-
step and supply me with what I need so your plan for me becomes
a reality.

February 23

*Lord, you have probed me, you know
me: you know when I sit and stand; you
understand my thoughts from afar.*

— Psalm 139:1-2

God is all-knowing and ever-present. We belong to the Lord and nothing separates us from his love. Do not try to hide from him. He knows our every breath and thought. Do not fear his intimate awareness. He views us through the eyes of grace.

God speaks to us through the intricacies of our minds and whispers messages to our hearts. He leads us as we journey on earth through good times and bad, through dark valleys and on clear mountaintops. Our longing to stay on the mountain top is good and natural. But at times, we fall into darkness and move away from God, succumb to sin, or attempt to control situations on our own. We are lost in the valley of darkness.

We forget we have no power of our own. Our strength comes from God. Turn back to the Lord. Fix our eyes on the light and stay close to God through prayer. Ask him to guide our steps when the going gets rough and the path is rocky and steep. He loves us and carries our burdens when they become heavy. Be still and know God can do anything.

Hold tight to his hand and follow the path he selects. Watch God's perfect plan unfold. Remember trials bring unforeseen blessings. Trust there are blessings waiting around the bend. Have faith in God.

Isaiah 43:1; Jeremiah 1:5
Point to Ponder: God knows your heart and cares for you.

Pray: Thank you, Lord, for making me your child. Touch my heart and free me to follow you.

February 24

Know that I am with you; I will protect
you wherever you go, and bring you back
to this land. I will never leave you until
I have done what I promised you.

– Genesis 28:15

God is our shield and protector. In times of trouble, people experience all sorts of emotions: conflict, pain, confusion, and fear. Some become dysfunctional. Problems become the focal point instead of God. Some fail to reach out to him.

God created us in his image. He knows when we are vulnerable and when we are strong. He knows our thoughts and fears. When we lack courage or our faith falters, simply pray, "God, I need you. Come to me." Never far away, God meets us in the stillness of our souls.

Trust the Lord, who is our refuge and strength. Walk hand in hand with him on life's journey. Trust his timing and look for signs of change controlled by God.

Focus on the present and do not worry about the future. God guides us through each day. He has a plan for us before we wake each morning. We draw closer to God by simply whispering his name. The more aware of his presence we are, the safer we feel. Concentrate on trusting God and building a relationship with him. He protects us.

Psalm 56:10-12; Nahum 1:7
Point to Ponder: Call out to God for guidance and protection.

Pray: Lord, help me turn to you throughout the day in prayer and be more content to let things unfold according to your will.

February 25

The favors of the LORD are not exhausted,
his mercies are not spent; they are renewed
each morning, so great is his faithfulness.

– Lamentations 3:22-23

The Lord wants us to seek him each day. Take time to be in his presence. Find a quiet place and whisper his name. Pray for his strength to guide and protect us. God knows what we think and feel in our hearts.

He wants us to overcome sin so we have victory over Satan. Sin, though sometimes subtle, creeps into our lives when and where we least expect it. Packaged in ways we do not recognize at first, Satan blinds us and ties us up in his embrace. He drives us away from God. Sin, a persistent enemy, causes us to do illogical things and robs us of the good God has planned for us.

Ask God to cleanse our spirit and teach us how to remain faithful throughout the day. God does not condemn us – he forgives us. His grace and power release us immediately, no matter how dreadful our sins. Seek his mercy and forgiveness.

Our deepest needs revolve around peace. To find peace of mind and peace of heart, reach out to God. We inevitably fall short of God's standard but continue to turn to him daily for renewal. He prepares us for each day. He shelters us. We have only to focus on God, entrusting our concerns to him. God's love and his faithfulness last.

Psalm 25:8; 1 John 1:9
Point to Ponder: Start each day with prayer.

Pray: Lord, forgive my sins. They block me from encountering you. Have mercy on me.

February 26

*Yet the L*ORD *is waiting to show you favor, and*
*he rises to pity you; For the L*ORD *is a God of*
justice: blessed are all who wait for him.

— Isaiah 30:18

Building a relationship with God is a priority. He should be the focal point of our lives. As the bond grows stronger and we spend more time with him, we begin to delight in the things God loves. We start to see things as God sees them. Our first thought in prayer should not be for ourselves, but for God's name to be exalted. Give him thanks and praise.

God continues to reveal himself to us according to his purposes. He designed us to need him continually. When we grieve, he comes to us as a comforter. When we are in need, he provides. When sick, he relieves our suffering. When we face a serious challenge, he is ever-present and delivers us from all evil.

Draw closer to the Lord daily. Our understanding of God grows greater with each passing day. We know him better now than we did five years ago. He personally brings us out of darkness into his light. He entrusts us to tell others about his awesome kingdom.

Think of every situation as a growth opportunity to know God better. Learn from each experience and reflect on his teachings. He accomplishes things through our lives we never dreamed possible. Wait for the Lord. Rejoice in his faithfulness.

Psalm 130:5; Psalm 37:3-4
Point to Ponder: God shows us great favor and blesses us with joy, love, and peace.

Pray: Lord, I want to grow closer to you day by day. Strengthen my resolve as I travel the path to a deeper union with you.

February 27

For while your obedience is known to all, so that I rejoice over you, I want you to be wise as to what is good, and simple as to what is evil; then the God of peace will quickly crush Satan under your feet. The grace of our Lord Jesus be with you.
— Romans 16:19-20

Satan lurks and temps man to follow his ways. He stirs up conflict, envy, jealousy, and mistrust. The evil one strives for a world full of corruption, chaos, and sin. Satan plays on our weaknesses and suspicions. Do not get ensnarled with the evil one whose purpose is to gather souls around him who have fallen from God's grace and who feel defeated and lost.

Call out for God. Allow him to adjust our lives so we follow his ways as his beloved children. When tempted by Satan, God waits for us to seek him.

The Holy Spirit, who dwells within our souls, prompts us to return to God. We have an arsenal of weapons: prayer, the intercession of saints, and the angels. Following God requires obedience. Sometimes we find this easy and have no questions. At other times, we are weak and tempted by Satan to strike out on our own.

Always choose God. Following him may be difficult and like a torrential storm, or he may lead us on a peaceful walk in a field of blue bonnets. Scripture promises if we obey the Lord, our lives will be a channel of his blessings. Our responsibility is to serve God. He sends his saving grace.

Revelation 12:9-12; Matthew 16:23
Point to Ponder: Stay alert. Be in God's presence daily.

Pray: God, help me wear my spiritual armor to defeat the temptations of Satan. Lead me.

February 28

Therefore, encourage one another and
build one another up, as indeed you do.

– 1 Thessalonians 5:11

As followers of Christ, we find he sends people into our lives for a reason. Sometimes the person is there for just hours and at other times it is for years. We discover God's plan for our lives through his activity and through the people he sends to share our lives.

God wants us to reach out to others and be interdependent. He holds us accountable as to how we relate to our neighbors. We have a responsibility to live without hurting others and avoid sin. Live to enjoy God's blessings.

Say yes to God and a resounding no to Satan. Ask God to take away selfishness and wrong doing, and cleanse our hearts. Practice kindness. Lift others up with encouraging words. Smile and see how God's light shines through. Filling our minds with God will dramatically affect the way we treat each other.

When we look at other Christians, see the face of Jesus. He works to restore mankind so we enjoy his blessings of beauty, peace, and love. He works through each of us so we use our gifts and talents to glorify him. We lift others up when we acknowledge God-given talents and treat them with kindness and respect. Be a positive influence and a powerful change agent to everyone we encounter.

Proverbs 3:1-2; 1 Corinthians 14:26
Point to Ponder: Spread God's love by encouraging others.

Pray: God, thank you for the many blessings you send each day. Guide me to assist others so they reach their potential.

February 29

*But you, L*ORD*, are a merciful and gracious*
God, slow to anger, most loving and true.

— Psalm 86:15

God created us in his image. He knows our full potential and provides opportunities every day for us to make choices pleasing to him. He gives each person the ability to reason. We can choose to live in a Christ-like manner, spotless in words, actions, and spirit. Or make poor choices and live with chaos, bitterness, anger, and sin. Those who love God, choose the former.

Some people focus on external beauty; this changes over time. Others choose internal beauty which is eternal. People who have external beauty are attractive to the world but may not have pure hearts. God wants us to have internal beauty. People who have beauty from within have open and pure hearts. They demonstrate kindness and a gentle calmness to everyone. No matter what earthly vessel our spirit dwells in, God loves us.

We have a responsibility to God to help others as we journey on earth. Simple acts of kindness are a saving grace to those who hurt or suffer. Laughter lightens the load and lifts the heart. God wants us to be happy.

Hope for God's love above all things. He created us to be at peace and bask in his love. Give thanks to God for we are wonderfully made. Be merciful, generous, loving, and slow to anger. Imitate God. Relax and enjoy his blessings.

Psalm 139:13-16; Job 34:19
Point to Ponder: God is gracious and merciful.

Pray: God, I believe in your mercy. I stand ready to advance your kingdom.

March 1

He said to them, "Go into the whole world
and proclaim the gospel to every creature."

— Mark 16:15

Strive to be an ambassador for God. Think of him as our greatest teacher. Grow in wisdom by reading and practicing the truths as found in the Bible. Embrace God's teachings and then share them. We come to know God through silent messages to our hearts and through our experiences.

God is ever-present in our lives. Our awareness of his presence is our greatest strength. He guides us to be knowledgeable about his truths, and fills us with wisdom so we show others mercy and love. God wants his peace to rule.

Model God's teachings. Run with endurance and meet the challenges and opportunities presented each day. Proclaim the gospel and God's ways as his peace strengthens us.

Strive to live righteous lives. Step out in faith to tell others about God. He sends us the tools we need. No one is perfect except God. We should consider ourselves works in progress. God performs his divine work and transforms us. Nothing is impossible for God.

Psalm 96:3; Jeremiah 1:5
Point to Ponder: Tell others of God's never-ending love.

Pray: Lord, teach me to proclaim the gospel and build your kingdom on earth.

March 2

O Lord, my God, I cried out to
you and you healed me.

— Psalm 30:3

God dwells within our souls. He waits for moldable, pliable, and willing followers. People have a natural tendency to turn to God when their lives are in shambles, or when they live in a dark place with no hope. At other times, we give thanks when we receive a miracle of healing or when we have prayers answered quickly to our liking. No matter the circumstances, God brings hope and salvation to us, to our friends and family, and to the world.

Those who experience God working in their lives typically want to build a closer relationship with him. Be persistent in prayer and persevere in faith. God responds in his time. He does not see time as we do. If answers to our prayers do not come quickly, have faith God has not forgotten. He finds ways to reach us at the perfect time.

God fits everything into a pattern of good. He may not remove all our barriers and troubles but he sends ways to cope. He ceaselessly works on our behalf. We change on the inside with his guiding touch, and believe anything is possible with God leading us.

Make him the focal point. Invite him to heal us from the inside out. Strive to honor and follow his teachings. Grow in knowledge and trust the Lord. He loves us unconditionally.

Hebrews 7:24-25; John 4:46-54
Point to Ponder: Christ heals those who call out to him.

Pray: Lord, build my faith as you cleanse my heart and make me pure.

March 3

*Can any of you by worrying add a
single moment to your life-span?*

— Matthew 6:27

Do not worry or be anxious. Sometimes we find this easier said than done. Whatever is pressing on our minds controls us. If we allow worry to consume our waking thoughts, havoc and confusion infest our lives.

Turn troubles and worries over to the Lord. Pray for God to intervene and break free from burdens. Every time worry interrupts our thinking, pause and whisper a short prayer, "Help me, Jesus," or "I trust you, Lord." Practice minimizing worry and increasing prayer.

The best direction for our thinking focuses on God. He sustains and sees us through every situation. He knows our needs. God desires us to follow his will. Do not worry that his path is too difficult. Take one step at a time. God leads the way. When we focus on following him, our cares and worries lose their hold on us.

God wants his children to live in peace. Trust him to find a way to send peace no matter the situation. Scripture tells us nothing is impossible, too difficult, too troubling, or too fearful for God (Mt. 19:26). Let his perfect peace guard our hearts.

Direct our worries to God. Although the situation may not change immediately, God sends enough strength to cope. He is pleased when we give him our worries. Remember, he works through us for the good of all his children.

Luke 12:22-26; Proverbs 12:25
Point to Ponder: Pray more and worry less.

Pray: God, I release my worries to you. Help me find peace.

March 4

Entrust your works to the L<small>ORD</small>, *and*
your plans will succeed.

               – Proverbs 16:3

We seek more than head knowledge about scripture to be effective and demonstrate God's teachings. God is not bound by earthly trappings and what feels good. He works through us to express his love and plan for our lives.

We seldom have the big picture of our purpose in life. But if we move forward and take the small steps in front of us each day with love in our hearts, we get an inkling of what God desires. Recognize the awesomeness of God and our littleness. Be persistent and model faithfulness. Pray often for direction and be aware of God's presence in our lives.

God cares about all our deeds. He wants to do more than make us obedient servants. Whatever we do for work, we do for the glory of God. He endows those who seek him with a sensitivity and awareness of his love. God wants us to succeed.

Focus on choices that provide an opportunity to contribute to the great works of God. When others see us face a crisis, do not crumble and fail. Seek the Lord's help as optimism prevails. Fill each day with intermittent prayers. Respond in a positive manner to show others love in our hearts. Listen to God as he guides us. Stay focused and energized to do God's will. Our plans succeed when God leads the way. Entrust our lives to him.

Psalm 145:14-17; John 5:30
Point to Ponder: Follow God's plan.

Pray: Lord, guide me to do your will. Keep working in me so I bring others to you.

March 5

If you remain in me and my words
remain in you, ask for whatever you
want and it will be done for you.

— John 15:7

The disciples learned to pray through Jesus's example. They saw him praying at different times during the day, at night, and always before difficult decisions. When Jesus selected his disciples, he prayed a full night to his Father to understand his mind. He made an extended effort to find a quiet place so he could clearly hear his Father's voice. Follow his example. Find a quiet place to pray and be alone with God. Listen for his voice to guide our actions, thoughts, and words. Resolve problems with God's intervention. Whisper, "Jesus, I need you. Help me."

Surrounded by crowds, Jesus remained obedient to his Father. Through prayer, Jesus could perform miracles. In addition, prayer gave him the strength to endure excruciating pain on the cross. He remained close to God throughout his life on earth and always said yes to him.

Whenever our minds wander, redirect our thoughts back to the Lord. Prepare our minds and hearts to hear God's message. Do not let static from the world and our busy lifestyles block God's messages. Tune in to him.

Worry is released when we pray, judgmental thoughts are unmasked and confused ideas are untangled. Encounter him daily through prayer. God is only a whisper away. Follow him.

Mark 11:24; Luke 18:1-8
Point to Ponder: Stay close to God through prayer.

Pray: God, hear my prayers and keep me close. I surrender to you. Bless me in your mercy.

65

March 6

*When the just cry out, the L*ORD *hears*
and rescues them from all distress.

— Psalm 34:18

Why does God allow bad things to happen to good people? This has been a question asked for centuries. We will probably never know in this world why God works as he does. Scripture tells us, "I have told you this so that you might have peace in me. In the world you will have trouble, but take courage, I have conquered the world" (Jn. 16:33). He did not say we might have trouble but that we will. God promises to rescue us.

Some people do not trust God and have chosen to turn away and reject him. Often disgruntled, these people demonstrate characteristics that do not honor the Lord. They exhibit selfishness, arrogance, hatefulness, jealousy, envy, and other abusive behaviors. When people turn from God and let down their guard, Satan finds a way into their souls. He snares unsuspecting and spiritually unhealthy people and throws them into darkness and hell. Sinful ways become the norm for those living far from God.

Always have faith in God. He waits for us to return to him. No one wants a life filled with suffering and pain. God is more powerful than Satan and breaks his hold. Cry out to God. Draw closer to him through prayer. He sharpens our character and energizes us to do the right thing. God provides refuge and strength.

Prepare for troubles now and then. God never promised a carefree life without hardship. Reach out in faith for the gift of forgiveness and mercy. Trust God to rescue us from all distress.

Numbers 6:24-26; Psalm 13:2-6
Point to Ponder: The Lord rescues those who seek him.

Pray: Lord, lead me and build my faith.

March 7

*Be brave and steadfast; have no fear or dread of
them, for it is the LORD, your God, who marches
with you; he will never fail you or forsake you.*
                                   − Deuteronomy 31:6

Many Christians pray multiple times a day. Others turn to God
only during times of trouble and distress. God blesses us every day
even if we do not pray.

Unforeseen events in life may humble us: when death comes
unexpectedly to a loved one, or when we suffer a job loss,
foreclosure on a house, or a diagnosis of a terminal illness. When
loss occurs, we worry and fear the unknown. When there is no
immediate comfort, anxiety abounds, and we forget about the
other blessings and good things remaining. Our troubles rise to the
forefront of our minds; they consume us. We question if God has
forgotten us.

God knows our pain and hurt. Be willing to give back gifts and
blessings from God. Never become so prideful and self-important
that we forget who sends the blessings. God gives us sufficient
strength to take the next steps with him. We have only to ask and
then receive his goodness and mercy. Those who wait for the Lord
and pray grow stronger. Persevere and never give up on God. Be
brave and steadfast. Count on God to bring good out of all situations.
He heals the brokenhearted and gives them peace (Ps. 31:18).

Matthew 9:4; Luke 7:6-7
Point to Ponder: God never forsakes those who love him.

Pray: God, you are my salvation. Hear my prayers. Help me rejoice
for all that remains.

March 8

"For I will forgive their evil doing and
remember their sins no more."

— Hebrews 8:12

Sin seeks to rob us of good things. Evil creeps into our being and
overtakes our souls. We become enslaved and our lives change.
Unable to fulfill God's plan for us or hear his voice, we find
ourselves locked in Satan's clutches. We grow distant from God
and walk in darkness.

Stop, call out to God. Do not allow Satan and his demons to
rob us of our spiritual power from God. He knows when we sin
and incur debts against him. Seek the Lord and ask for forgiveness.
God is merciful.

He cleanses us from all unrighteousness (1 Jn. 1:9). He frees
us from Satan's entanglements. Jesus told his disciples to ask for
forgiveness every time they prayed. We should do the same. God's
grace, mercy, and power abound.

In order for us to be forgiven, we must forgive others who have
sinned against us. Anger rules when we choose not to forgive. Rid
our souls of evil thoughts. Give the anger and resentment to God.

Just as God has mercy so should we. Open our hearts to
God and remember the salvation he won for us on the cross. Our
awareness of the need for forgiveness puts the offenses of others in
their proper light. Ask God to strengthen and relieve us from the
burden of guilt. There is no limit to what God can accomplish.

Psalm 51:4-5; Mark 11:25
Point to Ponder: God is merciful and forgives your sins.

Pray: God, remember me. Have mercy on me. I seek your
forgiveness.

March 9

Fear not, I am with you; be not dismayed; I am
your God. I will strengthen you, and help you,
and uphold you with my right hand of justice.

— Isaiah 41:10

God has promised to never abandon us in times of confusion, fearfulness, and discouragement. He sends us grace and the resources we need to conquer our weaknesses.

When fear takes hold and our faith crumbles, God watches over us. He walks beside us or sometimes carries us when troubles become too difficult to bear. Even when we cannot hear him and prayer does not come easy; he weaves grace into our lives.

God comforts us with his strong presence. He carries us as we journey down the path that passes through dark valleys and horrendous pain. Otherwise, we may find the walk too difficult and give up all hope. During times of grief, we experience his love and compassion in a deeper dimension than ever before.

Aware when we experience difficulty and fear, the Lord sees all our actions. Call on God for direction. Cry out to him or softly whisper his name; he hears us. God heals and rejuvenates our souls. Trust him to show us the way. Believe in God, our refuge and our strength, and fear nothing.

Psalm 23:2-6; John 8:12
Point to Ponder: Have no fear. God is a whisper away.

Pray: Help me, Lord, to trust in the strength of your love.

March 10

God's way is unerring; the LORD'S *promise is tried
and true; he is a shield for all who trust in him.*
— Psalm 18:31

God uses ordinary people to do extra ordinary things. He uses
people with all sorts of gifts, talents, and abilities to advance his
gospel. All of us regardless of race, gender, educational level, or
status can be mightily used by Christ.

Many examples appear in scripture where God chose humble
men and women to testify to his grace. For example, Jesus selected
uneducated men for his disciples and to spread the gospel (Acts
4:13). The Lord sent word to a maiden woman, Mary that she
had been chosen to be the mother of his only Son (Lk.1:38). God
humbled Isaiah, a man of unclean lips, and cleansed him of his
wickedness and sin so he could testify to God's grace at work in
his life and in others (Is. 6:7). He used these humble people in
extraordinary ways.

Think of a favorite biblical character or person from church
history. Before they came to prominence, they were nobodies. God
made them somebodies by his grace.

He cares about our growth in wisdom, knowledge, and
understanding. Do not turn away from God. Instead, ask him for
the resources to perform a daunting task or for the energy to serve
in unfamiliar situations. God leads the way and his blessings follow
in our wake. Watch how God uses us and energizes us for his glory.
Trust his promises and work to build his kingdom on earth.

2 Peter 3:17-18; Isaiah 6:3-10
Point to Ponder: God, never changing, hears your call to serve.

Pray: Here I am, Lord. Use me to glorify you. Keep me in your
loving presence.

March 11

*Lord, who may abide in your tent? Who may
dwell on your holy mountain? Whoever
walks without blame, doing what is right,
speaking truth from the heart.*

— Psalm 15:1-2

We do not understand the mystery of how God chooses each of us
and knows us by name. We accept this by faith. Those who have
strong faith often have a close relationship with God and readily
believe his truths.

God gave us prayer so we would have a way to communicate
with him, encounter him, and listen. Prayer enables us to
experience God more intimately. Our relationship with God
changes as we grow closer to him. The activities he commands
provide opportunities to enhance our love relationship with him.
Take time to be alone with God. Find a place to rest in the stillness
of his love. Time alone with God is not wasted.

Do not get caught up in religious activities which do not praise
and honor God. People go through the actions of worshiping our
Savior by praying, attending church services, or giving an offering
without feeling God in their hearts. Guard against following others
who perform rituals without the Lord being present.

God's presence makes things happen in our lives. Dwell and
pray with him daily. Go out and exclaim to others his goodness and
love. Speak his truths from the heart.

Matthew 18:1-5; 1 Corinthians 6:19-20
Point to Ponder: God resides in your heart.

Pray: Lord, send me grace to live in the fullness of your love.

March 12

Enter the temple gates with praise, its courts with
thanksgiving. Give thanks to God, bless his name.
– Psalm 100:4

Praise God continually for giving us the opportunity to have him live in our thoughts, words, and actions. God frees us from self-centeredness and reorients us to service. Faith in God allows us to experience the world in the light of his presence.

Glorify and give thanks to the Lord. Thankfulness puts us in proper alignment with Christ. The way we interact with others is a direct reflection of our love for him. If we take his name in vain, we show no respect or love for the Almighty. On the other hand, when we act in the name of Jesus, we make him proud and pleased to join in what we accomplish. He watches as we work cooperatively with others, care and teach our children about his unending love, and pray to him unceasingly.

By choosing God as our Savior, we learn to follow his will. Start simply by saying, "Thank you, Jesus." Repeat this throughout the day. Take time to pray multiple times as we go about our business. Simple prayers during the day keep us close to God.

Our supreme desire should be to glorify God by the way we live, giving him thanks and praise joyfully every day. His grace flows to us in ways that transcends our understanding. He loves us deeply and completely.

Psalm 136:1-3; Hebrews 13:15-16
Point to Ponder: Give thanks to God throughout the day in quiet prayer.

Pray: Thank you, God, for the faith planted in me. May your ways be written on my heart.

March 13

And let the peace of Christ control your
hearts, the peace into which you were also
called into one body. And be thankful.

        – Colossians 3:15

Our lives change when we encounter God. He removes impurities from the heart that get in the way of praising him and following his will. It takes a pure heart to have God dwell in the soul. He sends us joy and happiness when our hearts are receptive to his love. Real peace is found only in the presence of God.

He places us where we need to be to serve him and our neighbors. God calls us to be a channel of his loving peace. Put him first. We honor God by being consistent with our behaviors, attitudes, and words. Do not value worldly goods and material riches above the Lord, because they are temporary. The Lord's love and peace are ever-lasting.

Know that the Lord forgives us our sins and pardons us when we repent. He has no anger and instead shows mercy. Trust him to extend a helping hand full of grace. We simply have to ask. God sends abundant blessings to those who believe in him. Our impact has no boundaries when Christ controls our hearts. Pray and receive God's peace.

John 20:19-23; Psalm 32:10-11
Point to Ponder: Give thanks to God. Rejoice in his love and the peace he sends.

Pray: God, let your love burn in my heart. Cleanse my heart and make it pure. Send your joy and peace to me so that I inspire others.

March 14

The Advocate, the holy Spirit that the Father will
send in my name – he will teach you everything
and remind you of all that [I] told you.

– John 14:26

God gives us the Holy Spirit at baptism to dwell within our souls. The Spirit begins the divine work of guiding and teaching as we journey on earth. The fruit of the Spirit: love, joy, peace, patience, kindness, generosity, faithfulness, gentleness, and self-control fills us (Gal. 5:22). We, as children of God, want to demonstrate these traits to others.

The Spirit prompts us to do the right thing. Working all nine traits into our lives may seem challenging and at times impossible. How quickly we adopt these gifts depends on how we live. Be alert to the Holy Spirit's promptings instead of being caught off guard and succumbing to sin.

If we live in sin and disobey the Lord's commandments, we quench the Spirit's activities. Our hearts harden. God's word does not come to mind, and prayers are limited or nonexistent.

Listen to the Holy Spirit's gentle voice, and reflect on the resources and promises God makes to us as his children. The Spirit continues to prompt us to be watchful and attuned to what God has in store for us. He reminds us of God's greatness and helps us grow in righteousness. Listen for the quiet voice from within. Welcome the Holy Spirit and be guided to abundant life.

1 Corinthians 3:16-17; Romans 8:26-27
Point to Ponder: The Holy Spirit is your advocate and a gift from God.

Pray: Holy Spirit, guide me with your counsel and burn in my heart.

March 15

For I know well the plans I have in mind for you,
says the LORD, plans for your welfare, not for
woe! Plans to give you a future full of hope.

— Jeremiah 29:11

God has a plan for us before birth. In his perfect design for our lives, he places his Son in our hearts. He gives us what we need to carry out his assignments and mission to save mankind and build his kingdom.

In the busyness of our daily routines, many people become disoriented to the ways of God and focus on earthly things such as sports, work, and acquiring new possessions and worldly riches. They do not form an intimate relationship with God, a relationship strong enough to withstand all onslaughts.

Satan constantly bombards man. He tries to wear us down and convince us God has turned away. Satan's temptations always look inviting at first. Demons whisper we no longer need God. They suggest we do not turn to God because his plans are too difficult. The evil one wants us to hide from the Lord and take an easier path to acquire riches. Satan's temptations are filled with lies and contrary to God's plan for us.

Stop and pray before acting impulsively. Ponder outcomes. God knows our hearts and waits for us to call out to him. God's power defeats the evil one every time. All things work together to bring about God's perfect plan. Never be separated from God. Reach out to him through prayer.

John 6:40; 2 Corinthians 5:17
Point to Ponder: Follow God's plan. Trust him to send perfect blessings.

Pray: Lord, I want to follow your plan. Give me a future filled with hope.

March 16

Rid yourself of all malice and all deceit,
insincerity, envy, and all slander; like newborn
infants, long for pure spiritual milk so that
through it you may grow into salvation, for
you have tasted that the Lord is good.

— 1 Peter 2:1-3

Be sensitive and aware to the times we live. Keep God as our central focus. This may be difficult for many who find themselves dependent on work, possessions, status, and money to make them feel successful and worthy. Our busyness sometimes keeps us from living in a spiritually healthy state.

Be careful how we handle the gifts and successes God gives us. What we value in life is a window to our hearts. As we enjoy our blessings, keep in mind we are instruments in the Lord's hands. God controls all things. He loves us but may choose at any time to make changes in our lives. Circumstances change in the blink of an eye.

God takes pleasure in worthy sacrifices. It pleases him when we surrender and commit wholeheartedly to doing his work. We belong entirely to God. Seek ways to honor him by giving of our time and serving others. Get to know him through prayer, and look at all the possibilities he puts before us. Then act.

God sees all we do. Nothing separates us from his presence. As we sacrifice and respond to others, we experience a profound joy and security only God sends.

Mathew 6:33; Psalm 119:105-107
Point to Ponder: Seek to be spiritually healthy. Pray often and read scripture.

Pray: Lord, show me how to magnify your life for the benefit of others.

March 17

Be my rock and refuge, my secure stronghold;
for you are my rock and fortress.

– Psalm 71:3

No one is beyond the saving power of God. He created us in his image and made himself human so we might respond to his divinity. He works through us. Listen and hear his call. Christ cares and liberates us so we reach our fullest potential.

He comes to unbind and free us from sin. Do not allow Satan to rob us of our happiness and God's presence in our lives. Sin invades our souls when we let down our guard. Evil spirits take over our thought processes and control our actions. We can never run the race God has planned entrapped in sin.

Grow in virtue by practicing spiritual and moral concepts as written in scripture. These truths are timeless. Build a foundation based on these eternal laws and grow closer to the Lord. Have faith. Stand before God and repent. Seek forgiveness. He is all-powerful and all-knowing, and he sends his grace to untangle the snares of sin. God releases us immediately. Never take God's forgiveness and mercy for granted. He wants us to learn from our mistakes.

Walk in a manner worthy of God's love. Devote time and effort to loving him, helping neighbors, and caring for the less fortunate. When we focus on God's truths, our heavenly Father takes care of everything else. God is the rock of our salvation.

Romans 10:9-12; Acts 22:16
Point to Ponder: God is your rock and your salvation.

Pray: God, I believe in your promises. I choose to rejoice in the blessed life you have given me.

March 18

*Wait for the L*ORD*, take courage; be stouthearted, wait for the L*ORD*!*

— Psalm 27:14

We are people of action in our fast-paced society, moving from one activity to the other without delay. No one likes to wait. We study time management to boost our productivity and prioritize events. We expect things to take place on time, with little thought as to what God has planned. When our schedules are interrupted because of unexpected situations, we become impatient, frustrated, and sometimes angry.

We need to reflect on our level of patience while waiting. Many find waiting difficult. At times in life, we have to wait: in traffic, at a busy restaurant, at the doctor's office, to graduate from high school, to get married, or to have a baby.

Use times of waiting to draw closer to God. This requires training to reframe the situation from one of frustration and impatience to one of focus. Say simple, one sentence prayers such as, "Come to me, Jesus," or "Send me patience, please," or "Help me slow down, Jesus." Practice these prayers and build an arsenal. Make time waiting the most valuable time we have each day.

God is with us every moment even when forced to wait. He cares about our frustrations and teaches us patience. God has perfect timing and a plan full of good for us. Wait for the Lord. He is always worth the wait.

2 Peter 3:9; Isaiah 58:11
Point to Ponder: Wait for the Lord. Learn to be patient.

Pray: God, draw me near to you when I become impatient. Teach me to wait and focus on you with a glad heart.

March 19

For God did not give us a spirit of cowardice,
but rather of power and love and self-control.

— 2 Timothy 1:7

We strive to be a role model for our families and others who seek God. Our Father wants us to serve others rather than be served. He wants us to have humble hearts and serve the poor and needy. God desires us to have self-control. These attributes and activities are difficult, and many in society show indifference to them.

We observe individuals who hold powerful jobs. These people may be friends, neighbors, well-known athletes, actors, or television personalities. They seem to have self-control and everything going for them. But do not be fooled by outward appearances. Some of these people hurt inside, have little hope, or feel inferior. They hide their real personalities and have accepted their false image as one that others want to see. Their fame and status belong to this world. Earthly riches, money, and position cannot buy them a place in heaven.

God created us in his image and guides us as we build character. He desires that we live righteous lives. The Holy Spirit guides us (Jn. 14:26). He wants us to experience and demonstrate love, kindness, generosity, peacefulness, and self-control.

Seek a closer walk with God. Pray for his presence to be powerfully real. He sends us grace and the resources needed to live righteously. Stay connected to God through prayer, praise, and worship.

1 Corinthians 9:24-27; Proverbs 25:28
Point to Ponder: Say yes to God's plan to send love and teach you self-control.

Pray: God, I want to have self-control and live a righteous life. Help me.

March 20

God will rescue you from the fowler's snare,
from the destroying plague, Will shelter you with
pinions, spread wings that you may take refuge;
God's faithfulness is a protecting shield.

— Psalm 91:3-4

When challenges weigh us down and we face worries and doubts, be still and pray. Take time to find the Lord, our great intercessor, in the midst of all the confusion. He fights for us and protects us from evil.

The temptation to sin is powerful when frustration and confusion abound. Satan is powerful and lures us into his realm of evil. He makes the pathway to sin look enticing and easy. We forget his ways turn us away from God. When we sin, we are not in union with God. Our relationship falters, and his goodness is snatched from us.

Jesus walked before us and faced troubled times. He experienced hunger and poverty and the temptations of Satan when he walked on earth. Rejected and shunned, he understood suffering and the pain of persecution, but he was without sin. Nothing happens to us that God does not understand.

God is faithful. When we confess our sins, he cleanses us and forgives us every time. He does not keep tally of our sins or our lack of faithfulness. Pray and ask God for assistance. Cling to faith. Call out to God no matter how difficult our suffering. Divine power flows from him. He offers his strength and mercy to his children. Grip the guiding hand others may not see. Hold tight, be steadfast, and believe God's presence is a protective shield.

1 Thessalonians 5:14-15; Hebrews 9:24-28
Point to Ponder: Be faithful to God. He protects you.

Pray: God, hold my hand. I want to be your constant companion.

March 21

But now you must put them all away: anger, fury,
malice, slander, and obscene language out of
your mouths. Stop lying to one another, since you
have taken off the old self with its practices and
have put on the new self, which is being renewed,
for knowledge, in the image of its creator.

— Colossians 3:8-10

The Holy Spirit guides us and helps us eliminate sinful ways.
When we ask God for forgiveness, our impurities are removed.
God invites us to become involved in his work and follow his ways.
Walking closely with the Lord, guarantees we are right where he
wants us to be. We can seek his will in all situations.

The disciples followed Jesus and stayed by his side. His ways
became their ways. They asked questions but followed willingly.
They did not worry about where they would travel next. The future
held no concern because they knew God would provide for them
every day, all day.

God is pleased when we seek him each day. He wants to be a
part of our lives. Pray the Lord's Prayer daily (Mt. 6:9-13). When
we pray, focus on "your will be done, on earth as in heaven." We
need endurance to follow the will of God.

Pray, "Here I am Lord. Where will you lead me today?" In
order for us to know God's will, cultivate a relationship with him.
Be alert. Listen closely for his voice. He does not hide his will.
When we follow God's plan for us, we witness things happening in
our lives only explained by his powerful presence.

Matthew 6:9-13; James 4:15
Point to Ponder: God renews you to imitate his ways.

Pray: Lord, teach me to recognize your voice. Open my heart.

March 22

But without faith it is impossible to please him, for
anyone who approaches God must believe that he
exits and that he rewards those who seek him.

— Hebrews 11:6

Our relationship with God must have a foundation of faith. When we pray, believe in God Almighty as revealed to us in the Bible. God responds when we earnestly seek him.

The mystery of faith is God. Follow his ways and teachings. No excuses. Build faith in God, realizing that faith does not eliminate problems. We face challenges in our daily walk with God. Faith keeps us in a trusting relationship. With strong faith, we know God is in the midst of our problems. He never abandons us or lets us fall from his grace.

Faith has to do with our relationship with God, not our situation or trials. Fashion a life filled with faith, love, and many good works. God knows our hearts. He is in our midst when we experience real joy and peace as well as frustration and impatience. Trust him to be with us every moment of our day and live in harmony with him. Be persistent in prayer. Place our faith in God and then strive to please him by our ready obedience. God rewards those who are faithful. Our faith matters when we go out to be "doers of the word and not hearers only" (Jas. 1:22). Honor God. Develop great faith in his ways to lead a righteous life. Build his kingdom on earth.

Psalm 119:108-112; Psalm 16:9-11
Point to Ponder: Grow in faith each day. Honor God.

Pray: God, strengthen me to be more faithful. Clarify your plan for me.

March 23

They that hope in the L<small>ORD</small> will renew their strength,
they will soar as with eagles wings; they will run
and not grow weary, walk and not grow faint.
                                        – Isaiah 40:31

Sometimes we feel worn out and exhausted from the busyness of work, taking care of family and other tasks which require our time and energy. At times, in the rush to mark off tasks, we pace ourselves to race ahead of God. We forget to wait for him. We focus on meeting self-imposed demands. When we feel stressed and rushed to the point of exhaustion, pause and find a few minutes to pray. Evaluate our activities and pray for guidance. Ask God for the strength to move forward at a more realistic pace. Do everything for the glory of God (1 Cor. 10:31).

When we pray, we cease our own pursuits and turn our attention to God. Be patient, slow down, and watch for God's response. He shows us what to do and what resources we need. Ask him to renew our tired minds and cluttered hearts. God sends hope and encouragement, and whispers words we most need to hear. Give worries to God and rest in his love. Our problems fade in significance as God's love and grace give us renewed strength to carry-on.

James 1:16-17; 1 John 14-15
Point to Ponder: God renews your energy and calms your soul.

Pray: Lord, I open my heart to you. Whisper the words I need to hear. Slow my pace so I hear your voice and follow your plan.

March 24

I give you a new commandment: love
one another. As I have loved you, so
you also should love one another.

— John 13:34

God's love endures forever and has no limits. God wants us to
love our neighbors (Rom. 13:8-10). Love assumes the best about
others. When someone offends us, do we immediately seek revenge
instead of choosing to believe the offense might be unintentional?
Do we judge others by how they look – by their race, gender,
religion, or homeland? Do our friends and relatives know they can
do foolish things and make mistakes, and yet we still love them?

No one who knows God's love should say, "I don't have that
kind of love in me." When negative thoughts enter our minds, turn
back to God for guidance. Whisper his name. Draw closer to him
for strength. The love we feel for others may not be perfect at first,
but our hearts soften. We grow to be more accepting if we practice
and imitate God's love. Our actions should always honor him.

Ask God for understanding in regard to unconditional love. He
teaches us. Only God who created us, who knows us completely,
shows us how to love unconditionally. Hold onto Christ. He shows
us repeatedly how much he loves us. God sends us forth in his
image as his disciples. We are never separated from his love.

Romans 13:8-10; Luke 6:35
Point to Ponder: Practice loving one another.

Pray: Lord, may I seek to love others as you love me.

March 25

*All scripture is inspired by God and is useful
in teaching, for refutation, for correction,
and for training in righteousness, so that
one who belongs to God may be competent,
equipped for every good work.*

— 2 Timothy 3:16-17

God's word goes out and never fails to accomplish his will. We cheat ourselves if we do not access, study, and act in accordance with his word. The Bible references God's desires for us and his commandments. We find direction and answers in scripture.

Become an avid reader of the Bible. Every verse is important. None should be skipped especially those verses that convict us to walk with God daily. Read with a holy expectation, listening for the life-changing words God has for us. Practice God's teachings. Times may be different now, but we still apply scripture in our lives. By reading, we learn what God expects of a righteous person. Scripture equips us to do good work and walk in the ways of the Lord.

As we fill our minds with truths from the Bible and as we obey his instructions, God guides us through all our trials and tribulations. His word transforms us. We grow in righteousness. With growing knowledge of God's ways, we better understand and find the wisdom we need to carry out his plans for us. With an open heart and mind, embrace God's word today.

Joshua 1:8; 2 Thessalonians 2:15
Point to Ponder: All scripture is inspired by God. Encounter him in the Bible.

Pray: Teach me and guide me, Lord. Help me grow in wisdom and knowledge.

March 26

The name of the LORD is a strong tower;
the just man runs to it and is safe.

— Proverbs 18:10

At any time, call on the name of the Lord and be heard. Give thanks and praise to him for considering us his children and fellow heirs to his kingdom. We are not his equal. He is God Almighty and we are not. Seek to imitate his ways.

When we enter church, we may encounter God. There is no guarantee. We walk on holy ground and rest in a safe place. Most people still their hearts and receive God and his messages in the peace and quiet of church. Ask him to cleanse our hearts.

The Holy Spirit guides us and instills a proper reverence for the Lord. Worshiping God and having the freedom to attend church are privileges we should seize with gratitude. Treasure our prayer time with God. Seek his peace. Meditate on his goodness and mercy, and his awesome holiness. Set our hearts on loving God. He leads us to live righteously. Give him thanks and praise.

The true quality of our prayers rest within us. God hears our prayers and answers them in his time, not our time. He gives us what we need even if the answer is not what we imagined. Be in his presence and feel safe. God is a whisper away.

Psalm 11:4-7; John 3:21
Point to Ponder: God provides a safe haven. Spend time worshiping him.

Pray: God, you are my strength. Keep me safe and secure in your love.

March 27

Merciful and gracious is the Lord, slow to
anger, abounding in kindness. God does
not always rebuke, nurses no lasting anger,
has not dealt with us as our sins merit,
nor requited us as our deeds deserve.

— Psalm 103:8-10

Hope in the Lord's steadfast love. He sends blessings every day. Some people do not realize where all the goodness in their lives comes from; they are content with life and feel they need little help from God. They merely take these acts of goodness, God's blessings, and material success for granted. Some only seek God when things do not go as they want. They receive God's love and kindness and answered prayers without knowing the provider.

Others see God's miracles and daily blessings. They want to get to know him intimately and grow closer to him. Believers open their hearts to God and communicate their needs to him. They are thankful and praise his name. He has promised them everlasting love and compassionate treatment.

Have hope in the Lord our God and seek him in all circumstances. Allow him to guide and be our strength every day. He blesses us with his nearness and never forsakes us. Persevere in hope of Christ's perfect love and abounding kindness. Thank him. Praise him. Worship him. Give Christ our lives today because he gave himself to us by death on a cross. Rejoice in his mercy and love.

Psalm 71:5-6; Psalm 33:18-22
Point to Ponder: Give thanks to your gracious God.

Pray: God, I want to stay in your guiding light. I need your perfect love and kindness.

March 28

Love is patient, love is kind. It is not jealous,
love is not pompous, it is not inflated. It is not
rude, it does not seek its own interests, it is not
quick-tempered, it does not brood over injury,
it does not rejoice over wrongdoing but rejoices
with the truth. It bears all things, believes all
things, hopes all things, endures all things.

— 1 Corinthians 13:4-7

Never lose hope in those we love. Many different kinds of love exist: love for a child, for a spouse, for country, for freedom, and love of God. All love comes with sacrifices and compromise.

Sometimes we find that people who hurt us are difficult to love. We want to turn away from them and not forgive their transgressions. We hold a grudge. God wants us to respond differently. Though difficult, God desires us to forgive and be merciful, and love our neighbors.

Realize that we all make mistakes. Be patient and allow God time to teach and discipline those who stray from his word. Do not be quick to anger or to judge. Turn burdens over to God. Allow his loving touch to heal.

Spend time with the Lord in prayer every day, listen to his voice while reading scripture, and experience his presence. Seek God's transforming grace. Rejoice! His love endures forever.

Psalm 118:4; 1 John 3:1
Point to Ponder: God never runs out of love. His love has no barriers.

Pray: God, teach me to love as you do. Your love is never-ending and perfect in every way.

March 29

Like golden apples in silver settings are
words spoken at the proper time.

— Proverbs 25:11

God wants us to minister to those he sends us. He directs us to be kind and utter encouraging words. When others need us we sometimes become tongue-tied and cannot find words to comfort those who suffer. We falter and cannot retrieve words that lessen the burden or lead the individual to God. We become keenly aware of our weaknesses.

At these times, pause and ask God why he put this person in our lives. Pray and listen. Allow God to help us see beyond the material needs of a person. Look for what he wants to accomplish in this individual. He chooses us deliberately. Act with guidance from the Holy Spirit. These actions may take us out of our comfort zone.

Sit quietly with the needy person and witness his pain and suffering. Pray together and remember sometimes our messages to those suffering are spoken through our actions instead of words. These acts of kindness give immeasurable comfort to the needy person.

Spiritual depth and maturity do not come without constant effort. Our relationship with God makes us want to understand his truths. God teaches us to become more Christ-like in our ways and have a deeper dependence on him. He resides in the deepest depths of our being in union with the Holy Spirit. Rejoice in his loving presence deep within our souls. He gives us courage to speak the gospel and hold out a helping hand to others at the proper time. Trust God.

Psalm 118:17; Mark 16:20
Point to Ponder: Words spoken at the proper time heal and give comfort.

Pray: God, direct me in your ways. Teach me to share words of comfort.

March 30

But as for me, I will look to the Lord, I will put my
trust in God my savior; my God will hear me!

— Micah 7:7

God seeks a real and personal encounter with us. Sometimes this encounter is an invitation to follow him. We seek him and desire his love and compassion. Listen, watch, and feel God's presence. Never turn away from him.

Continually cultivate our hearts and minds so they are receptive to God. Prepare for and welcome his powerful presence. When we open our hearts to him, we are never the same. We experience a complete change in our minds and our behavior. We are transformed.

To draw closer to God, read the Bible. Ponder the words and reflect on how to apply the information. Pray for understanding. Then, attend church, hear others worshiping God, and join in the singing and praise. Be open to receive his fresh messages. Wait in hopeful anticipation. Serving God and carrying out his mission lead us to him.

When called by God to follow him, we realize his holiness and great strength. A sense of peace prevails and a confident expectation of how God might choose to use us evolves. He transforms us to reflect his character. We find ourselves being more joyful, peaceful, loving, kind, generous, faithful, and in control. By his grace, we become imitators as he performs his divine work in our lives.

1 Corinthians 11:1-2; 1 Peter 2:20-21
Point to Ponder: Place your trust in God.

Pray: Here I am, Lord. Help me follow you. Build my trust.

March 31

*Do to others whatever you would have them
do to you. This is the law and the prophets.*

— Matthew 7:12

Say yes to God and allow him to make our hearts receptive to his word. The purity of our hearts will determine our faithfulness. If our hearts are troubled and struggles abound, we are not attuned to God. We may read or hear his words, but they do not penetrate our souls. Our earthly issues get in the way of acting in a righteous manner.

The condition of our hearts varies depending on our closeness to the Lord. He knows when we are weary and when our strength runs low. He sees our lack of patience and our desire to throw up our hands and walk away from difficult situations. God wants us to repent our bitterness, anger, and non-belief so that our hearts are open to his teachings.

How do we soften our hearts to treat others better? Ask God to be with us every moment each day. Pray for his guidance. Read the Bible and ponder his word. Act on God's messages. Give thanks when God works through us and we sense his hope, peace, and conviction. He remains our companion in joy and in sorrow. He softens our hearts and fills us with love.

Our yes to God unleashes a tidal wave of grace to those around us. We find ourselves treating others with love, kindness, and patience. We follow the Golden Rule: Do to others whatever you would have them do to you.

Psalm 46:9-11; Philippians 4:1
Point to Ponder: Treat others with love and kindness.

Pray: God, take my hand. Lead me. I trust you to show me the way to righteousness.

April 1

Finally, all of you, be of one mind, sympathetic,
loving toward one another, compassionate, humble.
Do not return evil for evil, or insult for insult; but,
on the contrary, a blessing, because to this you
were called, that you might inherit a blessing.

— 1 Peter 3:8-9

Seek unity with God and honor him. Scripture states each of us will give an account of himself to God (Mt. 14:12). He gives us free will to follow his teachings. The Lord sits in judgment upon us. This should motivate us to please him with our words, actions, and deeds.

Fashion a life filled with kindness and gentleness, love, generosity, patience, and righteousness. We do not have to be perfect, but we need to be persistent with our character. Strive to be compassionate, sympathetic, and humble. Lend a helping hand. God treats us with the same grace or severity with which we treat others.

Being in union with God requires hard work. Seek physical and emotional strength from him. Whisper brief prayers throughout the day, "Show me your way, Jesus," or "Show me what you would do."

Pleasing God is important and a barometer for happiness. Make sacrifices in order to be obedient and follow his will. When we stand in front of God and give an account of our lives, his judgment matters more than anything else. Dare to live the way God desires, confident of salvation and eternal life with him.

2 Corinthians 5:6-19; John 3:11-15
Point to Ponder: Live a righteous life and inherit blessings from God.

Pray: Unite me in your peace, God. Give me the grace I need to persevere.

April 2

Indeed, the word of God is living and
effective, sharper than any two-edged sword,
penetrating even between soul and spirit,
joints and marrow, and able to discern
reflections and thoughts of the heart.

– Hebrews 4:12

God sends blessings to us. We are a new creation each day, loved and cherished by him. Sometimes God's words fill us with joy and affirmation. At other times, they cause us discomfort. He knows our needs and speaks to us in different ways. His messages come to us through: reading scripture, listening to sermons at church, gazing at a picture, repetitive words in a song, or through the voices of friends, and the promptings of the Holy Spirit.

We believers may feel anxious and inept before encountering God. Afterward, we have a sense of hope, peace, and conviction. God's timing is always perfect. Do not try to escape, hide, or avoid hearing him speak. He waits for us with patient arms open for comfort. We have a responsibility to make the connection between our lives and what God expects from us. Above all, God wants us to return to him and love with pure hearts.

Learn to discern his voice. Choose to uphold the truths in the Bible. Trust God to mold us into his likeness and meet the needs in our lives that only he can. Refuse God nothing. Do everything through love and for his glory. He sends his grace to those who serve him. Stay connected through prayer.

Proverbs 28:26; 1 Corinthians 1:25
Point to Ponder: Believe in the word of God.

Pray: God, open my heart and teach me to love and grow in wisdom.

April 3

*He said to them, "Why are you terrified, O you
of little faith?" Then he got up, rebuked the
winds and the sea, and there was great calm.*
— Matthew 8:26

When Jesus lived on earth, he often taught his disciples by
performing miracles. For example, we have the following accounts:
the calming of the storm at sea (Mk. 4:35-41), when people
witnessed Jesus healing a woman with a hemorrhage (Mt. 9:20-
22), and cleansing the ten lepers (Lk. 17:11-19), and raising Lazarus
from the dead (Jn. 11:38-43).

Jesus expected his disciples to adjust their lives, be obedient,
and live according to his teachings. He taught them to trust him
implicitly. Despite demonstrating his miraculous power, the
disciples did not realize who Jesus was. Their faith was challenged.
Followers of Christ still have difficulty today.

At times we doubt, and our faith falters. We grow weary and lose
heart. We pray, but answers to our prayers do not come quickly. We
forget God provides according to his plan and brings good from all
things. He answers our prayers in his time according to our needs.

We do not understand God's ways. Often when we work on
one thing, God is doing something else in our hearts, creating
something new we cannot recognize until time passes. Hold fast
to faith and look to God first. Have confidence in his plan for us.
Practice his truths and do not fear the outcomes. We get answers
when God wills them. He blesses us with goodness, grace, and
love. God sends exactly what we need.

Psalm 34:9; Mark 16:17-18
Point to Ponder: Have faith in God. Trust his timing.

Pray: God, fill me with faith. Anchor my soul in your love.

April 4

*One thing I ask of the L*ORD*; this I seek: To dwell*
*in the L*ORD*'s house all the days of my life, To*
*gaze on the L*ORD*'s beauty, to visit his temple.*
— Psalm 27:4

What requirements are placed on us to be assured a place in heaven and dwell with the Lord forever? First, trust God in every situation and do not rely on human strength. Sometimes we get over confident, and feel we have the knowledge and strength to solve any problem. God has a way of humbling us and bringing us back to trust him. His power and knowledge far surpasses any human strength. Second, seek the favor of God at all times. Turn to him in prayer. Spend time in his presence to strengthen our relationship with him. He speaks to us through scripture and songs, through words from friends and our pastor, and through the Holy Spirit who dwells within us. Listen for him.

Surrender to the Lord. Depend on his strength to make all things good through our weakness. He controls all things on earth and in heaven. Ask God to cleanse our hearts and souls. Have no regrets as we follow his will. Trust him to show us the path to eternal life. Those who do the will of the Lord remain forever in his light and dwell in his house forever.

James 1:5-8; 2 Corinthians 12:9
Point to Ponder: Fix your eyes on the Lord. Follow him.

Pray: God, help me listen closely to your voice. Thank you for the gift of prayer to keep me close to you so I follow your truths.

April 5

Happy those whom you guide, LORD,
whom you teach by your instruction.

– Psalm 94:12

Call upon the Lord often throughout the day, especially when troubled. This gives God an opportunity to guide us as we draw closer to him. Build a relationship with God based on love, obedience, and trust. If he never allowed us to experience need, people around us would have little chance to witness God's provision in our lives. They might ascertain we do not need God's intervention. Christians believe God is everywhere at all times, working on our behalf.

Pride might tempt us to act without seeking God's assistance, but be on guard. Self-sufficiency hinders our ability to see God in the midst of a situation. Do not allow pride to take what rightfully belongs to God. Be humble and give thanks through prayer for all of his gifts and blessings.

Pray often and wait for God to instruct us in his ways as he works through us. Trust him to send the resources we need to face any circumstance.

Give God the glory he deserves. At times we may find communication with God dulled, but strive to be grateful for lessons learned through hardships. Lean on him. Realize God calls us to do something special with our lives and talents. We have direct access to him. Bask in God's presence and rejoice in his love.

Proverbs 21:11; James 1:22-25
Point to Ponder: God is your guide and protector.

Pray: God, instruct me in your ways. Build my faith to trust you in every situation.

April 6

*Now the Lord is the Spirit, and where the Spirit
of the Lord is, there is freedom. All of us, gazing
with unveiled face on the glory of the Lord, are
being transformed into the same image from glory
to glory, as from the Lord who is the Spirit.*
— 2 Corinthians 3:17-18

The Spirit dwells within our souls and is always teaching and showing us how to have pure hearts. He helps us find hope and stay close to God. Our bodies are the temple of the Holy Spirit. The Spirit is a gift from God, one in being with the Father and the Son. He guides us to do the right thing and honor God through our actions.

When sin enters our being and we act against God's truths, pause and pay attention to the promptings of the Holy Spirit. Trust the Spirit when things get confusing. Disobedience angers the Lord. His anger is aimed against our behaviors, not against our hearts. The Spirit teaches us how to untangle the web of destruction and sinfulness.

Many people live in darkness and sin. They do not know which way to turn. Some corrupt their temples and do not heed the promptings from the Spirit.

Reach out to those who are hurting, beginning with family and friends, and show them how to encounter God. Help others so they experience his love, grace, compassion, and guidance, not his wrath. Rely on the Holy Spirit to make our lives extraordinary. God has abundant treasures to share. He is always on our side.
John 14:26; Ephesians 1:13-14
Point to Ponder: The Holy Spirit is God within your soul.

Pray: God, restore me to joy and wholeness. Guide me toward your light.

April 7

Happy those who observe God's decrees,
*who seek the L*ORD *with all their heart. They*
do no wrong; they walk in God's ways.

— Psalm 119:2-3

God gave us the Ten Commandments, through Moses on Mount Sinai, to show us our need for him to teach us his ways. In summary, the Ten Commandments follow: you shall not have other gods besides me; you shall not carve idols for yourselves; you shall not take the name of the Lord your God, in vain. Remember to keep holy the Sabbath day. Honor your father and your mother. You shall not kill. You shall not commit adultery. You shall not steal. You shall not bear false witness against your neighbor. You shall not covet (Ex. 20:1-17).

Review and follow the Ten Commandments – no excuses. God wants to form us into a people who instinctively follow his commands. He asks us to be kind, loving, generous, and merciful. Christ hears what we say and observes our actions. He judges our habits and our hearts. We have no place to hide from him.

The Bible is inspired by God. Scripture comes alive and transforms us. Reading, reflecting, and following God's word develops our spiritual instincts. The more scripture we have in our minds, the more grace God gives us. Strive to understand God's teachings and his commandments. Walk in his ways. He works through us to build his kingdom.

Exodus 20:1; Proverbs 2:1-5
Point to Ponder: Read and meditate on Bible passages and the Ten Commandments.

Pray: Lord, send me courage to follow the Ten Commandments and receive your blessings.

April 8

So submit yourself to God. Resist the devil, and
he will flee from you. Draw near to God, and he
will draw near to you. Cleanse your hands, you
sinners, and purify your hearts, you of two minds.
– James 4:7-8

There may be times when God seems far away. When we feel distant from God, we fail to self-evaluate and question our behaviors and attitudes. Ask ourselves whether we have lost God as our focus; or has Satan entered our being and separated us from him? Are we searching for a quick fix? How often do we pause and pray?

God does not change; he remains the same yesterday, today, and tomorrow (Heb. 13:8). We change. Sometimes we get caught up in the busyness of life, and we forget to be still long enough to pray. We do not worship the Lord as we should. Sometimes he takes a back seat to other worldly activities, and we forget about him. We become so enthralled with material riches that we find ourselves worshiping worldly things. We strive to please ourselves and impress others. Christ is no longer central in our lives.

God gently disciplines us. He allows us to tremble to remind us of our limitations and need for him. He warns us we cannot have two masters. We cannot put earthly treasures or money before him. God humbles us. Pray and ask him to unravel the ties which bind us.

Make certain our attitudes and motives are right in God's eyes and in harmony with his commandments. Seek him first above all else. Grow in faith and receive his abundant love.

Psalm 145:18; 1 Timothy 6:18
Point to Ponder: Love the Lord. Seek him throughout the day.

Pray: God, thank you for the countless times you have forgiven my sins. Keep me close to you.

April 9

Since the LORD, your God, is a merciful
God, he will not abandon and destroy
you, nor forget the covenant which under
oath he made with your fathers.

– Deuteronomy 4:31

Christ wants us to imitate him. Though it is difficult at times, follow his example and show mercy to others and forgive them. Take one step at a time to control thoughts. Practice reframing biases so we do not judge and condemn people. Come to God with contrite hearts and allow the Holy Spirit to work freely within us.

Practice forgiving others. God desires we hold no bitterness and grudges. Jesus spoke to his disciples at the Sermon on the Mount and told them to forgive others their transgressions, and God would forgive them. But if they did not forgive others, neither would the Father forgive.

Forgiveness does not come easily for most people when the hurt runs deep. Remember that we are all sinners. We have been freed of sin through God's love and mercy. He died to pay the penalty for our sins.

Mercy is a gift and often not deserved. If not for God's mercy, we would be punished each time we sin. God does not let us bear the full punishment we deserve when we sin. Honor him and be merciful. He smiles on our efforts and knows our hearts.

1 Peter 1:3; Matthew 5:7
Point to Ponder: God is merciful. Imitate his ways.

Pray: God, teach me to forgive others as you have forgiven me. Have mercy on me.

 April 10

Do not store up for yourselves treasures on
earth, where moth and decay destroy, and thieves
break in and steal. But store up treasures in
heaven, where neither moth nor decay destroy,
nor thieves break in and steal. For where your
treasure is, there also will your heart be.
— Matthew 6:19-21

What do we treasure? Do we value and treasure our status at work, our position? Do we treasure a beautiful family and material riches? Do we attempt to impress God with all we do for him and his church?

Sometimes we become too enamored with our own plans and achievements. We never set a goal so big or attempt a task so significant that God does not have something far greater he could do in and through our lives.

Be in constant contact with God. Find a quiet place and pray. Have communication with him and always listen. He sees the big picture. God's power far exceeds our limited imagination. He calls us according to his plan, not our plans.

Be willing to put aside our agenda and dreams. Follow God's plan, and witness things happening in our lives only explained by his awesome presence. Seek God's guidance every day. Stay in close contact with him. He guides and protects us. When we keep our hearts fixed on the Lord, we find abundant treasures. He graces our lives with blessings of love, peace, and deliverance.

Peter 3:15; Psalm 66:8-9
Point to Ponder: Store up treasures from God.

Pray: God, guide me and teach me your ways. I trust you.

April 11

For thus says the Lord God; I myself will
look after and tend my sheep. As a shepherd
tends his flock when he finds himself among
his scattered sheep, so will I tend my sheep. I
will rescue them from every place where they
were scattered when it was cloudy and dark.
— Ezekiel 34:11-12

Sometimes we succumb to Satan's temptations. When our hearts harden toward God because of sin, stop and reflect. Are we tired of living with vengeance, retribution, and anger? Do we want to mend our ways and not allow sin to break or weaken our relationship with God? If we answered yes, repent and seek God's forgiveness.

When we ask, God stands ready to forgive and release us from guilt and sin. He separates us from the influences destroying us. Seek the ability to hear him more clearly. He cleanses our hearts of evil and wrongdoing. His grace builds our devotion to him. He never wants us to fail, but instead become faithful followers. The more we imitate Christ, the more we experience hope and love.

Remain with the Lord. He protects us from evil. He pours his love into our hearts offering his grace, forgiveness, and peace. His face shines upon us, beaming out love. Walk with God, dwell in his love, and do not fear the future. Experience life enveloped in his care one day at a time. God eases our burdens and carries them for us if the weight gets too heavy to bear. Follow God and find joy in our hearts.

Romans 5:1-2; Psalm 50:22-23
Point to Ponder: God rescues you from sin.

Pray: God, shelter me from all evil.

April 12

Praise the Lord, all you nations! Give glory, all
you peoples! The Lord's love for us is strong;
the Lord is faithful forever. Hallelujah!

— Psalm 117:1-2

We worship God and sing hymns of praise to him. The quality of our worship is not based on our activities but on our character. God responds to those who follow him by cleansing our hearts and teaching us how to live righteously. He graces us with his love. He guides us away from sin so our lives are not burdensome and filled with stress and confusion.

Today, many people believe external trappings enhance our worship. People mistakenly assume churches that have better music, an impressive building, and dynamic speakers are superior and provide a more spiritual experience. If our relationship with God is not healthy, these things have little influence and are nothing more than religious pageantry. Attending a religious service does not guarantee an encounter with God, especially if our hearts and minds are not open to him.

Commit to prayer as a priority. Be still and thank God for the blessings he sends. Let his voice penetrate our hearts. Listen and wait for his guidance. Read scripture and apply the messages to our daily activities. Let him fill us with confidence so we go out and tell others about his love, his peace, and his kingdom. The Lord remains with us, faithful in his love. Praise him so his presence within us becomes stronger. When we do this, we grow closer to God.

Proverbs: 9:10; Matthew 9:5-8
Point to Ponder: God loves you unconditionally.

Pray: Lord, take away my insecurities and give me courage to tell others of your goodness.

April 13

But you will receive power when the Holy
Spirit comes upon you, and you will be my
witnesses in Jerusalem, throughout Judea
and Samaria, and to the ends of the earth.

– Acts 1:8

Jesus empowers us through the Holy Spirit. The Spirit is the love of God within our souls. Jesus told his disciples to remain in Jerusalem until the Holy Spirit came upon them. When he did, they became new people – courageous, zealous, and ready to die for Jesus. The Spirit told the disciples to carry the Gospel to every nation and gave them the ability to speak in different languages (Acts 2:4). In preparation, the disciples prayed and followed their hearts to tell everyone about the glory of God.

Discern God's voice and realize the impossible is possible. Be moved by scripture. We do this through prayer, church attendance, reading the Bible, and speaking God's word. We become like the first disciples. God sends us where we need to be, at the time we need to be there, and gives us the right words to use to tell others about his kingdom.

Adjust prayers to be more aligned to God's plan, which is extremely personal and exactly what we need. The fullness of God dwells within each person. He invites us to join him in working out the details of our lives. God wants us to stay close, listen, and open our hearts wide to family and neighbors so they encounter him. Follow the promptings of the Holy Spirit to receive God's love and peace.

John 16:13; Proverbs 10:22
Point to Ponder: The Holy Spirit guides and protects you.

Pray: God, please open my eyes and my heart to fill me with the Holy Spirit.

April 14

Have no anxiety at all, but in everything, by
prayer and petition, with thanksgiving, make
your request known to God. Then the peace
of God that surpasses all understanding will
guard your hearts and minds in Christ Jesus.

– Philippians 4:6-7

God cares for us at all times. We are his children. As such, he wants to be close to us no matter our situation. Some envision our journey on earth as a swing through luminous events and sorrowful ones. They see life as a roller coaster ride, filled with ups and downs. Others seem to coast along in calm seas. No matter where our journey takes us, God dwells within our souls. His gifts of peace and love spill over into our relationships with each other.

When circumstances occur that are out of our control and feel burdensome, we often lose hope and feel trampled and alone. Whenever we face difficulties or experience injustice, find a quiet place and pray. Focus on God. He understands our troubled hearts, and waits to be our refuge. Stay close to him. Pray without ceasing (1 Thes. 5:17). Talk to God as a friend.

Feel the Lord ease our burdens as he answers our prayers. Feel strength return as he energizes us. God may not take our troubles away, but he helps us carry our burdens. He gives us peace beyond our understanding. Nothing is too difficult, too troubling, or too fearful for God. Let his peace reign in our hearts for all eternity.

Psalm 62:6-9; Matthew 11:28
Point to Ponder: God's peace and love is available to everyone.

Pray: God, I trust you. Never allow me to be separated from your love.

April 15

The Lord's *throne is established in heaven;*
God's royal power rules over all.

— Psalm 103:19

Heaven is real. God created heaven and the earth. Some wonder what heaven looks like. We read about heaven in the Bible: "Then the angel showed me the river of life-giving water, sparkling like crystal, flowing from the throne of God and of the Lamb down the middle of its streets. On either side of the river grew the tree of life that produces fruit twelve times a year...Night will be no more, nor will they need light from lamp or sun, for the Lord God shall give them light, and they shall reign forever and ever" (Rev. 22:1-5). Heaven has a beauty beyond our imagination.

Not everyone goes to heaven and experiences God's eternal presence. Those not worthy, go to hell. Heaven holds no sin, no sickness, no anger, and no hurt. Love abounds.

God calls his children to be with him in heaven. He desires us to live righteous lives and always worship him, practice and obey the Ten Commandments, and imitate God's great works while on earth. When we stand before God face-to-face on judgment day, we dwell in the midst of God and his Son, Jesus Christ, in perfect fellowship. His glory will be revealed in its fullness in heaven. No one on earth has ever seen the ecstasy of an unhindered view of God. Those who love and serve him dwell in heaven for all eternity with him.

Revelation 21:1-8, 18-19, 21; Luke 23:43
Point to Ponder: Seek eternal life in heaven with God.

Pray: Save me, Lord. Open my heart to be touched and transformed by your presence. Call me to heaven.

April 16

*In my misfortune I called, the L*ORD *heard*
and saved me from all distress.

– Psalm 34:7

People suffer loneliness, sickness, pain, and regret at times. How we react to these issues is based on our understanding of God's saving grace and our relationship with him.

God sent his only Son, Jesus, to walk the earth as a man. Jesus suffered the full brunt of temptation, pain, and death. He humbled himself, taking all the characteristics of human flesh. Jesus felt tired, hurt physically, thirsted, and had little food in order to experience all the limitations we have – yet he was without sin. He experienced the struggles of living a righteous life and the difficulties of resisting Satan's temptations. He suffered greatly on the cross and died a painful death so our sins would be forgiven.

Through Christ, we have been given the Holy Spirit who dwells in our souls and guides us in our decisions. Call out to the Spirit. Be still and listen for his voice throughout the day in prayer, in the words of a friend, in our conscience, or out of the blue. Be receptive to the promptings of the Spirit.

Choose not to dwell on past mistakes or struggles but instead, focus on the present. Refuse to be discouraged. Wait for God with hopeful anticipation of what he will do. We find our struggles do not seem so overbearing when we trust God. Pray for an open and humble heart. God sends peace and renewed strength to those who believe.

1 Peter 3:18; Hebrews 12:1-5
Point to Ponder: God saves you from all distress.

Pray: God, thank you for the Holy Spirit who guides and protects me. The Spirit works freely in my soul.

April 17

*Many are the plans in a man's heart, but it
is the decision of the Lord that endures.*

– Proverbs 19:21

We make important decisions and plans every day. When we pray
to God and listen and wait expectantly, rest assured he sends us
the strength and courage to move forward. He gives personally and
individually because of his great love for us.

Sometimes we make snap decisions when tasks appear easy.
We fail to pray or take time to be with God. He sees our minds
slip into neutral as we go about our day unchallenged. There is
no hiding from God. He knows our thoughts and actions before
we make them. Pray often. Be reassured God is our constant
companion.

Pray the Holy Spirit comes in wisdom and brings
understanding of God's ways. This is the same Spirit who guided
Jesus and enabled him to see through the evil one's deceptions.
The Spirit abides in us as comforter, advocate, and master teacher.
Make full use of this amazing source of strength. God fills us with
his Spirit of wisdom. The Spirit helps us live our lives filled with
the fruit of the Holy Spirit: love, joy, peace, patience, kindness,
generosity, faithfulness, gentleness, and self-control (Gal. 5:22).

Stay alert and pray continually. Never lose focus on God's
ways and his plans for us. His light and presence shine upon us
as we journey toward heaven. Be filled with peace, hope, and
encouragement. Trust the Lord.

Isaiah 12:2; John 10:27-30
Point to Ponder: The Holy Spirit guides, protects, and teaches you.

Pray: Lord, thank you for the Holy Spirit dwelling in my soul to
teach, guide, and comfort me.

April 18

I sought the LORD who answered me, delivered me
from all fears. Look to God that you may be radiant
with joy and your faces may not blush for shame.
— Psalm 34:5-6

What triggers our fears? People fear different aspects of life: marriage, commitment, and having children. Others fear surgery or the loss of a loved one. Still others fear bugs and spiders, thunder and lightning, or driving through a dark tunnel, or crossing over a high bridge. There are really too many fears and anxieties to name here. Often fears occupy our thinking and make us weary.

Fear, a natural response to the unknown, enters our thoughts and causes anxious moments, and makes situations seem insurmountable. Like a deer caught in the headlights, we feel movement impossible. We are stuck and do not know which way to turn. Remember we choose what thoughts to dwell on. Turn these stressful incidents and worrisome fears over to God.

When fear holds a tight grip, call out to God to open our eyes to the reality of the situation. Whisper short prayers like, "Help me, Jesus," or "Send me courage," or "I trust you, send me strength." If God leads us to an uncomfortable situation, he sees us through the experience and sends us what we need to live without crippling fear and stress.

Fix our eyes on God. He knows our needs. He puts our fears in perspective and gives us strength. Trust him implicitly. God is the answer.

Proverbs 29:25; Romans 8:14-17
Point to Ponder: God delivers you from your fears. Seek him always.

Pray: God, release me from my fears. Drive them away with your perfect love.

April 19

For the wages of sin is death, but the gift of
God is eternal life in Christ Jesus our Lord.

— Romans 6:23

We have many choices each day. First and foremost, choose God as our Savior. As we devote ourselves to following his ways, we draw closer to him, develop a sound relationship, and feel his love more deeply.

If we choose not to follow Christ and strike out on our own, Satan waits to draw us into wrongdoing, evil, and sin. Realize that we have all sinned and fallen short of God's glory. People get caught up in worldly vices such as adultery, gambling, alcoholism, and disrespect for family and friends. Poor choices become the norm. When caught in Satan's evilness, people see no end to sin and no path to return to God.

But wait. God remembers us. No one escapes his attention. He never abandons us, so whisper his name. He hears our pleas. His Almighty power is far greater than Satan's clutches.

The wise man does not choose to stay in the darkness of sin. Ask God for forgiveness and the strength to say no to sin. Follow God. Listen to the gentle promptings of the Spirit. Be persistent in prayer. Leave the darkness behind and walk joyfully toward the light.

In scripture, Jesus said to a woman accused of adultery, "…Neither do I condemn you. Go, [and] from now on do not sin any more" (Jn. 8:11). Trust God to forgive us our sins and cleanse us of our iniquities. Choose to follow Jesus Christ.

Deuteronomy 30:15-18; John 12:44-50
Point to Ponder: Seek forgiveness from God. Ask for his mercy and love.

Pray: God, let the light of your salvation lead me out of darkness. Free me.

April 20

Cast your care upon the LORD, who
will give you support. God will never
allow the righteous to stumble.

– Psalm 55:23

How we spend our time says a great deal about what we value. Invest time and energy encountering God. Let go of wasteful pursuits. Satan knows that blatantly tempting us with evil appears too obvious, so he lures us with distractions. His goal is to separate us from the love of God, and shatter our relationship. Be on guard. Cast our cares to God. He leads us out of sin and into the light of his presence.

Pray often throughout the day and stay close to God. He works through us in a seemingly ordinary and insignificant way. He fills our hearts with love and our minds with wisdom. We have everything we need to live joyful and abundant lives.

Do not let depression and worry rob us of gifts from God. Our journey through this world does not have to be wearisome. Have faith. Cast negative thoughts aside. If we look at our own skills, knowledge, and resources, we may become discouraged. Stop. Strike negative doubts away. God knows each of us. We are reminded, "Do not let your hearts be troubled. You have faith in God; have faith also in me" (Jn. 14:1).

Seek God every day. Focus on him. He never lets go of our hand. God cares about us and lightens our burdens. He sends grace and blessings to those who love him.

Psalm 89:16; Proverbs 2:6-8
Point to Ponder: Depend on God for support. Increase your faith in him.

Pray: God, guide me through my journey. Teach me to dwell in your presence.

April 21

Observe what is right, do what is just; for my
salvation is about to come, my justice, about to be
revealed. Happy is the man who does this, the son
of man who holds to it; Who keeps the Sabbath free
from profanation, and his hand from evildoing.

— Isaiah 56:1-2

When we walk in faith each day and follow God's word, we are a living testament to him. He fills us with grace. God wants us to be exactly where he places us. He works through us to build his kingdom.

Some people have difficulty hearing God's voice. When disoriented and unable to hear him, pause and pray. Ask for a better understanding of what God wants us to accomplish. Have faith. He leads us step-by-step.

Ask the Holy Spirit to help us navigate our way while building our relationship with God. The Spirit knows our hearts. He sees the small steps we take to draw closer to God. When we come with humble honesty about how we have fallen short, God takes care of the rest.

He is sovereign over every aspect of our lives. When life gets rushed and consumed with busyness, remember to find time to pray. No situation is too desperate for God to overcome. He shines his light on those who follow him and knows each person by name. Glorify the God of hope. Take refuge in him. Our hearts and love for God burns a little more brightly each day.

Psalm 2:11; John 14:1-3
Point to Ponder: Righteousness leads to happiness. Feel God's love in your heart.

Pray: God, my hope and salvation, bless me with happiness.

April 22

God created man in his image; in the divine image
he created him; male and female he created them.
– Genesis 1:27

This does not mean a man or a woman can be God. We are unique individuals born with a conscious that gives us a sense of right and wrong. We are stamped with the image of God.

When Jesus walked on earth, he was holy and without sin. He was a great teacher, a prophet, and a miracle worker. God wants to shape us to carry-on his divine work. He blesses people who are moldable and totally submissive to him.

God desires us to be compassionate and forgiving. He commands us to love our neighbors as he loves us. We have the capacity to relate both to God and to others. If our neighbors see his actions through us, they get a glimpse of his holiness, and that makes them want to find out more. God has the master plan. He wants us to bring others to him.

Yield to God. He plans to transform and free us from sin so we have eternal life with him. As we imitate Christ and pray faithfully, believe he hears us and responds. Live close to God, our heavenly Father, and draw strength from him. He leads us all the way to eternal life.

Proverbs 16:2; Galatians 3:26-29
Point to Ponder: God created you to be righteous. Imitate him in all your ways.

Pray: God, help me be more Christ-like. Give me a heart of humility and service.

April 23

Let love be sincere; hate what is evil, hold on
to what is good; love one another with mutual
affection; anticipate one another in showing honor.
                                            – Romans 12:9-10

God's love is unconditional and never ending, and it has no limits.
Man has difficulty understanding this type of love in his human
reasoning.

When life is good and we receive lots of earthly signs of God's
love, we feel and witness joy and peace. But in the stormy seas of
life when we doubt and during troubled times, we feel confused
and lost. Hold onto faith, persist in prayer, and seek God's mercy
and love. His love follows us to the depths of our troubles until
he reclaims us. The closer we draw to God and affirm our trust
in him, the more we find hope in his unfailing love. He sends his
selfless love to us over and over again.

As the authority on love, God enables us to love our parents,
our spouses, our children, or our enemies in a deeper way then we
could ever love them on our own. Remember, God is love (1 Jn.
4:16). Every day be persistent and spend time in prayer with him.
Ask God to fill us with love until our cups run over. Have a tender
heart and share love with others. By accepting God's love, we have
a greater sense of belonging. His love sets us free to love through
words, deeds, and in truth. Our happiness comes from loving God.

1 John 3:16-18; Psalm 145:14
Point to Ponder: Love one another as God loves you.

Pray: God, teach me your ways so I am a reflection of your love.

*Since we have gifts that differ according to
the grace given us, let us exercise them: if
prophecy, in proportion to the faith; if ministry,
in ministering; if one is a teacher, in teaching; if
one exhorts, in exhortation; if one contributes, in
generosity; if one is over others, with diligence;
if one does acts of mercy, with cheerfulness.*

— Romans 12:6-8

God has blessed us with unique gifts and talents. He wants us to inspire others. When we encounter a new situation, our first thoughts are not typically of God. We wonder how to address the unfamiliar. Rather than thinking about what God intends to do through this new circumstance, we personalize and question the particulars. When we remain focused on ourselves, we miss so much of what God could do through our experience, both for us and the others around us. God gives us the resources and the grace to tackle any issue and serve others, but we hesitate to move forward into the unknown.

Ask God to make us aware of our gifts. Are we blessed with healing power? Are we able to teach a child to read? May we minister to the sick through visitation and prayer or cook a meal for an aging relative? Whatever our gifts and talents, God works through us. He uses different settings to demonstrate his saving power. Let others see God's presence as he fills our hearts with peace and joy. Work is no longer burdensome. Do everything for the glory of God.

1 Peter 4:10; James 1:16-17
Point to Ponder: Use your gifts and talents to serve others.

Pray: God, help me enter into the spirit of love and share my gifts with others.

April 25

*No trial has come to you but what is human. God
is faithful and will not let you be tried beyond your
strength; but with the trial he will also provide
a way out, so that you may be able to bear it.*

— 1 Corinthians 10:13

Strive to follow God's commandments. We train our minds to think the thoughts of God instead of worldly happenings. Be still in God's presence. Pray often and grow closer to him. Be faithful to the roles God has given us. We are uniquely blessed.

Sometimes barriers get in the way of our pursuit to place God first in our lives. Our journey takes twists and turns, and our relationship with God falters. We find ourselves struggling with indecision and irritated with challenges.

Seek God and profess hope through prayer. Call out to him with a pure heart. Be patient for God to intervene. Realize that sometimes there is not instant relief. A painful silence may continue. Be persistent in prayer. He leads us through trials and in his time shows us a way out. His timing is best. How glorious to hear God say to us, "Well done, my good and faithful servant. Since you were faithful in small matters, I will give you great responsibilities. Come, share your master's joy" (Mt. 25:21).

If we never stop believing in Christ and always trust, then we experience great blessings. God has everything in place for us. He has the master plan. Believe and trust God.

Psalm 145:17-21; Proverbs 21:21
Point to Ponder: God is faithful. He rescues you from evil and sinful ways.

Pray: Lord, I trust your plan for me. Show me how to live righteously.

April 26

Safety comes from the Lord! Your
blessing for your people!

— Psalm 3:9

The key to knowing God requires us to communicate and build a relationship with him. Be in communion with the Lord daily. Begin each day with prayer. God opens our hearts and minds to understand scripture (Lk. 24:45). Read it often. Search for God as for hidden treasure.

Do not become prideful of accomplishments for each day brings new opportunities. Sometimes we assume God is pleased with us when our work is difficult and challenging. We believe we have reached our maximum potential. This is human thinking. Unless we hear from God, press on. Avoid making assumptions or take work accomplishments for granted.

We cannot imagine what our lives could become or all that God could accomplish through us. His power exceeds our limited imagination. Never become satisfied and boast about accomplishments. Our dreams are finite. Ask God to open our eyes so we see his plan more clearly. Let go of any sense of self-sufficiency. Strive for perfection that only Christ sends.

Do not be afraid to try new things. Go and be the person God wants us to be. The Lord provides a safety net through the Holy Spirit. The Spirit guides and protects us so we become vessels of his grace. Take refuge in God. Hold fast to the hope that lies before us. Never underestimate our potential to have him do mighty works through us.

John 15:9-10; Ephesians 3:20-21
Point to Ponder: God keeps you safe. Count on him.

Pray: I trust you, Lord. Here I am ready to do your will. Show me your ways.

April 27

Jesus Christ is the same yesterday,
today, and forever.

— Hebrews 13:8

Christ protects us throughout our journey on earth. Circumstances change all the time, but he does not change. No human comprehends God's love. We find it hard to fathom even after we have sinned, ignored, disobeyed, and rejected God, he still loves us.

God never gives up on us. He asks us to be obedient and follow his commandments. Our love for God does not grow unless we spend time with him and listen to his voice. We flounder and become irritable when things do not go our way. Prayer seems useless because answers elude us. Worry sets in. When this happens, take time to be still. Reach out to God through prayer. Open the Bible and read a few verses.

God watches over us and provides stability and direction in our lives. He sends us messages through scripture. When we spend time with God, listen for his voice, and receive his love, we feel peaceful. He wipes away tears and heals the brokenhearted.

Have faith in God's healing touch and his never-ending love. Accept his forgiving nature. Realize we all make mistakes on our earthly journey. God's grace sets us free to enjoy the numerous expressions of love he showers upon us each day. God is love. Rejoice!

Isaiah 41:13; Psalm 96:1-3
Point to Ponder: God never changes. His love is constant.

Pray: God, my heart is in your hands. Direct me and keep me safe. Grace me with your love.

 April 28

> *Good is the Lord for the one who waits for him,*
> *to the soul that seeks him; it is good to hope*
> *in silence for the saving help of the Lord.*
> — Lamentations 3:25-26

We all experience difficulties periodically: illness, broken relationships, sorrow, injuries, heartache, and death. Tragic stories of pain, hurt, and loss appear daily in the news. Many of us are preoccupied with our troubles. The impact hardships have on our lives can be debilitating.

God teaches us through the circumstances we encounter. He shows great compassion and gives us hope through our difficulties. He wants to change our focus from dwelling on our burdens to living one day at a time. God wants us to fix our minds and hearts on the present.

The Lord's restorative process requires us to slow down and listen. Accept God's offer to quiet our hearts and minds. Sometimes the Lord sends relief through our brothers and sisters. Be open to a warm smile, a gentle touch, and words of compassion. Ask God for his healing grace. Move forward walking hand in hand with Christ. Let go of past hurts. Try today to willingly part with whatever may be weighing us down.

Over time, we feel God in our midst. He strengthens us spiritually, emotionally, and physically. Develop an intimate and personal relationship with God. Rejoice in his goodness and faithfulness. Encounter God through prayer every day. Hope for his loving grace.

Isaiah 40:31; Psalm 16:11
Point to Ponder: Wait for God with hope in your heart.

Pray: God, be my constant companion, my rock and my salvation.

April 29

I, the Lᴏʀᴅ, alone probe the mind and test the heart, To reward everyone according to his ways, according to the merit of his deeds.

— Jeremiah 17:10

Some Christians experience great accomplishments but do so without the knowledge of God's presence. They take a worldly view and assume their good health, position and status at work, and family successes are due to their hard work and innate intelligence. They have inadvertently chosen worldly accomplishments over their walk with God, and they have forgotten how quickly worldly achievements come and go.

As we meet challenges and successes day after day, remember to thank God for his constant support. Pride tempts us to think we are capable and do not need to thank him or seek his assistance. Self-sufficiency greatly hinders our relationship with him. Worldly riches, power, and wealth should not take the place of an intimate relationship with God. Never allow material riches to overshadow him. Keep God first.

Today, take time to pray. Stay in close communication with God. Our security comes from having him in our lives at all times. For every work we attempt, God promises to give us the grace we need to complete the task. Like an upward spiral, each step of obedience opens up new opportunities for us to work with God, our true benefactor. Our union with the Lord is the greatest achievement we experience in the world. Yield in obedience and watch him work through us. He blesses us abundantly. Give the Lord thanks and praise.

Romans 8:28; 1 John 4:8-10
Point to Ponder: God tests you. He rewards you for your worthy deeds.

Pray: God, never let me stray from your love. Be with me always.

April 30

The way of the just is smooth; the path of the
just you make level. Yes, for your way and your
judgments, O LORD, we look to you; Your name and
your title are the desire of our souls, My soul yearns
for you in the night, yes, my spirit within me keeps
vigil for you. When your judgment dawns upon
the earth, the world's inhabitants learn justice.

— Isaiah 26:7-9

God has given us a treasure of infinite value: the gift of himself to dwell within our souls. We are constantly renewed. Everything available to Christ dwells within us.

God teaches us. He is endlessly patient. Our wisdom increases as we change and grow closer to him. God fills our hearts with love and probes our minds. We are precious in his eyes.

Journey with God along the path he has mapped out. There are stops along the way where we serve others and bring them to Christ. God rids us of sins and burdens that pull us down.

Persevere in running the race that lies before us keeping our eyes fixed on God; the leader and benefactor of faith. Communicate through prayer. Listen for his response. Do not grow weary and lose heart if he does not answer prayers immediately. Instead, seek him and his strength. God works in his time, not our time. He has prepared a place in heaven for all his children. Honor him daily through prayer and praise.

Ephesians 2:8-10; 2 Corinthians 4:6
Point to Ponder: God blesses you with knowledge, wisdom, and understanding.

Pray: God, I stand ready to journey with you. Lead me in the path of righteousness.

May 1

Not that anyone has seen the Father
except the one who is from God; he has
seen the Father. Amen, amen, I say to you,
whoever believes has eternal life.

— John 6:46-47

People believe what they see, touch, and hear. Unable to see God and witness his almighty power face-to-face, causes some people to turn away. When we hesitate and do not seek God, he chooses to intervene in our lives at the most opportune time.

Messages from God are everywhere and revealed to us in unexpected ways. For example, promptings from God may come to us in dreams or through quiet whisperings from our hearts. We may hear him speak in the words of a friend or through the lyrics of a song. Messages come through overheard conversations, an article, or even a billboard. Pay attention to these murmurings and signs.

Does God want us to react in a certain way and respond to his truths? We may hear scripture in church that touches our hearts and prompts us to change. Prophecy in scripture is nothing more than getting a message from God. Ponder his messages.

Our encounters with God are emotionally powerful and always defining. He gets our attention and reveals his heart. Respond to his divine power with trust and faith. Believe and watch how our lives change.

2 Timothy 3:16-17; Proverbs 16:20
Point to Ponder: God is everywhere. Believe in him.

Pray: God, open my eyes and heart so I feel your presence. Increase my belief.

May 2

My foes turn back when I call on you. This
I know: God is on my side. God, I praise
your promise; in you I trust, I do not fear.
What can mere mortals do to me?

– Psalm 56:10-12

Fear not, God protects us from adversity. Stay alert. Do not let the busyness of life get in the way of righteousness. Have faith and feel secure in God's loving presence. Practice truths from the Bible. Let God become the focal point of our lives.

When we study God's word and practice his teachings, a light surrounds our souls. We reap his blessings of grace. We have nothing to fear. God has given us an advocate, the Holy Spirit, who guides and protects us. He reads the heart and knows the honest pursuit of those calling on God and searching for him. The Spirit opens our minds and our hearts to better understand God's ways.

When we find ourselves or friends confused and disoriented and our thoughts linger on worries, return to the Bible. Read scripture. Seek God in quiet prayer. He opens our eyes to the truth. Turn fears over to him. Allow God's perfect peace to guard our hearts. When he works through us, others see his powerful presence. God is on our side and brings good from every situation. Trust him always. Fear not.

Romans 8:38-39; Psalm 1:1-6
Point to Ponder: God cares. He is on your side and wants good for you.

Pray: Lord never abandon me or allow me to be separated from your love.

May 3

The powerful grow poor and hungry, but
those who seek the Lord lack no good thing.
— Psalm 34:11

Do not be content with what we know about God, even if we know a lot. Be like a baby learning more with each passing day. Seek out more insight and revelation. Regularly take inventory of our relationship with God to grow spiritually.

God reveals himself by working mightily through us. He orchestrates each action. Stop and reflect on the number of people we encounter as we go about our day. Think about interactions with family members, business associates, friends, neighbors, a clerk, the postman and more. The fullness of God dwells within each person.

Imitate his ways. God guides, comforts, and encourages us. He shows steadfast purposefulness. Demonstrate to others through kind words or acts (such as a smile) that God's light shines within. Model his perfect love. Invite friends to attend church. Give the gift of a Bible to someone searching for God. Allow the Holy Spirit to work through us and bind us together in love.

When we seek to open the eyes and the hearts of others to God's love, we always find an ample supply of his grace. God sends exactly what we need. He reminds us that a heavenly reward waits. He remembers everything we do to serve and honor him.

Ephesians 2:10; Proverbs 25:11
Point to Ponder: The Lord provides. Ask God for blessings and believe he answers prayers.

Pray: God, I offer myself to you. I need to model your love and peace.

 May 4

Magnify the LORD with me; let us exalt his name
together. I sought the LORD, who answered
me, delivered me from all my fears.

— Psalm 34:4-5

God tells us to not be afraid. Many people find it difficult to turn over problems and fears to God, but he lessens the burden and handles any trials we face. Christ may not take away all our issues. He does not differentiate between minor problems and those fears and concerns that are God-sized needs. Allow him to carry the weight of all our problems. He wants to lead us through treacherous waters. This only happens once we have formed a relationship with him, a relationship of trust. Believe in God enough today to take the first step and pray. Do this often each day.

After praying, we may feel as if a weight has been lifted from our shoulders. Our problems and fears seem less burdensome. Trust God to calm our fears and clear our minds. He touches our hearts first, and then our worries and fears shrink in importance. God desires us to experience peace.

Through God's perfect love for his children, his peace guards our hearts. He designed us to dwell in peace and draw ever closer to him. In the language of faith, leave our fears and worries with him. God's love is at work in every event of our lives. Embrace his love and peace.

2 Timothy 1:7; Isaiah 41:10
Point to Ponder: Give fears and worries to God.

Pray: God, build my trust in you. Cast away all my fears so I live in peace.

May 5

The law of the Lord is perfect, refreshing the soul.
The decree of the Lord is trustworthy, giving
wisdom to the simple. By them your servant is
instructed; obeying them brings much reward.

— Psalm 19:8, 12

Sometimes we ponder why God allows war, death, tragedies, and disasters. We cannot fathom his response to certain situations, but we follow him in faith. Understanding God's ways may cause confusion because we do not see clearly, and his voice may be muted during times of difficulty.

God has given us the Ten Commandments to be used as a guide to live an abundant life; they are a blueprint for righteousness. With faith, we Christians follow the commandments. We receive this gift by faith, not by works alone. Obedience to God's word is important.

"Therefore, confess your sins to one another and pray for one another, that you may be healed. The fervent prayer of a righteous person is very powerful" (Jas. 4:16). We have all sinned. Only God is without sin. We should remove iniquity from our souls quickly by seeking God's forgiveness and mercy.

Satan constantly leads us into temptation and wrongdoing. Say no to Satan. Follow God's law and stay away from sin. The Bible says, "If you keep my commandments, you will remain in my love, just as I have kept my Father's commandments and remain in his love" (Jn. 15:10). Pray for increased faith and abide by God's laws. Remove all sin from our souls. Let God's grace refresh our souls.

Exodus 20:1-17; Deuteronomy 5:6-21
Point to Ponder: The law of God is perfect. Follow his plan.

Pray: God, imprint your ways on my heart. Allow me to embrace your ways.

May 6

Let us not grow tired of doing good, for in due time
we shall reap our harvest, if we do not give up.
— Galatians 6:9

Do not become sluggish; instead, be imitators of those who, through faith and persistence, inherit God's promises. Christ, with his all-knowing power, gives us the resources to bring others to him. God places people in our lives that are searching and in need. He is aware of what they lack.

Even though we may feel inadequate and unsure of quoting scripture, God sends us grace and courage to speak on his behalf at the right time. He gives us words of comfort to echo and strength to help those carrying a heavy burden. Do not be concerned about quoting scripture word-for-word. It is more important to speak from the heart.

God chooses us deliberately. We have been handpicked, commissioned, and empowered by him. He wants us to lead others to him. The receptiveness of our hearts determines our response to God's word.

Always strive to be a powerful witness to God. Be faithful to him. Meditate on his word so when he does call on us, we apply his teachings. Prepare our hearts so we imitate God in thought, word, and deed. He graces us with all we need to build his kingdom on earth.

Proverbs 27:19; John 20:19-23
Point to Ponder: Be faithful. Follow God at all times.

Pray: God, your loving presence enfolds me. Lead me to do your will.

May 7

The crucible for silver, and the furnace for
gold, but the tester of hearts is the LORD.

– Proverbs 17:3

Jesus knows our hearts. When we grieve, he comes to us as a comforter. When in need, he demonstrates his ability to be a provider. If sick, he heals. When we face a serious challenge and fear all is lost, he reveals he is God Almighty. Nothing overpowers Christ.

As we grow in God's love, we form a relationship with him and learn to trust. Our hearts soften. We understand the Lord's ways better than when we first became Christians. We seek his guidance when a new circumstance develops that causes fear, confusion, or anxiety. Whatever situation we find ourselves facing, think of the experience as a growth opportunity. God teaches us through circumstances about himself and how to proceed.

Christ's presence makes a significant difference in our lives. When we open our hearts, he reveals himself so we appreciate the glory of his person and the marvelous riches he brings. We imitate God's love, kindness, and gentle spirit. Our actions should be a tribute to the matchless grace God has bestowed upon us. Allow him to see a heart full of love and peace. When we walk with God in this manner, he brings us to virtuous service. Our lives fall into harmony with him. We thrive in his presence.

Psalm 139:2-6; Luke 5:1-11
Point to Ponder: God has the master plan. Follow him.

Pray: God, open my heart to your transforming presence. Fill me with peace and love.

May 8

*For the Holy Spirit will teach you at
the moment what you should say.*

– Luke 12:12

The Holy Spirit works within our souls, prompting us to make statements filled with love and support. When we practice kindness, it becomes a habit. We find sharing God's love uplifting.

Jesus remained patient with his disciples when they questioned. He taught them through parables and stories. We Christians learn to be Christ-like in our behaviors from the Holy Spirit's nudges. Like the disciples, we question, reason, and pray as we learn to follow Christ. We strive to inherit the riches of God's kingdom.

Be alert, because Satan lurks. The evil one tempts us and catches us off guard. We succumb to sin. While floundering, the Holy Spirit's activities are muted or quenched. Sin rules and we dwell in darkness and negativity. Our hearts harden and grow dull. As time goes on, we move further and further away from God.

Stop wallowing in sin. No matter the difficulty, God is merciful. Pray and repent. God watches and waits for our cries for help. With perfect timing, he leads us one step at a time from darkness and evil to his light.

Pray every day, multiple times a day for his faithful guidance and protection. The Holy Spirit, God within our souls, refreshes us. With time and prayer, we return full of energy, ready to tackle whatever comes. Praise God.

Ephesians 3:14-19; 2 Peter 1:3
Point to Ponder: The Holy Spirit guides and teaches you.

Pray: God, open my ears to hear you. Open my eyes to see your glory.

May 9

*Whatever you do, do from the heart, as for
the Lord and not for others, knowing that you
will receive from the Lord due payment of the
inheritance; be slaves of the Lord Christ.*

— Colossians 3:23-24

God rejoices in the small things we do in his name. When we use our gifts and talents to help others, he is pleased. He watches us go about our labors motivated to serve. We see work as a labor of love for God. Doing a good job is a way of paying homage to him for giving us talents to share.

Mediocrity has no place in the life of a Christian. Some people disappoint, betray, and neglect us. These people forget about God's commandment to love our neighbors. When people disappoint us and do not measure up to our expectations, keep in mind we are toiling for the Lord. Let his peace rule in our hearts. Try to be less judgmental.

Believe that God wants to manifest his kingdom through us. Pray for those people who do not follow God's truths. Have courage and intervene to bring these people to him. Everything we do should be pleasing to God.

Psalm 113:1-9; Matthew 28:18-20
Point to Ponder: Do everything for God.

Pray: God, let my work be pleasing to you. Fill my heart with peace.

May 10

Do not neglect to do good and to share what you have; God is pleased by sacrifices of that kind.

– Hebrews 13:16

Be open-handed toward neighbors and the poor. This is often difficult and goes against our human nature. People choose to be in close contact with others who look like they do, and have the same beliefs and lifestyles. When God places us in an uncomfortable situation with people who speak another language, look different, or are poor and live on the margins, how we respond matters. Guard against bias and prejudice. Remember, that we are all made in God's image.

Collaborate with God through prayer. Feel his life merge with ours. He calls us his children. He blesses us with unique gifts so we can help our neighbors. We may use the gift of time to be with someone who needs comforting. Some may employ the poor or immigrants. Doctors and nurses cure the ill. Teachers teach children and prepare them for the future.

As we go about serving others, God directs our steps. He may be working to produce peace in our hearts, or he may be developing a forgiving spirit. Perhaps God is working to eliminate a particular sin in our lives. When we look to see what God is accomplishing through situations, we find his way is best.

God does things through our lives only he understands. Rejoice in his word and act on his promptings. We are guided by the truth of his love. Tell others about him. Our lives change when we have God first and share our gifts and talents.

Acts 20:34-35; 1 Peter 4:8-10
Point to Ponder: Share with others.

Pray: God, teach me to love as you love so I can reach out to others and hold back nothing.

May 11

Fathers, do not provoke your children
to anger, but bring them up with the
training and instruction of the Lord.

– Ephesians 6:4

A child is a gift from God. Many parents or caregivers find challenges in building a spiritual foundation and love for God in their children. Parents wonder where to start. In scripture we learn about inheriting the kingdom of God. We strive to acquire the fruit of the Spirit: love, joy, peace, patience, kindness, generosity, faithfulness, gentleness, and self-control (Gal. 5:22). Be alert and model these characteristics for children. Let God's light shine through our words and deeds.

Build a spiritual foundation by attending church with children. There is no better way to experience God than through church and being involved with peers as they learn to love him. Read stories from the Bible. Children listen to stories about Jesus's love, peace, gentleness, and kindness. They hear about miracles and his healing power. Young people grow in knowledge and understanding, and begin to see the world through the eyes of Christ.

Growing in spiritual knowledge is all about transformation to be more like God. Teach children to pray. When children learn about Jesus, they know he watches over them like an invisible friend and helps them. He is someone who is infinitely powerful, tenderly loving, and wise beyond all understanding. Teach them to love God.

Hebrews 13:20-21; Psalm 29:11
Point to Ponder: Teach children to know and love God.

Pray: Lord, direct my steps so I teach my children to love and trust you. Help me model righteousness.

 May 12

Then he said to the crowd, "Take care to guard
against all greed, for though one may be rich,
one's life does not consist of possessions."

– Luke 12:15

Our lives on earth do not exist to accumulate material riches and money. There is nothing wrong with having money, but beware. Money cannot buy a place in heaven. Many people get so caught up with possessions and status, that they forget when we stand before God on judgment day, he will not ask about riches. Instead, he will ask us to give a reckoning of our acts to love our neighbors, how we helped the needy and the poor, and how we served him.

When our awareness of God grows dim and we do not have him as our focal point, it is never too late to turn back to him and seek righteousness and spiritual riches. He is continually at work in our lives, but he waits for the perfect opportunity to draw us closer. It does not cost money, but does take focus and persistence. "For everyone who asks, receives; and the one who seeks, finds; and to the one who knocks, the door will be opened" (Lk. 11:10).

Sometimes our prayers are not answered immediately. Do not lose heart. Keep on praying. Search scripture because it permeates, guides, and enriches our lives.

When we stand before God on judgment day, have an arsenal of spiritual riches that glorify him. Develop a relationship with the Lord and an unbreakable bond. Praise God's holy name. Always have God first in our lives.

Colossians 3:1-11; Proverbs 4:23-27
Point to Ponder: Guard against greed. Spiritual wealth matters to God.

Pray: Lord, teach me and show me your ways. I want to serve you.

May 13

*In the same way, the Spirit too comes to the
aid of our weaknesses; for we do not know
how to pray as we ought, but the Spirit itself
intercedes with inexpressible groanings. And
the one who searches hearts knows what is the
intention of the Spirit, because it intercedes
for the holy ones according to God's will.*

– Romans 8:26-27

The moment we become Christians, God sends the Holy Spirit to
dwell in our souls. He teaches us self-control and guides us so we
have the strength to say no to Satan and his evil ways. Satan is
powerless when challenging God.

We travel through life with the aid of the Spirit nudging,
guiding, and teaching us to follow Christ. We pray, study, and
meditate on scripture to understand God's will for us.

At times, temptation causes us to lose sight of God's ways.
Satan confuses, misleads, and tries to separate us from God's love.
If we continue to sin, we do not really know Christ. Pray for God's
intercession every day. He is never far away. Seek him. Confess
and repent. Hold on to his guiding hand, which others cannot
see. Even though we cannot see clearly, he feeds our souls. Allow
the Lord to eradicate every trace of sin in our lives. Learn from
mistakes and do not repeat sins. Once again, experience victory
over sin. Praise God!

Romans 5:5; John 3:5-8
Point to Ponder: The Holy Spirit is your advocate and friend.

Pray: Lord, awaken the Holy Spirit in my soul.

May 14

My son, when you come to serve the LORD, prepare
yourself for trials. Be sincere of heart and steadfast,
undisturbed in time of adversity. Cling to him,
forsake him not; thus will your future be great.
Accept whatever befalls you, in crushing misfortune
be patient; for in fire gold is tested, and worthy men
in the crucible of humiliation. Trust God and he will
help you; make straight your ways and hope in him.
— Sirach 2:1-6

God makes good out of all our experiences. Consider each day
he gives us as an adventure story waiting to happen. Do not let
fear and worry overtake the excitement of a new day. We worry
about our health, lack of money, our job, and our children. Not
to mention our concerns about national issues: natural disasters,
global warming, war, deportation issues, and terrorists' attacks. We
instinctively worry.

We ease these natural worries by calling on God. Scripture says,
"Then call on me in time of distress; I will rescue you, and you
shall honor me" (Ps. 50:15). We deny the Lord honor when we fail
to call upon him. Sometimes God allows us to reach a point of need
so desperate we cry out as a last resource. Why wait? Call on God
when trials first evolve. When he intercedes, he demonstrates to the
world the difference he makes in the lives of those who follow and
believe in his almighty power. We need God in our lives daily. Seek
him and give him all the glory. Hope in the Lord our God.

Proverbs 8:17-21; Psalm 41:1-14
Point to Ponder: Wait patiently for God. He wants only good
for you.

Pray: Lord, help me glorify your name with a thankful heart.

May 15

And the king will say to them in reply, 'Amen,
I say to you, whatever you did for one of these
least brothers of mine, you did for me.'

– Matthew 25:40

Power, status, and money mean everything to some individuals. God is more interested with the number of people we serve and not our bank accounts. God reassures and strengthens us to serve others.

Filled with pride and self-importance, many people find service a struggle. Their hearts may have shifted away from God. Others are capable of serving and look past personal biases. God honors those who serve. When he sees us investing time to serve others, we experience his unfailing love and the full dimensions of being children of God.

Pray daily. Have an open heart to receive God's message. Ask the Holy Spirit to prompt us to reach out and befriend the less fortunate. Ask him to teach us selflessness. Take steps to help the poor and needy, and strive for a humble attitude. Like God, have a kind and generous spirit.

As Jesus did, make a point to be present to all people. The Bible states, "Should anyone press you into service for one mile, go with him for two miles" (Mt. 5:41). Christ invites us to join in serving others. Be thankful for these opportunities. Embrace the peace that transcends on those people who help the less fortunate.

Sirach 2:7-11; Isaiah 26:4-13
Point to Ponder: Serve God first. Never doubt his power.

Pray: Jesus, fill my heart with love to share.

May 16

But the wisdom from above is first of all pure, then
peaceable, gentle, compliant, full of mercy and
good fruits, without inconstancy or insincerity.
– James 3:17

God blesses us with wisdom as we learn to follow his teachings. Human reasoning does not make us wise, and in some cases, it causes us to reject the ways of God. He wants us to trust, persist, and follow him.

The Holy Spirit abides in our souls to guide and prompt us. The Spirit opens our eyes to knowledge and the truth of scripture so we see things from God's perspective and better understand his ways. Take small steps and listen for the promptings of the Spirit.

As we follow God and experience life, he guides us to make the correct choices. We need God's help with the decisions we face. Sometimes God allows us to fail. In actuality, he has given us an opportunity to learn and acquire knowledge from our missteps. The path might be confusing and obstructed, but God moves us forward as we face obstacles.

At times, God says no and we lack the wisdom to accept his decision. He is in control; we are not. God's wisdom far outweighs any understanding we may have about a decision. It is an affront to God when he says no to continue pleading with him. He has a different plan for us. Trust God to bring good out of all things. Give thanks to him for sharing his wisdom, knowledge, and understanding. Believe in his almighty power.

James 1:5; Colossians 4:5-6
Point to Ponder: Seek wisdom from God.

Pray: God, teach me your ways. Open my heart to the day's opportunities.

May 17

No foul language should come out of your mouths,
but only such as is good for needed edification,
that it may impart grace to those who hear.

– Ephesians 4:29

Sometimes we lose our temper and spout out offensive words. This kind of destructive outburst is often the result of frustration and anger. We lose self-control and say things that are mean-spirited and hurtful. Anger does not bring about God's redemptive work; instead it hinders God's efforts to get things done. Scripture tells us, "Give up your anger, abandon your wrath; do not be provoked; it brings only harm (Ps. 37:8). Count to ten and whisper God's name.

Examine anger that lingers. Ask God to remove any sinful attitudes, thoughts, and expressions. Releasing anger does not mean we cease to have strong convictions about a situation or lose our quest for justice. It does mean others are not going to pull us into sinful ways with them. Letting go of anger is a choice where we consciously turn over our bitterness to Christ and allow him to carry the weight of our problems. Though difficult, this requires us to trust the Lord. Our minds keep returning to the issues. Stress levels and anxieties increase when anger prevails.

Refocus and turn to God. Let him fill our minds with positive thoughts so we experience calm. Choose to leave anger, foul language, and bitterness behind. The Lord transforms us. Trust him in all situations to have answers and to heal those in need.

Proverbs 16:24; Psalm 51:10
Point to Ponder: Speak kind words to be uplifting. Never use foul language.

Pray: God, take away my anger and hurt. Thank you for teaching me how to forgive others.

May 18

*Say not: "I have sinned, yet what has befallen
me?" for the LORD bides his time. Of forgiveness
be not overconfident, adding sin upon sin. Say
not: "Great is his mercy; my many sins he will
forgive." For mercy and anger alike are with
him; upon the wicked alights his wrath.*

— Sirach 5:4-7

Sin affects all of us, both when we succumb to sin and when others sin. We recognize the driving force emanating from Satan as sin leaves tarnish on a person's mind and soul. Some people continue to sin even after struggling and refusing temptation for a while. They feel ill at ease and unhappy, but gradually their consciences adjust to sinful ways. Each sin makes the next one a bit easier. Eventually they sin without a qualm. Evil ways become addictive, like a drug.

Not until we see sin has battered, bruised, and driven us to despair, do we want a way out. Not until we grasp that sin has arrested, imprisoned, and condemned us, do we think of reaching out to Christ. He is our only hope. Death and hell are the alternatives.

Say yes to God. Trust God to send grace and strength to overcome sin. Pray every day. Scripture says, "Whoever sins belongs to the devil, because the devil has sinned from the beginning. Indeed, the Son of God was revealed to destroy the works of the devil" (1 Jn. 3:8). Walk with Christ in holy trust. He leads us to truth, and walks with us out of darkness.

Psalm 1:4-6; Mark 9:42-48

Point to Ponder: Follow God in glory. Avoid sin and Satan's temptations.

Pray: God, keep me in your grace. In your mercy, remove sin and cleanse my heart.

May 19

*A kind mouth multiplies friends, and gracious lips
prompt friendly greetings ... A faithful friend is
beyond price, no sum can balance his worth.*

— Sirach 6:5, 15

Faithful friends maintain a closeness and awareness of desires, beliefs, and promises. Every so often, God places someone in our lives to encourage us and lovingly challenge us to be the best we can be. God does nothing by accident.

In the spiritual sense, a true friend leads us closer to God. They tell us the truth even though the words may be painful to hear. This is done in love and with our best interests at heart. A faithful friend is always just a call away, no matter the time passing between visits.

We should not expect every person to be a true friend even though God asks us to love our neighbors. We have a responsibility to live in such a way as to not intentionally hurt others. Face neighbors with a cheerful heart and a smile. Remember that they are all equally loved by God and deserving of dignity and support. Strive to put away the natural inclination to be self-centered. Listen and respond to others with words that do no harm.

Be cautious when you select faithful friends, as Jesus was with his disciples. He did not look for perfect people, but instead chose those whose hearts were in the right place. Be receptive to how these friends help us grow to be a better person. See God working through them. Open our hearts to the gift of true friendship.

Proverbs 17:17; Luke 6:31
Point to Ponder: Faithful friends are gifts from God.

Pray: God, send me a faithful friend. Thank you for allowing me to love.

May 20

See what love the Father has bestowed on us that we may be called the children of God. Yet so we are. The reason the world does not know us is that it did not know him. Beloved, we are God's children now; what we shall be has not yet been revealed. We do know that when it is revealed we shall be like him, for we shall see him as he is.

— 1 John 3:1-2

Our lives have been set apart and made holy by God; made in his image and filled with his divine presence. God loves us unconditionally. We are the crown of his creation.

God knows everything about us. He knows our feelings, how we think, and if our intentions are pure from the heart. There is no point in trying to fool God. Stay in union with him. He leads us. "In his mind a man plans his course, but the LORD directs his steps" (Prv. 16:9).

God does not probe to point out flaws. He gently disciplines us and calls us back with no condemnation when we sin. Draw closer to him. Make God the focal point of our lives. He hears our prayers and responds. God's love and mercy heals. He never abandons anyone. He calls us by name.

Remember to raise our hearts and voices in praise and gratitude. He makes every moment of our lives meaningful as he embraces, forgives, and heals us. Walk with him all the way to eternal life.

Psalm 103:13-18; Acts 17:24-28
Point to Ponder: We are all God's children.

Pray: God, help me imitate you, see the resemblance, and understand who I really am.

May 21

*Be patient, therefore, brothers, until the coming
of the Lord. See how the farmer waits for the
precious fruit of the earth, being patient with
it until it receives the early and the late rains.
You too must be patient. Make your hearts firm,
because the coming of the Lord is at hand.*

– James 5:7-8

God is omniscient. He sees us running from one appointment
to the next, and he knows how we fill our time with earthly
endeavors. God wants to strengthen us and renew our spirits so we
enjoy the abundant life we have carved out. Never become too busy
to have God in our lives.

We live in a society which expects instant gratification and
results, and so we often find waiting difficult. We rush through
each day without taking time to reflect or evaluate our activities.
We do not pause long enough to pray or listen for God's voice.

Sometimes we race ahead of God knowing we deal with time
in twenty-four-hour segments. Slow down and find time to be still.
Scripture tells us, "Be still before the LORD; wait for God. Do not
be provoked by the prosperous, nor by malicious schemers" (Ps.
37:7). When we are still, we feel his grace and peace.

The Lord dwells in timelessness with no beginning or end. He
is the alpha and the omega. God wants us to be happy and impart
love. Count on him to send us blessings in his time. Be patient and
wait for God. He wants good for all of us.

Isaiah 40:31; Revelations 1:8
Point to Ponder: Learn to wait for God. Be patient.

Pray: Thank you, God, for loving me. Teach me to be patient and
wait for you.

May 22

Consider this: whoever sows sparingly will
reap sparingly, and whoever sows bountifully
will also reap bountifully. Each must do
as already determined, without sadness or
compulsion, for God loves a cheerful giver.
— 2 Corinthians 9:6-7

When we hear a call from the Lord to perform a service for others, press forward and meet the challenges with joyful hearts. God provides the gift of grace to go about our work and build his kingdom.

Some may try to convince us to give up on our mission to serve God. His grace enables us to forgive our accusers and sense his pleasure, even when others are critical of our efforts and do not understand. When we make mistakes while doing God's work, he picks us up and sets us on a righteous path. He wants us to try our best to use our gifts and talents in ways that glorify him and lift up others. When the work is finished and no one expresses thanks for what has been done, God's grace surrounds us. He reminds us we have a heavenly reward.

Christ does not promise worldly riches and great success in all our works. He blesses us according to how we respond to his tasks. Our relationship with God is deeply affected by what we do to serve. Let us serve generously in everything we do in our lives. God sees all we do and remembers. Do God's work with joy and a gentle heart.

Colossians 3:17; Ephesians 2:8
Point to Ponder: Develop a generous heart. Be a giver.

Pray: Lord, my Savior, I lift up my heart and works to you. I love you.

May 23

Be imitators of me, as I am of Christ. I
praise you because you remember me in
everything and hold fast to the traditions,
just as I handed them on to you.

— 1 Corinthians 11:1-2

We read in scripture about Jesus. "Then he said to all, 'If anyone wishes to come after me, he must deny himself and take up his cross daily and follow me'"(Lk. 9:23). When we follow Christ, we practice obedience and trust. We should not complain about our lives. God does everything for a reason, and places us where he wants us to be to do his work.

Obedience to God comes from the heart. If we are struggling with God's plan for us, then maybe we have shifted away from him. Have we been too busy to pray? Have we lost interest in reading scripture? Do we feel going to church an obligation? Has our faith in God's goodness and mercy changed? Are our hearts troubled?

Genuine love for God leads to obedience, a joyful attitude, kindness toward others, peacefulness, and generosity. Nurture genuine love for God as he transforms us to imitate his ways. God is not satisfied with partial love or disobedience.

God looks beyond our godly habits, beyond our lifestyle, and beyond our church environment to focus on our hearts. If we have wandered away from Christ and have little hope, pause, reflect, and then turn back to him. Pray and listen for his voice. Obey God and wait hopefully in his presence. Affirm trust in him to see his perfect plan unfold. God's love for us endures forever.

Psalm 79:9, 13; Micah 7:7
Point to Ponder: Hold fast to God. Trust him to lead the way.

Pray: Lord, teach me to be a loyal servant. Thank you for guiding me.

May 24

Sing to God a new song; skillfully play with
joyful chant. For the LORD's word is true; all his
works are trustworthy. The LORD loves justice
and right and fills the earth with goodness.

– Psalm 33:3-5

God loves us with a love beyond our human understanding. He never gives up on us, even though we may forget to praise and thank him. We allow God to slip from the center of our minds to the periphery. When this happens, be still and focus on him.

Sometimes Christ gently disciplines us. We may get angry or resent him. At times he says no to our prayer requests. This causes us to feel we have lost favor, or he does not care about what we want. When these feelings enter our hearts, we need to pray.

Scripture says, "The LORD watches over the way of the just, but the way of the wicked leads to ruin" (Ps. 1:6). Christ suffered rejection and pain. He understands disappointments and feelings of worthlessness. Even when we suffer and experience negativity, trust that God sends grace and love to strengthen us. Pray to God with all the more vigor.

When we turn to God and seek help, he delights in us who are created in his image and likeness. God loved us first. Return to him. Open our hearts to his will and love. If we follow God, the future will be forever bright. Be prepared to receive abundant joy, love, kindness, gentleness, and peace. Walk along our life-paths with him to eternal life.

Proverbs 22:2; 1 John 4:12-16
Point to Ponder: Praise God for his trustworthiness and goodness.

Pray: God, thank you for loving me first. Keep me in your loving presence.

145

May 25

*All of us, gazing with unveiled face on the
glory of the Lord, are being transformed
into the same image from glory to glory,
as from the Lord who is the Spirit.*

— 2 Corinthians 3:18

Our spiritual maturity is deeply affected by what we do and how
we imitate Christ. He is generous to his children who willingly
and freely give to others and convey their spiritual beliefs. When
we continue to pray when praying is difficult, God sees this
and rewards us with a deeper more powerful prayer life. When
we focus on being patient and waiting for God, he blesses us in
unexpected ways beyond our understanding. When we express
kindness to our neighbors, God fills our lives with joy and peace.

God's kingdom has no room for selfish, miserly people.
He blesses us with gifts and talents unique to each individual.
Scripture says, "Do not be deceived, my beloved brothers: all good
giving and every perfect gift is from above, coming down from the
Father of lights, with whom there is no alteration or shadow caused
by change"(Jas. 1:17). God asks us to give our possessions as freely
and as willingly as we receive them. Be a conduit through whom
the Lord pours his blessings. If we struggle to give to others freely,
we have become attached to worldly possessions. Work on God's
plans for us and be generous in every situation.

Take time away from the glitter and gloss of earthly treasures.
Open our hearts to God. Thank him for all his blessings. Draw
closer to him and be filled with joy and peace.

Psalm 46:9-12; Proverbs 21:2-3
Point to Ponder: Imitate Christ in all you do.

Pray: Lord, teach me to be generous especially with spiritual gifts.

May 26

I make a solemn vow to keep your just
edicts. I am very much afflicted, LORD; give
me life in accord with your word.

— Psalm 119:106-107

As we read the Bible and grow closer to the Lord through worship and praise, we hope others see God's powerful presence in us. His presence changes our lives. People draw closer to us as we exhibit: a joyful and generous attitude, a calm and peaceful nature, and an understanding of God's word, his mercy, and his love. Always model these blessings.

God blesses us as we strive to live according to his laws. Those friends who have children want them to play and socialize with our children because they are raised in a godly manner. Employers enjoy having us work for them because of our nature and persistence to get the job done, and because of the encouragement we give others. We model family life by joining together in unconditional love for special occasions and by worshiping God through prayer and church attendance. We have discovered that the more we allow God to make his presence known in our lives, the more people draw near to us.

God wants us to help others find him. He opens his arms wide to those searching for meaning in life. Christ wants us to devote ourselves to knowing and loving him with all our hearts. His kingdom is open to everyone. Let God probe, test, and lead us to eternity.

Matthew 7:7-8; Proverbs 24:3-4
Point to Ponder: Follow God's ways. Learn from scripture.

Pray: God, help me imitate your love so others will be drawn to you through my actions.

May 27

Faith is the realization of what is hoped
for and evidence of things not seen.

– Hebrews 11:1

Our relationship with God is largely determined by our faith in his goodness and mercy, not by our circumstances. With strong faith, we trust him to be there when troubles abound. Faith does not mean God eliminates our problems, but he extends a helping hand. He never abandons us. Believe and seek him. Look for his response and be faithful. God sends hope.

He wants us to trust and build our faith. Scripture tells us, "But without faith it is impossible to please him, for anyone who approaches God must believe that he exists and that he rewards those who seek him" (Heb. 11:6).

When we face difficult situations, we sometimes qualify our beliefs in God and lower our expectations of how he might help us. It is uplifting to read about miracles in the Bible. Jesus performed wonders when he walked the earth. He still has the power to perform miracles. The more faith we have in God, the more we recognize his works and experience his presence.

God provides for our needs often without us asking. He lifts our burdens from our shoulders and takes away our worries and anxieties. We experience God in our lives working through us. God directs our steps. Expect a miracle!

1 Corinthians 3:16-17; John 5:24
Point to Ponder: Have faith in God. He never abandons us.

Pray: Christ, increase my faith.

May 28

When you call me, when you go to pray to
me, I will listen to you. When you look for
me, you will find me. Yes, when you seek me
with all your heart, you will find me with you,
says the Lord, and I will change your lot ...

– Jeremiah 29:12-14

People have called out to God from the depths of their being for eons. The practice of calling out to the Lord began with the earliest generations of mankind, recorded in the Bible. Today we call out in times of trial or delight, in despair or in rejoicing, and in an attempt to draw near to God. Whatever the reason, calling out to God is universal and is observed in cultures around the globe.

When we call on the Lord, we want to feel his divine presence. Speaking his name out loud renews and enhances our communication with him. Prayer, both verbal and silent, is a form of calling on the Lord. Scripture tells us spoken words are important to God. "For, if you confess with your mouth that Jesus is Lord and believe in your heart that God raised him from the dead, you will be saved" (Rom. 10:9).

This verse points to two actions that produce two different results. Believing is a function of the heart and is silent and righteous. Confessing and calling out to God is vocal resulting in salvation. Both lead to a richer experience with Christ. Call on the Lord. Pray throughout the day. Build a relationship with God because he cares about each of us as his own.

Psalm 121:1-2; Proverbs 15:22
Point to Ponder: Call on God daily.

Pray: Lord, hear my silent prayers and verbal calls.

May 29

May the God of hope fill you with all joy and
peace in believing, so that you may abound
in hope by the power of the Holy Spirit.

— Romans 15:13

The Holy Spirit controls our innermost feelings. When baptized, the Holy Spirit works to transform and guide us to demonstrate Christ-like character. The Spirit is the best teacher in the world. He teaches us about: love, joy, peace, patience, kindness, generosity, faithfulness, gentleness, and self-control (Gal. 5:22-23).

By faith, trust the Holy Spirit. Receive his divine dynamic life within us. We feel love when God touches our lives. Love melts our hearts and overtakes us. We experience joy in the presence of God when we realize he never abandons us. Peace enters our souls as we learn God is in control. His plan for us is good. He gives us the Spirit to guide and protect us.

The patience Jesus had for his disciples, who denied him and would not believe without seeing, is like the patience the Spirit develops for us. Our hearts soften as we build our knowledge base and understand who God is. We find kindness easier to share and pass on to others. The Spirit guides us to be generous with our time, talents, and treasures and we exude self-control. Our faithfulness to God increases as we follow his ways. We find ourselves more obedient to him.

Learn something new each day and prosper as we journey through life. How quickly this happens depends upon how completely we yield to God's grace by the power of the Holy Spirit.

Galatians 5:19-26; Isaiah 42:5-9
Point to Ponder: God fills my life with goodness.

Pray: God, teach me to be like you. Help me listen more carefully to the Holy Spirit.

 May 30

Make known to me your ways, Lᴏʀᴅ; teach me
your paths. Guide me in your truth and teach
me, for you are God my savior. For you I wait
all the long day, because of your goodness, Lᴏʀᴅ.
Remember your compassion and love. O Lᴏʀᴅ; for
they are ages old. Remember no more the sins of
my youth remember me only in light of your love.

                             – Psalm 25:4-7

The same God who created the heavens and the earth, and who gave Moses the Ten Commandments, resides within us. No power defeats God.

Following Christ is hard work. We systematically need to implement the truths of scripture into our lives. We strive to acquire grace that empowers us to accept God's calling and wisdom. When we first hear his voice, and he asks something other than what we expect, we tend to block out the murmurings. Pause and remember that God needs us to build his kingdom and do his work. Use the gifts he has given us, and trust him to lead us in the right direction.

Spiritual depth and maturity come only after we have consistently served God. Following God, reading scripture, giving thanks and praise, praying with a pure heart, and serving others are pleasing signs to him. He remembers all we do to grow closer to him and serve. God has a place for us in his kingdom. Eternal life awaits those who serve the Lord.

Joshua 1:9; John 15:1-8
Point to Ponder: Allow God to be your master.

Pray: God, teach to discern your plan. Remember me. I want to be with you in your kingdom.

 May 31

Every word of God is tested; he is a shield
to those who take refuge in him. Add
nothing to his words, least he reprove you,
and you be exposed as a deceiver.

– Proverbs 30:5-6

We followers of Christ seek his approval in all we say and do. We turn to God with confident expectations. He provides for all our needs.

As adults we seek the opinion of friends, colleagues, family members, and employers. At times, we allow the praise of others to affect us to the point of measuring our self-worth by what is said. Self-approval and praise from others often come routinely. Receiving God's approval is a far greater accomplishment. His evaluation of our actions matters.

The pleasure our lives give to God should be our motivation to live righteously. God tests us as he prepares us for eternal life. His plan for us may be different than the plans we have selected. We find ourselves questioning God. Our faith and trust may waiver.

God sees every hardship and temptation we face. He is always faithful and ready to deliver us and intercede on our behalf. God wants to know us and have a personal encounter with us. Turn to him and seek his strength. He has overcome Satan's evil in the world. God remains even when everyone else abandons us. We count on him to be our refuge. Obey his word, wait for him, and have hope. Receive his peace.

Philippians 4:19-20; 2 Corinthians 6:1-11
Point to Ponder: Look for God in the midst of your life. Trust him.

Pray: God, let your loving presence enfold me and renew my strength. Increase my faith.

June 1

Keep me safe, O God; in you I take refuge.
— Psalm 16:1

Stay connected to the Lord. Our spiritual growth comes from him. We need to be filled with his vitality, energy, and wisdom. Many people appear to be close to God, quote scripture, and have a surface knowledge of the Bible, but they never practice his truths or demonstrate them to others.

In order to build a relationship with God and take refuge in him, be faithful to daily prayer. Set aside time away from distractions to focus on him. Nourish the soul by reading scripture. When we abide in God's presence, we do what he would do. When we turn to God and practice his teachings through our actions and words, we give him the freedom to shape us. Embrace God's ways.

He places us right where he wants us to be. Scripture says, "Remain in me, as I remain in you. Just as a branch cannot bear fruit on its own unless it remains in me" (Jn. 15:4). Take time to cultivate a relationship with the Lord. Learn to recognize his voice and find joy in his plan for us. He speaks into the gentleness of our hearts. Seek him with a hunger and desire, and feel his presence. He uses every moment to shape us. He softens our hearts and fills our minds with his love. As we grow spiritually, we can watch as God does amazing things through us. Take refuge and rest in the assurance of his unfailing love.

Proverbs 19:1; Philippians 4:12-13
Point to Ponder: God is your safety net and refuge. Trust him.

Pray: God, keep me connected to you so we grow closer each day. Be my refuge and strength.

June 2

*Sing a new song to the L*ORD, *who has done*
marvelous deeds, Whose right hand and holy arm
*have won the victory ... Before the L*ORD *who comes,*
who comes to govern the earth, To govern the
world with justice and the peoples with fairness.

— Psalm 98:1, 9

Followers of Christ operate in a world of revelation. God reveals his will and plan for us in a myriad of ways: through scripture, through our pastors' and friends' voices, and through our prayers. Turn to God and trust him as we move into the future, ready to face whatever comes. We have nothing to fear.

Some people choose not to live by God's commands and his plans. They have a vision for life and organize their activities accordingly. They function with their own goals and aspirations, and they do what feels good and right in their eyes. Some pray only when troubles abound or when darkness enters their souls. These people are easily tempted by Satan and distracted by fears and temptations, and they fail to grasp God's life-giving truths. They live outside God's will. They do not seek him until they have nowhere else to turn.

God wants to watch over and protect us every day. We are saved by his grace, and he offers us an abundance of wisdom, insight, and guidance. We have only to ask for his help.

The Bible says, "We know that all things work for good for those who love God, who are called according to his purpose" (Rom. 8:28). The all-powerful God wants to make us an instrument of his grace. Be happy and follow his will.

Proverbs 1:32-33; John 20:29
Point to Ponder: God is fair and just.

Pray: God, hear my prayers. Never abandon me. I need you.

June 3

"If you love me, you will keep my commandments.
And I will ask the Father, and he will give you
another Advocate to be with you always, the Spirit
of truth, which the world cannot accept, because
it neither sees nor knows it. But you will know it,
because it remains with you, and will be in you."

— John 14:15-17

God sees all we do to live by his commandments. He looks beyond our rituals of worship, beyond our moral lifestyle, and beyond the time we use to evangelize. The Lord focuses his penetrating gaze to look upon our hearts. God sees our obedience to his ways if our hearts are pure.

He sends an advocate, the Holy Spirit, to help us return to him with a teachable spirit. Cooperate with the Spirit who moves freely within us to guide us as we seek forgiveness and mercy. He purifies our hearts and fills us with love.

Saying and believing we love God requires us to be obedient in good times and in bad. During times of difficulty, when we question God's love, pause and remember when God has intervened and sent us strength and his grace. Think about all the blessings he has sent before.

Make a conscious effort to stop, move away from distractions, and seek God in the quiet of our hearts. Call his name in confident trust, and wait patiently. God hears our prayers and responds in his time. He blesses us with love and peace and fills us with hope. Count on God.

John 15:12-17; Matthew 5:17-20
Point to Ponder: Follow the Ten Commandments. Practice righteousness.

Pray: God, keep me in your loving embrace.

June 4

Bear one another's burdens, and so
you will fulfill the law of Christ.

– Galatians 6:2

God places people in our lives for a reason. Some have emotional or physical needs, and others are searching for peace and contentment. God knows our needs and gives us the right words to use so others draw closer to him. Accept the invitation from Christ to serve others. He gives us blessings and opportunities to carry the burdens for those in need.

God helps us make comments filled with wisdom, understanding, and encouragement. When we speak from the heart, God sends his grace so we say and do the right thing. When we live what we have learned, we spread his message. Uplifting, gentle words and kind actions lessen the burdens for those who are weary.

God enlists us to bring others to him. Often we do not understand or realize the impact our actions and words have on others. Consciously strive to be imitators of Christ so our labors come to fruition. The more we grow in righteousness, the stronger we become to bear another's burden.

People seek those who love God because they present themselves in a joyful and blessed manner. They face life's challenges with an upbeat attitude. Seek God's perfect peace with every new encounter. Let love rule our hearts so we joyfully serve others.

Colossians 3:11; Matthew 6:1-4
Point to Ponder: Bear the burdens of others.

Pray: God, help me interact with others in an upbeat manner. Send me your grace so I spread the gospel in simple and meaningful ways.

June 5

*Bless the L*ORD*, my soul; all my being, bless his holy name! Bless the L*ORD*, my soul; do not forget all the gifts of God, Who pardons all your sins, heals all your ills, Delivers your life from the pit, surrounds you with love and compassion, Fills your days with good things; your youth is renewed like the eagle's.*
— Psalm 103:1-5

Each day we are a new creation in Christ. He invites us to draw closer to him, live in his presence, acknowledge our neediness, and pray continually for his never-ending love and renewal. Strive to experience God himself, not just his activities and blessings.

Every person starts with a clean slate each day. God is merciful, compassionate, and committed to us. He walks with us until the end of time and onward to eternity. Give thanks for God's blessings: answered prayers, the providential care over our families, our homes, and our jobs; and our emotional and spiritual health.

At any time, God may call us to do something completely new. Consider each opportunity as a great adventure and an invitation to follow his will. When we take steps to find God's presence, we also find ways through challenges. He sends all the resources we need to be in union with him. God fills our days with good things. Have faith. God's love is always available and flows out of us as it did for Jesus. The future is bright with God in our hearts.

Isaiah 25:1; Colossians 2:2-3
Point to Ponder: Be in union with God. Follow his ways.

Pray: Lord, thank you for the abundant adventures provided to me. Lead me to eternal life.

June 6

For this very reason, make every effort to
supplement your faith with virtue, virtue with
knowledge, knowledge with self-control, self-control
with endurance, endurance with devotion, devotion
with mutual affection, mutual affection with love.
If these are yours and increase in abundance,
they will keep you from being idle or unfruitful
in the knowledge of our Lord Jesus Christ.

— 2 Peter 1:5-9

Turn to God with great faith. Let him purify our hearts. As Christians, we have everything we need to live abundant lives. Our material wealth, intelligence, and family background do not determine our holiness. Ask God to bind our hearts to his and unite with him more fully as our faith in his goodness and mercy increases. Take every opportunity to grow closer to our Savior. Watch how he transforms our hearts and minds to be more Christ-like and holy.

Knowing God's love, we learn of the advocate who dwells within us. The Holy Spirit teaches us about love, joy, peace, patience, kindness, generosity, gentleness, faithfulness, and self-control. Christians by faith have access to the Holy Spirit and receive these gifts freely. Allow the Spirit to teach us to relinquish attitudes or actions not in keeping with God's truths in scripture. Let go of prejudices, racism, materialism, and consumerism. Follow the ways of God, not the ways of the world.

Be alert for opportunities to supplement our faith with knowledge. Trust God to walk with us each step on our earthly journey and on to eternal life. Feel joy in our hearts.

Galatians 2:15-21; Psalm 32:1-2
Point to Ponder: Grow in knowledge of the Lord.

Pray: Lord, increase my faith. Lead me to be more Christ-like.

June 7

Blessed are the merciful, for they will be shown mercy.
— Matthew 5:7

Scripture teaches us not to be judgmental of others. "Stop judging and you will not be judged. Stop condemning and you will not be condemned. Forgive and you will be forgiven. Give and gifts will be given to you; a good measure, packed together, shaken down, and overflowing, will be poured into your lap. For the measure with which you measure will in return be measured out to you" (Lk. 6:37-38). Be merciful to others to be shown mercy.

Our merciful God withholds the punishment we deserve for our sinfulness. He gives us every opportunity to repent and receive his forgiveness. Christ Jesus is merciful and kind, not quick to anger or judge. Strive to imitate him.

Forgiveness entails having mercy for others. When we cannot forgive, we hurt far more than the person who is not forgiven. Our bitterness turns to anger, which eats away at our souls. Our instinct for revenge is powerful, but an eye-for-an-eye attitude does not benefit anyone. Not forgiving someone is Satan's most clever and common temptation. Satan wants us to remain in sin and not follow Christ's teachings. The evil one wants to separate us from God.

Be alert and stay vigilant to God's commands. Pray for direction. Ask the Lord to help us forgive those who trespass against us. Do not underestimate the positive effects our merciful attitude has upon those whom we encounter. God sees all we do and say. He knows our hearts. Practice mercy. God's mercy and peace free us to enjoy every good thing he has given us.

Luke 6:36-38; Matthew 5:43-48
Point to Ponder: Be merciful. Forgive others as God forgives you.

Pray: God, help me show others mercy as you have shown me. Teach me to forgive.

June 8

*Therefore, putting away falsehood, speak
the truth, each one to his neighbor, for
we are members, one of another.*

                       – Ephesians 4:25

Our lives should be permeated with truth. God put the Holy Spirit of truth within each person when we proclaimed him as Lord and Savior. Every action and word spoken should be truthful with no shades of gray. White lies spoken are not the whole truth. The Lord teaches us through scripture, "Let your 'Yes' mean 'Yes' and your 'No' mean 'No.' Anything more is from the evil one" (Mt. 5:37).

What we say and do reflects the state of our hearts. When Satan tempts us and we succumb to sin, we live a lie filled with deception, and our mouths often speak falsehoods. We focus on worldly efforts to please others. We become filled with pride and self-worth. The world tempts us to compromise the truth. Satan's ways seem pleasing and feel good at first, but this quickly passes. Evil ways lead us to be cynical and eventually to despair.

Stay focused on our Savior, Jesus Christ. Nothing is too difficult for him. Call on Christ with confidence and determination to unbind us and set us free. His truth never restricts us. God is aware of our circumstances, and he sends his grace and strength. Our lives fall into harmony with him as we receive his abundant blessings. God's truths set us free.

Psalm 52:10-11; Deuteronomy 31:6
Point to Ponder: Speak only the truth with no shades of a lie.

Pray: Lord, teach me to speak the truth in every situation. Be with me.

June 9

Therefore I tell you, all that you ask for in prayer,
believe that you will receive it and it shall be yours.
When you stand to pray, forgive anyone against
whom you have a grievance, so that your heavenly
Father may in turn forgive you your transgressions.
— Mark 11:24-25

Sometimes God does not answer our prayers as we expect. He does not give us what we want, but rather what we need to do his will. When this happens, we evaluate what we have asked God to send us.

Some people find prayer difficult during times of sorrow and when faced with life changing situations. When our thoughts churn and confusion sets in, pray the Lord's Prayer (Mt. 6:5-13). Many know this prayer from memory. We can pray as we rush to the next event, or in our homes, at church, and in other social settings at any time of day or night. Jesus taught his disciples these words; they have remained with us through time.

This short prayer teaches us to seek first the kingdom of God and his righteousness. Then we ask God to "forgive us our debts, as we forgive our debtors; and do not subject us to the final test, but deliver us from the evil one" (Mt. 12-13). We pray God forgives us of any sinful acts. When we say The Lord's Prayer, a sense of peace and a confident expectation of God's goodness and mercy fill our hearts. Prayer transforms our lives. God hears every prayer. Reach out to him and whisper his name. Remember, prayer gives us a foretaste of heaven.

Psalm 111:1-4; Matthew 6:5-13
Point to Ponder: Pray every day for God's guidance.

Pray: Jesus, teach me to pray often throughout the day. I know you will lead me.

June 10

*The lamp of the body is the eye. If your eye
is sound, your whole body will be filled with
light; but if your eye is bad, your whole body
will be in darkness. And if the light in you is
darkness, how great will the darkness be.*
— Matthew 6:22-23

Our eyes and brain allow us to read and interpret God's word
through scripture. Strive to practice his teachings and experience
his presence in activities around us.

Our eyes filter the images we see daily. There is a radical
difference between seeing with eyes from a human perspective and
seeing life through spiritual eyes. Spiritual sensitivity to God is a
gift. We have choices as to what we perceive and what we focus on
with our thoughts and actions. Do we look for Jesus in our daily
routines?

Seek his gift of spiritual sight and hearing. Guard against
watching violence and hearing foul language on television or at the
movie theatre. Supervise the video games children play. Violence,
hatred, racism, and terrorism continue in this imperfect world, but
unhealthy images do not have to play over and over in our minds or
in the heads of our children.

Do not allow Satan to rob us of joy and God's peace. Sin
dulls our senses and leaves us spiritually blind. God said what
we see through our eyes shapes the focus of our hearts. Pray God
sensitizes us to see with spiritual eyes and hear with spiritual ears.

Proverbs 20:12; 1 Corinthians 6:19
Point to Ponder: Focus my eyes on the images of Christ.

Pray: God, sharpen my spiritual eyesight so I see clearly your
works and blessings.

June 11

Finally, brothers, rejoice. Mend your
ways, encourage one another, agree with
one another, live in peace, and the God
of love and peace will be with you.

— 2 Corinthians 13:11

God provides for us in every situation. Spiritual wisdom comes from knowing God and trusting him. Scripture comes alive as we grow in wisdom. We strive to understand things from God's perspective.

Only God sees the future. Trust him to lead us to encourage one another, make the right decisions, and live in peace. People who do not know him and have a surface relationship with God, may find our devotion and love for him unreasonable and confusing. Fear not, because the Holy Spirit guides us and remains in our souls as we journey on earth. The Spirit protects and prompts us to follow the will of God.

We grossly underestimate the God we serve. The Lord we serve today is the God who created heaven and earth. Almighty and powerful, the Lord of love and peace sends all the resources and grace we need to live joyfully.

Be obedient to God and watch how life changes. He teaches us to love our fellow man and be merciful and forgiving. Proclaim the word of God to others. Spread the gospel and remain faithful. Through trials and tribulations or in times of great joy, remain in God's presence and receive his peace and love.

Matthew 6:25-27; Psalm 34:2-3
Point to Ponder: Live in peace. Encourage one another.

Pray: Lord, send your blessings of peace and love to me.

June 12

Therefore, put on the armor of God, that you
may be able to resist on the evil day and, having
done everything, to hold your ground. So stand
fast with your loins girded in truth, clothed with
righteousness as a breastplate, and your feet
shod in readiness for the gospel of peace.

— Ephesians 6:13-15

Be self-controlled and alert to Satan's temptations. Sometimes the evil one uses others as unwitting instruments of deception and darkness. Never lose sight of the real enemy. Instead of turning away from an individual caught in the snares of Satan's grip, intervene for that person. Human nature tempts us to walk away from angry and conflicted people. Rather than walking away or retaliating, take steps to free the person from the bondage of sin.

God sends us the resources we need to help those ensnarled in sin. He has already defeated the evil one. He sends his angels to defeat spiritual warfare. We feel Christ living within us. He guides, protects, and reminds us to persevere.

When we consciously help another person turn from sin and find God, we receive grace from him. We have an opportunity to allow God to carry out his works through us. Wear the armor of God and stay vigilant in praise for him. He protects us and enfolds us in his radiant peace. Be his hands and feet on our earthly journey. Imitate him. Give glory to God.

Proverbs 16:3; Psalm 63:8-9
Point to Ponder: Do everything to resist Satan. Trust God.

Pray: Lord, you are my strong deliverer. In you I have all I need. Stay close to me.

June 13

The Lord is far from the wicked, but
the prayer of the just he hears.

– Proverbs 15:29

Prayer is a direct line to God. Encounter him every day through prayer. Begin each day with thoughts of thanksgiving and praise. Throughout the day, pray about safe travels and positive experiences for our family and friends, the leaders in the government, and on and on. End each day by giving thanks for God's continued love and blessings.

Every time Jesus faced a hard decision, he prayed. His life should provide a model for our prayer lives. Scripture tells us, "Rising very early before dawn, he left and went off to a deserted place, where he prayed" (Mk. 1:35). Jesus did this so he could clearly hear his Father's voice. Follow his example. Go to a quiet place, be still, and listen for God to speak.

Prayer is not so much what we say or how we express ourselves, but rather a matter as to what God does. He knows our hearts and thoughts and still loves us. We draw closer to God when we pray. Our relationship with him grows stronger. We cry and shout out to God what we want, but he decides what we need. Accept his will.

God answers all prayers. He sends his grace so we feel his presence. Remain alert in prayer no matter the circumstances. Reflect on the blessings God sends. He wants to feed and strengthen us, but most of all he wants to love us.

Philippians 4:6-7; 1 Thessalonians 5:17, 23-25
Point to Ponder: Be still and pray often. Stay close to God.

Pray: Help me pray and be in your presence, God. Teach me to listen more.

June 14

*When the L*ORD *is pleased with a man's ways, he*
makes even his enemies be at peace with him.

– Proverbs 16:7

The Lord commanded us to love our neighbors. Christians strive to imitate God's love and live in unity with those around them. Those who follow God's commandments are sought after and loved by their fellow man. Honor God by bringing others to him.

Others unconsciously disobey the second commandment, "You shall love your neighbor as yourself" (Mk. 12:31). Some people may ignore their neighbors or avoid the needy or those who are different. People may gossip and ruin an individual's reputation. These behaviors do not imitate Christ-like traits or love for our neighbors.

As followers of Christ, our actions should be permeated with kindness and expressed in practical ways. Consciously focus on how to lessen the burdens of others. When our neighbors experience sorrow, take time to listen and grieve alongside them. If someone verbally abuses you, and the action causes disruption, go to the individual and tell the truth. Face the fear and the outcomes. If you have unintentionally hurt people, and they feel betrayed, go immediately to them. Set aside the self-centered attitude and wear a cloak of humility. Clear the air. Ask God for a kind spirit, a tender heart, and a propensity to forgive others. These qualities build character. Our lives become pleasing to God when we reach out to love and serve others. He sends his peace.

Psalm 15:1-5; Matthew 7:12
Point to Ponder: Strive to please the Lord. Be gentle and kind.

Pray: Lord, live in me so I walk in your image. Let me be an instrument of your peace.

June 15

Attend, my people, to my teachings; listen to the
words of my mouth. I will open my mouth in story,
drawing lessons from of old. We have heard them, we
know them; our ancestors have recited them to us. We
do not keep them from our children; we recite them
to the next generation, The praiseworthy and mighty
deeds of the LORD, the wonders that he performed.
— Psalm 78:1-4

Scripture tells us to teach our children about God. As parents, we model for them; they mimic our smiles, words, and actions. When they see us reading the Bible and praying, they sense God's presence in our lives and want to know more about him. We help them learn about God's goodness and his unconditional love. We teach them to trust God and pray every day. Through stories and our responses to daily events, we teach children about God's never-ending love.

Children benefit from church attendance. They draw closer to God and learn of his mighty deeds. Children reflect on his presence in their lives and learn traditional prayers of praise and thanksgiving. Young people learning about Jesus feel his grace. They come to believe in his goodness and love for everyone.

Teach children to turn to God and rely on his faithfulness. Help them develop a relationship with him. Clarify the Ten Commandments. Building a foundation of God's truths, sets children on the pathway to eternity.

Isaiah 54:13; Ephesians 6:4
Point to Ponder: Teach children about our Lord and Savior and his mighty deeds.

Pray: God, send me grace so that I model your love to my children and all those around me.

June 16

Tell the rich in the present age not to be proud
and not to rely on so uncertain a thing as wealth
but rather on God, who richly provides us with
all things for our enjoyment. Tell them to do
good works, be generous, ready to share, thus
accumulating as treasures a good foundation for
the future, so as to win the life that is true life.
— 1 Timothy 6:17-19

When one accumulates a large amount of wealth, it is easy to go a little crazy and buy expensive things: homes, cars, clothes, and other furnishings. We often spend money with little regard for the needy. We get caught up with worldly riches and focus on ourselves.

The Bible warns us about storing up treasures for our own personal gain. "For the love of money is the root of all evils, and some people in their desire for it have strayed from the faith and have pierced themselves with many pains" (1 Tm. 6:10). Instead of worshiping what money buys, God wants us to serve others and be spiritually wealthy.

Our actions reveal the state of our hearts. When we serve others and impart the love of God, people see him working through us. It takes courage to be a giver. Jesus spoke of generosity and believed it to be more blessed to give than to receive (Acts 20:35). Be a conduit through whom the Lord pours his blessings. Resolve to give more as an expression of love and gratitude to God. Make a difference in the lives of others.

Psalm 18:21-31; Matthew 6:19-21
Point to Ponder: Be generous with all things. True wealth is from God.

Pray: God, give me a kind and generous heart to reach out to the needy and the poor.

June 17

Do not conform yourselves to this age but
be transformed by the renewal of your mind,
that you may discern what is the will of God,
what is good and pleasing and perfect.

– Romans 12:2

We want to follow God's will and strive to be obedient, but sometimes we find his ways hard to discern. When confused, ask the Holy Spirit for understanding in regard to the choices God has placed before us. By asking, we renounce our autonomous power and give God a chance to intervene.

Discuss changes and challenges with important people in our lives. Parents or a spouse often see situations differently. Listen and respect their comments, but know in the end that we are responsible for making choices which please God. Make certain the decisions align with his teachings.

Talk to God directly through prayer. Consult him when we plan a journey, change jobs, buy a car or home, select a vocation, or contemplate a marriage partner. Do not expect to receive a miraculous response or hear a voice telling us what to do. God answers us in his time and in his way.

Sometimes we must walk by faith and listen to others tell us we are crazy. God walks with us. He often stretches us beyond our comfort zone so we grow in knowledge, wisdom, and understanding. God works all things for good even though we may not understand outcomes for many years. The measure in which we fulfill God's will is the measure of our holiness.

Proverbs 16:17; Matthew 7:7-8
Point to Ponder: Discern God's will. Follow him.

Pray: Lord, help me remember to pray before all major decisions. Show me your will. Your plans are my plans. Guide me in my decision making.

June 18

This is how you are to pray: Our Father in
heaven. Hallowed be your name, your kingdom
come, your will be done, on earth as in heaven.
— Matthew 6:9-10

In The Lord's Prayer, Jesus gives us a blueprint of how to pray
and live righteous lives. Some feel overwhelmed and fear his
truths are too difficult to follow. How do we forgive those who
hurt or trespass against us? How might we believe without seeing
and commit fully to the will of God? When we question, do not
become disheartened with all God asks of us.

Do not fear. We belong to God. He cares and asks that we live
according to his plans. He wants us to use our unique gifts and
talents for his glory. Scripture says, "And whatever you do, in word
or in deed, do everything in the name of the Lord Jesus, giving
thanks to God the Father through him" (Col. 3:17).

God's kingdom constantly grows and adapts to answer the
needs and longings of all people of every age and place. His
kingdom grows stronger as we learn to follow his will and strive to
live righteously.

God calls us to give glory to his name and follow his ways.
When we live righteous lives, others observe our actions and
words. Christians, who reflect on the experiences God places
before them, see his hand at work. Trust God to provide for us each
day. Glorify him and draw closer through prayer. He is committed
to loving us.

2 Timothy 4:6-10; Isaiah 6:3-13
Point to ponder: Glorify God every day through prayer and praise.

Pray: Lord, here I am. Use me to build your kingdom. I want to be
like you in every way.

June 19

*I call upon you; answer me, O God. Turn
your ear to me; hear my prayer. Show your
wonderful love, you who deliver with your right
arm those who seek refuge from their foes.
Keep me as the apple of your eye; hide me in
the shadow of your wings from violence of the
wicked. My ravenous enemies press upon me.*

— Psalm 17:6-9

Trust God to intercede on our behalf. This is not wishful thinking but based on truth, as stated in scripture. "So shall my word be that goes forth from my mouth; it shall not return to me void, but shall do my will, achieving the end for which I sent it" (Is. 55:11). When God speaks, trust him. Even though we cannot see him, we know he is there.

At times, static blocks our hearts and minds. When we feel defeated and nothing seems to be going as planned, be still, listen, and call upon God. We allow sinful guilt, fears or anxieties, wounds from an old relationship, or preoccupation with worldly issues to be our focal point. Remove the static blocking God's voice. Every thought and prayer reaches God and he responds. He protects and delivers us from our foes and makes his will clearer to us.

The Lord promises to be there for us when we believe. He sends all the resources we need and teaches us to be flexible, creative, and resourceful. Scripture tells us, "God is our refuge and strength, an ever-present help in distress" (Ps. 46:6). Draw closer to him every day through prayer. Be ready to face what comes knowing he leads us on a path for good.

Mark 8:34-38; Proverbs 3:5-6
Point to Ponder: God guides and protects us.

Pray: God, give me courage to walk the path you have chosen for me.

June 20

*Learn then that I, I alone, am God, and there
is no god besides me. It is I who bring both
death and life, I who inflict wounds and heal
them, and from my hand there is no rescue.*
— Deuteronomy 32:39

Some believers have a surface understanding of God's power and glory. They are recipients of his goodness and mercy but do not know the provider. Some do not understand the importance of reading the Bible. Reading draws us closer to God. The Bible is not just a collection of stories, preventive warnings, or inspirational thoughts. Rather, it states God's word and his ways. Every time we read scripture, God speaks to us. Listen carefully to discern his words and live according to his teachings.

Do not be afraid to surrender to the Lord. Pray to be in his light and presence. Even though we do not know what will happen in the future, we count on God to be by our side. Scripture says, "I command you: be firm and steadfast! Do not fear or be dismayed, for the LORD, your God, is with you wherever you go" (Jos. 1:9). God loves us with an everlasting love that flows out from eternity without limits or conditions.

Take time to know God – really know him. He wants to give us everything we need. Make him the deepest desire of our hearts. Everything is possible when we believe in Christ.

Psalm 103:8-11; Proverbs 22:4
Point to Ponder: There is only one God. Trust him in all situations.

Pray: God, thank you for your compassion and mercy. Make me worthy of your love.

June 21

*For I am the L<small>ORD</small>, your God, who
grasp your right hand; it is I who say to
you, "Fear not, I will help you."*

– Isaiah 41:13

Fear is crippling. To ease the clutches of fear, engage the heart
and pray for a deeper union with God. He sends solace, strength,
and encouragement. Being close to God provides strength to face
all circumstances with a pure heart. At times, problems creep in,
and our faith dwindles. Confusion sets in about the choices to
make to lessen anxiety and worry. Our minds become fuzzy with
indecision. In our haste to fix the problem, do not race ahead of
God and make snap decisions.

The key to receiving God's blessings is to be patient. Pray
for his grace. Focus on prayer and not making hurried decisions
or lashing out at problems with quick fixes. Part of God's plan
requires us to slow down. He wants us to learn patience and how to
be still. His desire is for us to cast all our worries and fears to him.
That's right, *all* our cares. God is not bound by time. Wait for him.
In his time, he reveals his plan. Trust the Lord because he controls
all things.

God carries our burdens. He sends the resources we need to
deal with every situation. Be sensitive to his work. God gives
freely; receive his blessings with a loving and generous heart.
Observe how events change as we walk with him daily. God dwells
within us forevermore.

Psalm 26:1-3; 1 Peter 5:7-11
Point to Ponder: God lessens your fears. Hold tight to him. He
cares.

Pray: Lord, send your grace and peace. Teach me patience.

June 22

*Examine yourselves to see whether you
are living in faith. Test yourselves. Do you
not realize that Jesus Christ is in you? –
unless, of course, you fail the test.*

– 2 Corinthians 13:5

Christians walk faithfully with God every day. Do not lose hope; God wants what is best for us. He uses our activities and circumstances to shape our character to be Christ-like. For example, we proclaim the gospel in our own way, use uplifting words to encourage, and forgive others. With these actions and many others, we honor God.

Have faith and confidence that the Holy Spirit continually intercedes with God on our behalf. Be attuned to the Spirit's promptings in all aspects of life: our relationship with God, the way we deal with challenges, how we demonstrate our love for him, and build his kingdom on earth.

Scripture says, "But without faith it is impossible to please him, for anyone who approaches God must believe that he exists and that he rewards those who seek him" (Heb. 11:6). Have faith God acts on our behalf, whether or not we get exactly the results we desire. Be worthy of his love and devotion because he watches over us and sends what we need.

Believe and watch what God provides. He gives us a sense of balance, hope, and strength. Our encounters with God are always defining and increase our faithfulness and spiritual insight.

Psalm 30:5-6; John 14:6-14
Point to Ponder: Live in faith. Never lose hope.

Pray: God, I want to draw closer to you and be your faithful servant. Thank you for loving me.

 June 23

Do nothing out of selfishness or out of vainglory;
rather, humbly regard others as more important
than yourselves, each looking out not for his own
interest, but [also] everyone for those of others.
　　　　　　　　　　　　　　　　　– Philippians 2:3-4

Looking out for others is difficult, especially if the others look and act differently. Our interactions are a choice. Choose to honor God. Learn to accept and love our neighbors as God commanded. Strive to see God reflected in others.

We hold tightly to our beliefs. We feel weighed down and trapped in situations that require us to be open to others who do not have the same skin color, customs, or religion. We hold onto our pride and self-importance. This earthly tendency impedes us from building a strong relationship with God or serving others. Ask the Lord for help to cultivate humility, change our perspective, and treat everyone with dignity and respect.

Whisper a prayer, "Jesus, be with me." Scripture says, "Humble yourselves before the Lord and he will exalt you" (Jas. 4:10). Ask for guidance to remove prideful attitudes and loosen the bonds that bind us and prohibit us from understanding others. Take a humble stance, which may feel unnatural at first. Continually look to Christ for guidance. Search for ways to be kind, initiate a conversation, and reach out in friendship. God places the right words on our tongues, changes our interactions with others to be more Christ-like, and graces us with self-control when we ask for guidance. Be humble and bring glory to God.

2 Chronicles 7:14; 1 Peter 5:6
Point to Ponder: Accept others. Love your neighbor.

Pray: God, help me accept others and free me from negativity. Teach me to love.

June 24

The Lord will rescue me from every evil threat
and will bring me safe to his heavenly kingdom.
To him be glory forever and ever. Amen.

— 2 Timothy 4:18

Wait on the Lord. At times we may experience illness, broken relationships, sorrow, injuries, disappointments, and rejection. God knows our heartaches. We may pray for his intercession to change things but continue to experience hardships. It is difficult to remain faithful and hopeful when things do not go as we expect. Our journeys and trials become wearisome, but remember to pause and pray. Remain close to God and learn patience.

Waiting on God forces us to be still. He may not answer our prayers the way we expect, but he does send what we need. While waiting, trust God to love and care for us no matter the circumstances. By trusting, we grow and change. Our burdens ease, and we no longer feel bitterness and anger simmering in our hearts. Stay away from sin so evil forces do not rob us of joy and peace. Learn from experiences and realize God is the master teacher.

Pray with hope and faith, letting go of fear, anxiety, and worry. God walks with us step-by-step out of darkness. Give thanks to God for never abandoning us. Our lives are nurtured by him. Like the apostle Paul, we can say, "I have competed well; I have finished the race; I have kept the faith" (2 Tm. 4:7). Remember, God has prepared a place for us in his heavenly kingdom. Give him thanks and praise.

Psalm 27:13-14; Romans 12:12
Point to Ponder: The Lord rescues me from evil.

Pray: God, I put everything in your hands today. Teach me to wait for you. Praise to you, Lord.

June 25

Commit your way to the LORD;
trust that God will act.

– Psalm 37:5

Our relationship with God is meant to be love-filled and enjoyable. He is like a nurturing mother to her child. He provides comfort, hope, and healing. Like a mother who continually finds ways to care, our Lord is deeply committed to us. Be as committed to him. God looks at our hearts and knows whether we love.

Our relationship with God should be precious to us. Knowing him brings joy, hope, and great satisfaction. If any barrier ever keeps us from worshiping him, break it down. Return to him; spend time with God daily. Build a close relationship through prayer and praise. Give thanks to the Lord.

We experience blessings from God and feel his presence. He initiates the encounters and calls us by name. He fills our hearts with love. God wants us to share this love and his goodness with others. He reveals this through our relationships with family and friends. These blessings touch our hearts and renew our minds so that we start thinking more like him. When we sense him working in our lives, join in the activity so others see his goodness and mercy through our actions. Give God praise and glory.

Trust him to pour his love into us so we become a beacon and light to others. Reflect his goodness, mercy, kindness, and love. Commit our ways to the Lord.

Proverbs 3:5-6; Psalm 37:23-24
Point to Ponder: Commit to God and watch how he transforms your life.

Pray: God, I trust you to lead me as I draw closer to you.

June 26

*I love you, L*ORD*, my strength, L*ORD*, my rock,*
my fortress, my deliverer. My God, my rock
of refuge, my shield, my saving horn, my
*stronghold! Praised be the L*ORD*, I exclaim!*
I have been delivered from my enemies.

— Psalm 18:3-4

God wants a personal relationship with each of us. When we come to know him, we change. Friends see differences in our attitudes, words, and interactions with others. As he did with the disciples, God sends us out to teach and spread his gospel. We approach life without malice and look for good in all things. We do not judge our fellow man for only God's judgment matters. We develop strong faith and strive to have pure and generous hearts.

Some people do not know God. They yearn for his presence but do not know how to find him. There are levels of intimacy with God. People have memories of church attendance as children, but no one ever attempted to bring them back to the Lord when they were adults. Some pray infrequently, and only when they are struggling or when God's help is needed. Others have not opened a Bible in years. They lack knowledge of our Lord.

As Christians, we have only to invite our neighbors to seek Christ. If we bring them to him through our actions or words, God does the rest. He works in others' lives, even before we see anything happening. Trust him to be our stronghold, unseen but tenderly present and waiting to be a refuge for everyone. Trust God to act.

Hebrews 13:8; Psalm 18:3-4
Point to Ponder: Praise God. He is your refuge and strength.

Pray: Lord, thank you for always being a whispered prayer away. Let my knowledge of you increase. Remove my anxieties and fears.

June 27

"Stop judging and you will not be judged. Stop condemning and you will not be condemned. Forgive and you will be forgiven."

– Luke 6:37

God judges what we have done and contributed on earth when we stand before him on judgment day. The Bible says, "For we must all appear before the judgment seat of Christ, so that one may receive recompense, according to what he did in the body, whether good or evil" (2 Cor. 5:10). Do not judge our neighbors or throw the first stone when someone sins. We have all sinned. Ask God to use us as his ministers for those wallowing in sin. Pray they find God's light and seek his forgiveness. He forgives sinners over and over again when they repent.

Look at our neighbors through lenses of love. God knows each person's heart and motives. When someone hurts us deeply, it is easy to hold a grudge and not forgive them. There is something heady about not forgiving someone for the hurt and pain they caused. As time passes, the feeling of self-righteous pity fades. Left feeling powerless to change the past infraction, the unforgiving attitudes enslave us. God commands us to forgive. "Jesus answered, 'I say to you, not seven times but seventy-seven times'" (Mt. 18:22). Strive to forgive others to the point of it becoming second nature so we do not sin against the Lord. God's forgiveness toward us is limitless, so should ours be to others.

John 1:12-18; Psalm 18:16-20
Point to Ponder: Stop judging others. Look for God in every person.

Pray: God, have mercy on me and forgive my sins.

June 28

Be still before the Lord; wait for God. Do not be provoked by the prosperous, nor by malicious schemers. Give up your anger, abandon your wrath; do not be provoked; it brings only harm. Those who do evil will be cut off, but those who wait for the Lord will possess the land.

— Psalm 37:7-9

We pray for God to intervene when things do not go our way. By faith, we hope he hears our prayers and answers them according to our desires. God's powerful presence remains with believers.

Sometimes God's will is hard for us to discern. We pray and hope our situation changes in a certain way and then it does not. We plead with the Lord and continue to pray but get impatient if God answers our prayers differently than what we expect. When this happens, we feel abandoned, lose hope, and may express anger. Do not despise these feelings.

Call out to God. Go to a quiet place and communicate with him. Ask for the strength to know and understand his will. Seek patience and guidance. Have faith God works on our behalf. God's timing is perfect.

Being a follower of Christ is not easy. We continually make choices with struggles to overcome. God never leaves us. Seek his peace and refuge. God transforms our trials into blessings. Praise his holy name.

Proverbs 3:3-4; 1 Samuel 16:7
Point to Ponder: Draw closer to God through prayer.

Pray: Thank you for always watching over me and for loving me, Lord.

June 29

Know that the Lᴏʀᴅ works wonders for the faithful;
the Lᴏʀᴅ hears when I call out. Tremble and
do not sin; upon your beds ponder in silence.
Offer fitting sacrifice and trust in the Lᴏʀᴅ.

– Psalm 4:4-6

Those of us who live righteous lives have a special place in God's heart. We avoid sin because it separates us from God. We strive always to be godly people in every interaction and circumstance. We live by faith.

We have an intimate relationship with God and seek him through prayer without ceasing. Scripture says, "And we have this confidence in him, that if we ask anything according to his will, he hears us. And if we know that he hears us in regard to whatever we ask, we know that what we have asked him is ours" (1 Jn. 5:14-15). We have faith he stands ready to help us.

A righteous person's faith is not easily shattered. God hears our prayers and immediately responds. He is capable of sending miracles: healing the sick, feeding many people with little food, and calming the seas. The Lord never allows Satan to conquer our lives. Godly people have strong faith and believe the more we worship, glorify, and praise God, the closer we draw to him. God expects us to honor him wherever we go with our words, actions, and our lives. He sends blessings galore to those he loves. Honor God by trusting him in every situation.

Matthew 10:7-15; Mark 4:35-41
Point to Ponder: Thank God for his amazing grace. He works wonders.

Pray: Lord, strengthen my faith. Lead me always.

June 30

He said to them, "Because of your little
faith. Amen, I say to you, if you have faith
the size of a mustard seed, you will say to
this mountain, 'Move from here,' and it will
move. Nothing will be impossible for you."

– Matthew 17:20

Jesus spent time explaining things to his disciples because he
wanted them to understand the mysteries of heaven and why God
sent him to walk with men on earth. He often spoke in parables
and then answered questions. The parable about the mustard seed
is one Jesus used to teach about the importance of faith.

Our relationship with God is largely determined by our faith.
Even for those who feel they have strong faith, we are tested when
troubles and problems abound.

Faith grows only in response to a personal call from God. He
wants us to turn to him every day. We pray, perform good works,
attend church, encourage others and make sacrifices in the name
of God so all see our good works. But if we do not have faith and
trust that the blessings from God continue all the way to eternity,
we disappoint him.

Trust God. Faithfully communicate with him through prayer.
Be obedient. Ask him to show us the way and how to follow his
will. God sends his grace and makes us instruments of his peace
to bring others out of darkness and into his marvelous presence.
Encounter God in our hearts and feel the peace of his presence. Be
faithful to him always as he is to us.

Hebrews 11:6; Matthew 10:26-33
Point to Ponder: Nothing is impossible for God.

Pray: God, by your grace help me build strong faith.

 July 1

Hatred stirs up disputes, but love covers all offenses.
— Proverbs 10:12

Many people do not know God. Some live in a sinful state; they carry anger and hatred within their souls. The hate within is like a boil coming to a head, painful and festering. These emotions harden the heart and leave one with little hope for a better life.

In his grace, God has made a provision for those who turn away from him and dwell in a world of sorrow, hate, and darkness. He gives each person the Holy Spirit. The Spirit continues to prompt individuals to find a light to lead them out of darkness. This light may come from a person taking an interest in the hurting individual and talking to them about God, or through reading the Bible, or by focusing on others and their Christ-like behaviors.

We Christians cannot live as if we have no responsibility toward our neighbors. As people of dignity, made in the image and likeness of God, scripture tells us we should love our neighbors. Consciously reach out to people who are less fortunate. Encourage them by using uplifting words and kind actions. Model the love God has for us. He holds us accountable for how we relate to others.

Share the good news of God's love. We function as his voice on earth. Teach others to value God's presence and find their way back to him. Help them find hope in the light of Christ.

Isaiah 50:4-9; Psalm 105:7
Point to Ponder: Hatred stirs up trouble. Love is the way.

Pray: God, have mercy on me. Cleanse my heart of all hatred. Keep me rooted in the simplicity of your love.

 July 2

So let us confidently approach the throne of grace
to receive mercy and to find grace for timely help.
– Hebrews 4:16

All believers have sinned during their lifetime, but God is merciful and does not punish us as harshly as we deserve. Jesus told the crowds at the Sermon on the Mount, "Blessed are the merciful for they will be shown mercy" (Mt. 5:7). Mercy is a precious gift from God.

When someone hurts us and commits a wrong of sorts, there is a natural tendency to strike back and seek revenge – an eye for an eye. God wants us to turn the other cheek and try our best to forgive. He does not want us to compound the injustice. Showing mercy when the pain is deep is difficult. Call out to God for the grace to forgive and have mercy on our brothers and sisters. Trust he hears us and acts.

God asks us to show mercy. Follow his example. Extend the hand of forgiveness. Focus on building bridges to unite others and not walls or barriers to keep people away. Pray for God's help to see our own weaknesses and need for mercy so that we put the offenses of others in their proper light. Be like Jesus and whisper, "Father, forgive them, they know not what they do" (Lk. 23:34). God sends us grace to forgive others. Be merciful and forgive those who trespass against us.

Luke 6:36; Colossians 3:12
Point to Ponder: Seek mercy and forgive others.

Pray: Jesus, teach me to let go of my hurt and resentment. Help me forgive those who trespass against me.

July 3

*Let my cry come before you, Lord; in keeping with
your word give me discernment. Let my prayer come
before you; rescue me according to your promise.*
— Psalm 119:169-170

At times, our worries and fears take hold of every waking thought.
We become overwhelmed, lose sight of the big picture, and find
prayer difficult. We become lethargic and out of balance with the
demands of life.

When troubles and responsibilities get heavy and play havoc
with our emotions, we need to rest. The type of rest we need is not
just a good night's sleep but rest for our souls. We become fatigued
from carrying the weight of stress for ourselves and others. We
wear ourselves out beyond physical tiredness.

When this happens, find the rest that only God gives. Do not
try to cope alone. Break away and find a quiet place to pray. Go
to the inner room of our hearts and lean on Christ. Be like Jesus
and find time alone to pray. He rarely had privacy away from
the crowds. He sought rest and strength from his Father. Call out
to God.

Close communication with him eases our weariness. Spending
time alone with God invigorates us, restores our strength, and
recharges our souls like nothing else. He helps us find balance in
our lives. He responds with love, healing, and grace.

Proverbs 7:1-3; Matthew 11:28-30
Point to Ponder: God calms your soul.

Pray: God, your love is a stronghold. Help me grow in strength and
balance.

July 4

For my thoughts are not your thoughts, nor are your ways my ways, says the LORD. As high as the heavens are above the earth, so high are my ways and my thoughts above your thoughts.

— Isaiah: 55:8-9

The Lord increasingly calls us to follow him. We busy ourselves with ways to serve the Lord through prayer, service, and evangelization. We treat our neighbors with love, have an honorable work ethic, and even watch our actions in public. Yet we still have times of confusion and unrest.

Sometimes we let down our guard and fail to follow all of God's commandments. Aware of our weaknesses, we turn away. Our prayer life is minimal or nonexistent.

We have all sinned, but more important, believers return to Christ and seek his limitless power to forgive our waywardness. We realize the importance of God's mercy and love; without it, we are nothing.

Seek God's unconditional love. Work to fulfill the role Christ has given us. No matter how ordinary we feel, our lives are shaped to be extraordinary. No matter how slow the process, we do our part to have God's kingdom on earth grow stronger. God works in mysterious ways and with infinite wisdom. During times of change and growth, God moves in our midst. Draw closer to him, and give glorious thanks for his presence.

Philippians 4:19; 2 Timothy 2:1-7
Point to Ponder: Follow God's ways. Ask for help to follow his plan.

Pray: Lord, fill me with your grace. Guide me in all I do to serve you.

 July 5

*"My son, do not disdain the discipline of the
Lord or lose heart when reproved by him;
for whom the Lord loves, he disciplines; he
scourges every son he acknowledges."*

— Hebrews 12:5-6

At times, we become entangled in sin. Satan's temptations and evil
ways creep up on us. Sin is subtle and at first seems to be a bad
mistake. But then the evil one leads us further down his dark path.
We wallow in mistakes, weaknesses, and troubles. Satan distracts
us and moves us away from God.

The Holy Spirit prompts us to return to the light. He guides
us to seek God's grace. Through prayer and help from others, we
move slowly away from the grip of Satan and closer to Christ. The
journey out of sin is difficult. God removes the evil because he
does not want us to become defeated about our wrongful ways. But
he disciplines those he loves at the same time.

The consequences of sin may be unpleasant and not in the
likeness of our merciful and forgiving God. He wants us to
experience the negative consequences so we learn from them and
not repeat sinful acts. God disciplines us to gain our attention and
bring necessary changes to our lives. He warns us of the dangers
we face while living in sin.

God wants ultimate good for every person. Take small steps of
faith knowing he lifts us up and uses us in extraordinary ways for
his glory.

Psalm 103:19-22; Exodus 3:11-15
Point to Ponder: God gently disciplines those he loves.

Pray: Lord, help me sin no more. Purify my heart and strengthen
me in your love.

 July 6

*God is Spirit, and those who worship him
must worship in Spirit and truth.*

– John 4:24

We are taught from a young age to worship God, and we want to
draw closer to him and seek a personal and real encounter with
him. How do we have an intimate relationship with God?

The answer lies in faith and prayer. There is no escaping God.
He finds us and knows our hearts. He wants us to come face-to-
face with him when we pray. True worship means we have faith
and trust that he is there for us. We are his children. He leads us to
righteousness and away from our own sinfulness. He shows us how
to be joyful and express forgiveness for those who have trespassed
against us. The Holy Spirit, God in us, teaches us to pray.

True worship and knowing God is life-changing. We please
him when we love one another; feel joy and peace; show kindness,
gentleness, patience; and have generous hearts. We recognize who
God is: holy, almighty, our Savior, and our merciful Father.

Christians want to convey the love of Christ and put our faith
into action. We have a yearning in our hearts to bring others to
God. When we feel compelled to share with others all he has
given us, our faith is firmly grounded. By worshiping God daily,
we develop a foundation of peace and truth to weather any storm.
Build a personal relationship with the Lord and be transformed.
Encounter God and worship him in Spirit and truth.

John 14:6; Colossians 1:15-23
Point to Ponder: Be persistent. Pray every day.

Pray: Lord, you are my Savior. Help me bring others to you to
witness your love.

 July 7

Praise the Lord who is so good; God's love
endures forever; Praise the God of gods;
God's love endures forever; Praise the Lord
of lords; God's love endures forever.

– Psalm 136:1-4

We believers function best with love in our hearts. Love is a gift from God. Only as we grow closer to God and feel his presence, do we realize all we have comes from him.

We see love expressed through our actions and words. Watching a newly married couple being attentive to one another, or new parents caring for their baby, gives us glimpses of love. Our limited understanding of love hinders us. We fail to understand God's unconditional love. He loves us always without reservation. He cannot stop loving us.

No one is perfect. At times we succumb to Satan and find ourselves living in sin. Nothing seems to fall into place. While living under the influence of Satan, our happiness flees, and we find ourselves distraught. When this happens, stop and reflect on our actions and thoughts. Have we taken time to pray? Do we rush from one activity to another without much rest? Do we have love in our lives with God as our focus? If we answered no to any of these questions, we need to adjust our thinking and actions.

God's love follows us and endures forever. When we seek God and repent, he reclaims us. Ever faithful, ever patient, God never gives up on us.

Psalm 100:4-5; Proverbs 15:15
Point to Ponder: God provides love abundantly and forever.

Pray: Lord, have mercy on me and continue to show me how to love.

 July 8

Blessed be the God and Father of our Lord Jesus
Christ, the Father of compassion and God of
all encouragement, who encourages us in every
affliction, so that we may be able to encourage those
who are in any affliction with the encouragement
with which we ourselves are encouraged by God.

– 2 Corinthians 1:3-4

When tasks seem daunting, direct thoughts and works to God. Whisper, "Jesus, help me." God hears and responds. As we strive to complete difficult tasks with promptings from Christ, our work becomes less strenuous. God sends encouragement. He knows our needs.

Sometimes we forget about seeking God's help when tasks are mundane and less challenging. We feel less dependent on him on calm days. During these times, life holds many positive experiences. We get busy loving life and the blessings sent from God. As our minds slip into neutral, we forget to take time to give thanks and pray.

Gradually we find ourselves becoming less and less dependent on God – until we wake up one day and feel as if we live in a desert. Things begin to go opposite our plans. We feel sadness, doubt, or boredom. We have hit a dry spell. In times like these, pray more. God never abandons us, but he does remind us to depend on him.

Our happiness depends on our close relationship to the Lord. Remember to connect to him through prayer every day. Never stop starting over each day giving thanks and praise. His love heals and empowers us to press on.

Psalm 105:1-4; Proverbs 16:3
Point to Ponder: God is compassionate and loving.

Pray: Lord, help me give thanks and draw closer to you every day through prayer.

 July 9

Even a fool, if he keeps silent, is considered
wise; if he closes his lips, intelligent.

– Proverbs 17:28

Words have power. Multiple warnings appear in the Bible, cautioning us to watch our words so they do not come out as deadly shrapnel that pierces the heart. Sins of the tongue are like poison when spoken harshly and with little thought.

Some may be able to recall a time when harsh words impacted them to the point of causing real harm. Hurtful phrases such as: "You're a loser," and "I wish I never had you," or "You are such a disappointment to me," or "I'm sick of you," come to mind and linger as sad and hurtful memories.

The Bible says, "All bitterness, fury, anger, shouting, and reviling must be removed from you, along with all malice" (Eph. 4:31). God wants us to make truthful uplifting comments filled with hope and love. If our words are not such, we should speak less and listen more. Words spoken at the right time restore harmony. They have the ability to revive, heal, and change lives.

Countless times during the day we make choices. When faced with the choice of speaking godly kind-spirited words, or responding harshly, choose kindness or hold your tongue. Count to ten silently and listen without commenting. Ask God to soften our words so they are never hurtful. He fills us with grace as we become his voice on earth.

1 John 3:18; Ephesians 4:29-32
Point to Ponder: Think before you speak. Use kind words with a gentle tone.

Pray: God, place uplifting and healing words on my tongue. Send me the grace to listen more.

 July 10

Greet one another with a loving kiss.
Peace to all of you who are in Christ.

— 1 Peter 5:14

Throughout history man has greeted one another with a handshake or other gesture. Reaching out our hands to others is a welcoming gesture. Outstretched hands provide a warm touch of comfort or kinship to greet friends, neighbors, or family. Jesus used his outstretched hands to welcome his disciples. In church we use our hands in prayer, praise, and worship.

When we meet another person, we come face-to-face with Christ. How we greet our fellow man matters. Scripture tells us, "Amen, amen, I say to you, whoever receives the one I send receives me, and whoever receives me receives the one who sent me" (Jn. 13:20). This means we should be open and not judge others by their clothing, the color of their skin, or their ethnicity. First impressions are important, but if we have an unfavorable first impression, remember to not be quick to judge. Consciously give the person additional chances to change a negative impression. If we find ourselves uncomfortable and judgmental, pray for God's grace.

We Christians must be sensitive to the times in which we live. Extending our hands for a handshake or giving one another a gentle hug, shows the love Jesus wanted his followers to share. These actions should be viewed in light of how they affect others. Never intentionally make someone uncomfortable with an unwelcome touch. A smile and simple handshake are appropriate and customary. God sees all we do and hears our comments. Make him proud!

1 Timothy 2:8; Luke 4:40
Point to Ponder: Reach out to welcome others with a kind gesture.

Pray: Lord, teach me how to love. Show me your ways. Help me have a kind and gentle soul.

 July 11

Owe nothing to anyone, except to love one
another; for the one who loves another has
fulfilled the law. Love does no evil to the neighbor;
hence, love is the fulfillment of the law.
                                        – Romans 13:8, 10

Jesus has such love for us we cannot comprehend its power or depth. His love enriches our lives. As Jesus walked with his disciples, the Father's love filled his being. No ordinary love could keep Jesus obedient to his Father throughout his walk on earth. No other love could motivate him to suffer as he did and eventually die on the cross. Only God's love was powerful enough to compel Jesus to commit his life to the saving purpose of his Father.

Jesus wanted the disciples to have this kind of love in their hearts. We cannot be close to God without embracing his love. He desires us to go out and meet people, to touch them, and listen to their stories. That is how we break through our spiritual poverty and find the grace to love our neighbors as God commanded.

Many people find it difficult to love their neighbors or people who do not share the same values or traditions unless they have God's love in their hearts. Seek his love. Ask God for opportunities to give away this gift. Learn to encounter others with the right attitude. Accept them as a child of God. His love has no limits. Serve him by sharing love with others. He never stops calling us to love.

Matthew 13:24-30; Psalm 50:5-6
Point to Ponder: Love one another.

Pray: Jesus, put away my resistance to those who are different so I follow your commandment to love my neighbor.

 July 12

> *The Lord's Prayer: He was praying in a certain*
> *place, and when he had finished, one of his*
> *disciples said to him, "Lord, teach us to pray*
> *just as John taught his disciples." He said to*
> *them, "When you pray, say: Father, hallowed*
> *be your name, your kingdom come. Give us*
> *each day our daily bread and forgive us our*
> *sins for we ourselves forgive everyone in debt*
> *to us, and do not subject us to the final test."*
> — Luke 11:1-4

At times, we find difficulty in calling out to God because of hurt, fears, or troubles. When this happens, pause and repeat the prayers tucked in our hearts. Say the Lord's Prayer over and over. When we pray unceasingly, we feel God's presence.

God listens, forgives, and sends us his loving mercy. He has overwhelming compassion for those who suffer: the poor, the sick, the rejected, and those who live in sin and darkness.

Call on God. He hears our prayers and knows our suffering. Christ sends us strength to walk toward the light of eternal life. If too weak to walk on our own, God carries us. Remember that the Bible says, "Have no anxiety, but in everything, by prayer and petition, with thanksgiving, make your requests known to God. Then the peace of God that surpasses all understanding will guard your hearts and minds in Christ Jesus" (Phil. 4:6-7).

Pray unceasingly. God is forever faithful and answers our prayers.

Psalm 138:7-8; Romans 8:26
Point to Ponder: Never stop praying. He hears and responds.

Pray: Lord, allow me to draw closer to you through prayer. I have faith you hear and respond in your time.

July 13

Do not be deceived, my beloved brothers: all good
giving and every perfect gift is from above, coming
down from the Father of lights, with whom there
is no alteration or shadow caused by change.

— James 1:16-17

Our skills and talents are gifts from God. This knowledge frees us to use our unique gifts for his glory. We have the potential to help and bless everyone we meet.

Sometimes we may feel God expects too much from us. We often face tasks that seem impossible. When God places challenges before us, we should not turn away and treat his commands as implausible. The Bible says, "Jesus looked at them and said, 'For human beings this is impossible, but for God all things are possible'" (Mt. 19:26).

If God leads us to a situation and directs our actions, nothing is impossible. Our faith in him and his strength see us through any challenge. The Apostle Paul said, "I have the strength for everything through him who empowers me" (Phil. 4:13). Paul's faith in God never faltered. Neither should our faith falter.

God leads us to experiences which seem impossible to accomplish with our own strength. He sends the resources we need to meet success and accomplish his will. Be obedient and faithful. He wants us to use the gifts wisely. He asks us to show obedience, persistence, and faithfulness. Count on him to do the rest.

1 Peter 4:10-11; 1 Corinthians 12:4-11
Point to Ponder: Use gifts and talents from God wisely.

Pray: God, I want to be obedient and serve you. Send me your grace and strength.

 July 14

> *"Not everyone who says to me, 'Lord, Lord,' will*
> *enter the kingdom of heaven, but only the one*
> *who does the will of my Father in heaven."*
>
> – Matthew 7:21

Salvation is for everyone who believes and strives to implement the truths of God. Strive to be faithful and obedient to God. Seek to please him as we follow his will.

Some who attend church and proclaim to love the Lord, do not always follow what they hear and read. Scripture tells us to love our neighbors. Yet people hold resentment toward others because of skin color, their ethnicity, or their lifestyle. One may be kind to a person when speaking face-to-face but then gossips about the person behind his or her back. These types of behaviors do not honor God.

In the Bible we read, "There are six things the Lord hates, yes, seven are an abomination to him; Haughty eyes, a lying tongue, and hands that shed innocent blood; A heart that plots wicked schemes, feet that run swiftly to evil, The false witness who utters lies, and he who sows discord among brothers" (Prv. 6:16-19). If the Lord hates these things, we should also hate them. God lives and directs our paths. Seek his presence and his truths.

As we nurture our relationship with God and practice his life-changing words, we feel him working powerfully in our lives. Trust him. He leads us to eternal life.

Psalm 103:6-10; Matthew 13:36-43
Point to Ponder: Follow the will of God.

Pray: Lord, I will abide by your word as you lead me on a journey to heaven.

July 15

Everyone who acknowledges me before
others, I will acknowledge before my Heavenly
Father. But whoever denies me before others,
I will deny before my heavenly Father.
– Matthew 10:32-33

Believers surrender to the Lord and glorify his holy name. The Ten Commandments, developed by God and given to Moses, provide a roadmap for righteous living. We believe when we walk in close harmony with the Lord, every promise God made in scripture becomes available to us. When we seek the Lord and ask for something in his name, he gives us what we need. The Bible says, "Amen, amen, I say to you, whatever you ask the Father in my name he will give you. Until now you have not asked anything in my name; ask and you will receive, so that your joy may be complete" (Jn. 16:23-24).

If we do not receive answers to our prayers immediately, do not become discouraged. God may be preparing us to receive his truths and answers differently than what we expect. Be patient. Continue to build a relationship with God. He sends what we need in his time.

God sees all we do to serve him and others, as we spread his gospel. He restores our energy and strengthens us. God's way is best. Work diligently for him. Hear his gentle voice calling us. Thank him for answered prayers and for those answered differently than we expect. Acknowledge his goodness and mercy. God's power and presence are continual sources of joy.

Proverbs 28:5; Psalm 26:4-12
Point to Ponder: Acknowledge God's almighty power.

Pray: Lord, I trust and love you. Let your light shine on me. Open my eyes to your presence.

 July 16

Although you have not seen him you love him; even
though you do not see him now yet believe in him,
you rejoice with an indescribable and glorious joy.
— 1 Peter 1:8-9

We Christians love the Lord without touching or seeing him. We feel blessed when we move beyond our own limitations and reach out in faith to love and serve him.

In the Bible we read about Thomas, one of the twelve disciples. His doubting character followed him because he did not believe when the other disciples said they had seen Jesus. Christ allowed Thomas to touch his wounds. "Jesus said to him, 'Have you come to believe because you have seen me? Blessed are those who have not seen and have believed'" (Jn. 20:29). God wants us not to linger in doubt and confusion, but rather return to him in faith and hope. Believe in his love. God is present at all times. When confused and disheartened, be still and hear him whisper your name. Sense his presence in adversity. God works on our behalf to bring good out of chaos. Stay connected through prayer. Feel relief and peace when burdens lighten. Thank him.

Share the blessings we receive from God with others. Every day brings new opportunities and a fresh start. Rejoice in our choices to bring glory to God. Even though we cannot touch or see him, God lingers close to us. Do everything for his glory.

James 1:2-4; Acts 2:22-28
Point to Ponder: God is real. Believe in him.

Pray: God, fill me with your love. Teach me to demonstrate joy and peace to others.

 July 17

Call to me, and I will answer you; I will tell to you
things great beyond reach of your knowledge.
– Jeremiah 33:3

Preoccupied with our jobs, raising our family, and rushing from one event to the other, we have many people influencing our lives. We have limited opportunity to pray. We often operate on the shallowest levels of prayer, but God wants more from us. When we get too busy to pray or too tired, lift short prayers up to him. This brings God back into focus.

The life of Jesus provides a model for us. Often surrounded by people, he made himself go to a quiet place to pray. He prayed alone. Jesus listened to his Father as he revealed his will.

Imitate Jesus and not allow hectic schedules to interfere with our prayer time.

Our primary focus must be on God. Block out worldly distractions and reconnect with him. If we concentrate on people and their weaknesses at work or at home, and witness their negative attitudes, we become frustrated and pessimistic. Instead, remember to fix our eyes on God, and be persistent with short prayers. He knows us and what we need. God sends us the knowledge, the strength, and the patience to help ourselves and others. He lightens our burdens and lifts us up.

Have faith. God always answers our prayers. Live each day knowing and believing he directs our steps. Remember that prayer aligns our lives with God. He sees our imperfections and still loves us. Encounter God every day.

Matthew 6:7-8; Isaiah 61:10-11
Point to Ponder: Seek knowledge from God through prayer.

Pray: Lord, teach me to pray unceasingly and with a pure heart.

 July 18

The eyes of the Lord *are in every place,*
keeping watch on the evil and the good.

– Proverbs 15:3

God cares for us. We are his handiwork and affected by his love. No human love comes close to the love God has for his children. He watches over us and sends his strength, grace, and angels to protect us. We are the crown of his creation.

Follow God's will. This does not come naturally for many. Some days we fall short and step out on our own without him. We feel capable and able to handle any situation. Prayer ceases, and we no longer seek his strength. We turn our focus from God to earthly matters. Prideful ambition takes over.

In his mercy, God has made provisions for our weaknesses. We each have received the Holy Spirit at baptism. The Spirit is God in our souls. He prompts us to correct our wrongfulness. The reminder to seek God is like a thorn in our side. The thorn digs deep in us until we return to him, and ask for his mercy. We need to quiet our hearts and listen to the promptings of the Spirit.

The Bible says, "My grace is sufficient for you, for power is made perfect in weakness" (2 Cor. 12:9). When we are weak, Christ by his grace makes us strong. Build a shatterproof relationship with God. Make every effort to live close to him. Pray every day and follow his will. He is the God of love and peace.

Genesis 1:27; Psalm 97:1-6
Point to Ponder: God sees all you do and hears what you say. He protects us.

Pray: Lord, send your grace upon me. Help me gain the prize of salvation.

July 19

The Lord loves those who hate evil, protects
the lives of the faithful, rescues them from the
hand of the wicked. Light dawns for the just;
gladness, for the honest of heart. Rejoice in the
Lord, you just, and praise his holy name.

— Psalm 97:10-12

Ask God to purify our hearts, and watch as he transforms us. Be open to God's message and listen for him. Through prayer and praise, be in close communication with him. The truth does not penetrate our hearts and minds unless we surrender to God. We strengthen our relationship with him through prayer. Hear the Lord's messages through Bible readings, promptings from the Holy Spirit, words from friends, as well as in music and in worship.

Sometimes we fall short of following the Lord's ways, and our hearts harden. Repent and seek God's mercy. Meditate on his word until his teachings become part of our souls and our hearts. Allow God to show us his truths and then apply them to our lives. Let his teachings become our reality.

Be vigilant about praying unceasingly. Do not become overly concerned with worldly matters. God knows what we think. He knows our struggles and supports our efforts to love and serve. The Lord protects the faithful and the pure of heart. There are no barriers to him. Trust the Lord to rescue us and heal our hearts. Praise his holy name.

Jeremiah 29:12-15; Proverbs 4:18-19
Point to Ponder: The Lord loves those who hate evil.

Pray: Lord, never allow me to be separated from your love. Give me the grace I need to grow closer to you every day.

 July 20

Understand, then, that the Lord, your God, is God
indeed, the faithful God who keeps his merciful
covenant down to the thousandth generation toward
those who love him and keep his commandments.
                                        – Deuteronomy 7:9

God never tires of loving and rescuing us from our sinfulness. Repent and look to God for his forgiveness and mercy. He cleanses us from all unrighteousness.

The Lord knows us by name. He sees us worshiping, praising his holy name, and trying our best to follow his will. Ask him to allow us to make a difference in our homes and with our friends. He remembers us and the sacrifices we make, even the small ones we think go unnoticed.

God is the creator of wisdom and knowledge. There is no point in trying to fool he who is all knowing. God's opinions matter. When we do not follow his word, he allows us to fail. We suffer pain and disappointment before we remember to turn to our Savior. This brings us into a deeper relationship with God. He never leaves us in a hopeless state.

His truths never restrict us. God raises us up in his time and in his own way. Be faithful to God as he is to us. He is endlessly patient. Trust him to know how to lead us on a path that leads to him. Nothing is impossible for God. He asks us to be stewards of his word.

John 8:23-30; Psalm 106:6-12
Point to Ponder: God is faithful and unchanging.

Pray: Lord, thank you for your faithfulness to me. Teach me to always place my trust in your hands and rely on you. Increase my faith.

July 21

Give to the Lord the glory due God's name.
Bow down before the Lord's holy splendor!
— Psalm 29:2

Seek God through prayer. Give him all glory and honor, because he is our strength. He places us in the right setting so we follow his will. Through his guidance, we bring others to him. We walk by faith and know he intercedes at the appropriate time. We step out, sometimes hesitantly, to embrace opportunities presented to us. God works through us. His power is strong, steady, and unchanging. He leads us to live righteous lives.

The Lord clears out the clutter from our hearts and minds so we are receptive to follow his plan. Take one step at a time. God's grace and his faithfulness guide us. Scripture says, "Then you may securely go your way, your foot will never stumble; When you lie down, you need not be afraid, when you rest, your sleep will be sweet" (Prv. 3:23-24).

God has promised to provide abundantly. Rejoice in his vision for us as he sets a new direction with worthwhile goals. Step out in faith. God does not want us to fail; his plan is always for good. Worshiping him transforms us into the people he desires us to be. Go forward in trust to meet any challenge. God takes each step with us. Opportunities are endless with God by our side.

Proverbs 2:1-5; 2 Corinthians 6:14-18
Point to Ponder: Give God praise and all the glory.

Pray: God, help me look to you to provide for all my needs. I want to receive the peace and assurance you have promised to those who love you.

 July 22

I know indeed how to live in humble
circumstances; I know also how to live with
abundance. In every circumstance and in all
things I have learned the secret of being well
fed and of going hungry, of living in abundance
and of being in need. I have the strength for
everything through him who empowers me.
— Philippians 4:12-13

Trust God to guide us. Situations are presented daily where we feel challenged to reach out to others. Do not reject God's promptings when he presents opportunities. Remember, the situation is not about us and them, but more about God's strength being brought forth through us. We are his hands and feet on earth. God receives glory from his activity through our lives and actions.

God invites us to be involved in his activities. In order to receive his strength, we should practice obedience. He does not force us to accept all he has for us. We have the gift of free will to make choices every day. Pray for help to make Christ-like choices. Turn to him, surrender to his almighty power, and follow his commandments. They do not restrict us; instead they free us to experience his best.

In order to be content in every situation, abstain from evil. Train the mind to focus on God's ways. Slow down, find a quiet place to pray, and pay attention to the events of the day. Believe in Christ who empowers us to build his kingdom on earth.

Psalm 77:12-15; Matthew 16:24-28
Point to Ponder: God sends his strength to empower you.

Pray: Lord, stay in my heart. Give me what I need to build your kingdom on earth.

July 23

He gave them this command: "You shall act
*faithfully and wholeheartedly in fear of the L*ORD*."*
— 2 Chronicles 19:9

Faith in God is powerful. It is not easy at times; hold fast to faith.
Count on God to deal with us with abundance. God does nothing
halfway. He sends us grace to sustain us when challenged. God has
every resource we need to perform his will. When we work in his
name, he is pleased. We have nothing to fear. We may meet others
who criticize our work, but God's grace enables us to forgive the
naysayers. We sense God's presence directing us even when others
do not understand. Faith in God is rooted in our hearts.

When we complete our work and no one takes time to express
thanks, the Lord's grace reminds us we have a heavenly reward.
God sees everything and remembers those who have done good
works. Have faith. We will be rewarded on the final judgment day
when we stand before God and give an account of what we did and
did not do in his name.

It is better to be humble than prideful. All good things come
from the Lord including success and material wealth. As we enjoy
God's blessings, remember that money and material wealth can be
taken away in a heartbeat. Lasting riches include love and a solid
foundation of faith in God.

2 Corinthians 9:11-15; Psalm 112:1-4
Point to Ponder: Be faithful to God and follow his will.

Pray: Lord, be with me moment by moment. Help me be faithful to
you and your teachings.

 July 24

What good is it, my brothers, if someone says
he has faith but does not have works? Can that
faith save him? If a brother or sister has nothing
to wear and has no food for the day, and one
of you says to them, "Go in peace, keep warm,
and eat well," but you do not give them the
necessities of the body, what good is it? So also
faith of itself, if it does not have works, is dead.
                                         — James 2:14-17

With the gift of faith in God comes the responsibility to share his messages and riches. God takes our faithfulness and makes it a blessing to others through our works. For example, we may serve food to the poor or bring clothing to a shelter. This may seem insignificant in our eyes, but in God's eyes it holds much meaning.

Sometimes we question how best to use our gifts so others benefit and see God working through us. He has given us resources to use, such as the promptings of the Holy Spirit and the Ten Commandments, to establish boundaries and a strong faith foundation. We must ultimately use our consciences to discern what actions and works most glorify his holy name.

Take a leap of faith. Ask if the work conforms to God's will. Then try to do our best to complete the work at hand. Leave the rest to God. He is with us and guides us step-by-step. Even if we make a wrong decision, he finds a way to make good out of it. Count on God to lead the way. Have faith!

Hebrews 11:1; Psalm 37:27-28
Point to Ponder: Have faith in God. Follow him.

Pray: Lord, I trust your faithfulness. Increase my faith and remove my unbelief.

 July 25

The promises of the Lord, I will sing forever,
proclaim your loyalty through all ages. For
you said, "My love is established forever; my
loyalty will stand as long as the heavens."

— Psalm 89:2-3

Stay focused on what is important: our Lord and Savior. Each day when we awaken, whisper, "Here I am Lord. I need you today to guide my steps. Thank you for a new day." God wants to give us counsel, cheer us on in our successes, and teach us to live righteous lives.

Without the Lord in our thoughts each day and his helping hand to guide us, we may be consumed by jealousy, worry, anxiety, or by something else that immobilizes us. He has promised not to abandon us even when minor mishaps prevail. Petty annoyances, nagging doubts, along with self-condemnation, eat away at our peace. These little things irritate us. God is near so call out to him.

The Lord frees us from the snares of difficulty. When we pray in his name, he halts unbearable struggles and sends his grace. He fills us with his calm. We know his healing presence.

Nothing has power over the Lord – nothing in all creation. He gives us strength to live and spread the gospel to others. The glory of God is his presence. He wants to be our constant companion. He is committed and at work in us. Give him a sense of reverence and respect.

Deuteronomy 10:12-22; Proverbs 15:8
Point to Ponder: Trust in God's promises.

Pray: Lord, help me discern what truly matters. Teach me to focus on trusting you.

 July 26

*But seek first the kingdom of God and his
righteousness, and all these things will be
given you besides. Do not worry about
tomorrow; tomorrow will take care of itself.
Sufficient for a day is its own evil.*

– Matthew 6:33-34

When we seek the Lord, his truths set us free to live righteous
lives. Every time we pray, each time we say no to temptation, and
when we sacrifice even a small amount of time to help someone in
need, we practice righteousness and obedience to God.

Sometimes when troubles abound, we feel powerless to deal
with the issues facing us. Remember to call on God. Ask him to
send encouragement and strength. Whisper a simple prayer, "Lord,
be with me." God rejoices every time we come to him and say
yes to his will for us. No act of faith, no act of trust, and no act of
kindness escapes his notice.

When we seek God and his righteousness, we model for others
how to build a relationship with him. Others see us praying and
trusting him. He sends us the resources and grace we need to meet
challenges and bring others to him.

Strive to please the Lord. Such a mindset protects us from
temptations and focuses us on God and not our problems. Take one
day at a time and do not fret about tomorrow. God holds us with a
loving heart and keeps us from coming unraveled. Bask in his love and
his grace. We are never alone in our struggles. Rejoice in the Lord.

John 8:31-32; Colossians 3:23-24
Point to Ponder: Seek God first and then act. Give God the glory.

Pray: Lord, I seek you above all others. Help me make choices
pleasing to you.

July 27

> LORD, *your love reaches to heaven; your fidelity,*
> *to the clouds. Your justice is like the highest*
> *mountains; your judgments, like the mighty*
> *deep; all living creatures you sustain,* LORD.
>
> — Psalm 36:6-7

Delight in the Lord's blessings. If we take time to cherish God's gifts, we find great pleasure in them. Learn to wait on God. He sustains us.

The Lord reveals his character according to our needs and his purposes. He may send an angel in the form of a stranger to comfort us at a difficult time. If there is limited food to feed a crowd, he demonstrates he is a provider by making food enough for everyone. When a health issue develops, he sends a healer in the form of a doctor. He reveals he is God Almighty.

As we experience life and all its challenges, we come to know God intimately. Sadly, some people never grow in their knowledge of the Lord. They walk in darkness. They have the same basic knowledge of God as they had when they were a child. Pray for these people.

View God as our Savior. He provides opportunities to grow closer to him as we build our faith. Reflect on the circumstances presented to us. Question what the Lord wants us to learn. In this way, we begin to know God in dimensions we have never known him before. Be still, pray to him unceasingly, and be patient. He provides for us in his time. He is our refuge and strength.

Psalm 136:23-26; Joshua 24:14-15
Point to Ponder: God sustains you.

Pray: Lord, have mercy on me when I fail to learn what you have for me. Teach me your ways.

 July 28

> *"Now, therefore, fear the Lord and serve him*
> *completely and sincerely. Cast out the gods*
> *your fathers served beyond the River and in*
> *Egypt, and serve the Lord. ... As for me and*
> *my household, we will serve the Lord."*
>
> — Joshua 24:14-15

If we set our minds to serving the Lord, our example is a blessing for those around us. We practice God's ways and demonstrate to others his love, compassion, gentleness, and joy. These actions come from the heart. Give them away willingly. God replenishes them as we act as his voice, hands, and feet on earth.

Many young adults choose to practice the faith of their parents. Through modeling of scripture readings and a prayerful lifestyle, children learn the importance of trusting God. Families who pray together build a strong relationship with the Lord as a family unit.

When we place our trust in God, those around us see dedication and love for him. Reach out to those struggling with their beliefs. Suggest to them to look for God in unusual places. He may send a message through a television commercial, or posted on a billboard, or through the voice of another person. Trust him to reach out to those in need and those who seek to know him.

Celebrate life in God's presence as our awareness of him grows ever stronger. He wants to be in the midst of our challenges, working to make things better. When we trust and serve the Lord, we find peace, joy, and love. God never gives up on us. He equips us for whatever life brings. Praise his holy name.

Ephesians 5:15-20; Romans 8:1-9
Point to Ponder: As for me, I will serve the Lord.

Pray: May my words and actions please God. Help me find joy in all I do in your name.

July 29

By this I know you are pleased with me,
that my enemy no longer jeers at me. For
my integrity you have supported me and
let me stand in your presence forever.

— Psalm 41:12-13

Sometimes we make decisions that irritate others or cause confusion and ridicule. When this happens, we may find ourselves doubting our decision or walking alone in truth. After prayer and reflection, all we can do is maintain our integrity, trusting God to guide us. He may be the only one to understand.

Honor God by walking with integrity and doing what is right. The world considers truth optional. On the other hand, the Lord hates a lying tongue (Prv. 6:17). God watches over us and knows when Satan tempts us to lie and do evil. There is no hiding from God. He does not allow us to use deception to build his holy kingdom. If we have pure hearts and believe our actions are righteous, God does the rest in his time. He wants us to quiet our hearts so he can send his grace. He asks us to not dwell on what others think, and avoid sin and Satan's temptations.

Stand tall and endure the hardships that come with speaking out and working toward abolishing ungodly behaviors. Reject Satan and his evil temptations because he stands ready to devour us in our weaknesses. Seek deep faith and trust in God. Discern what is right and just. Pray for guidance. God calls us to be steadfast. He leads us on our journey to eternal life.

Hebrews 12:1-2; Luke 12:41-48
Point to Ponder: Live with integrity.

Pray: Lord, be with me as I serve you. Guide and protect me.

 July 30

*Give thanks to the Lord, who is good, whose love
endures forever. Who can tell the mighty deeds of
the Lord, proclaim in full God's praises? Happy
those who do what is right, whose deeds are
always just. Remember me, Lord, as you favor
your people; come to me with your saving help.*

— Psalm 106:1-4

With active lifestyles and busy schedules, we sometimes forget
to have God as our central focus. We live on our terms rather
than God's. We rush around busying ourselves with activities or
work responsibilities. Too tired to pray, we worship God at our
convenience and sometimes find church attendance a chore. Our
work is good, but we do not take time to cultivate our hearts and
minds with God's love. We fail to give thanks to him for sending
blessings our way. Sometimes we take our happiness for granted.
We reach out to God only when we need help and in times of
trouble.

When we feel we have not been as faithful as we should be
toward God, seek him and pray. Repeat simple prayers and find
time alone to read the Bible. Ponder his Word. Be alert to a sense
of wonder and reverence toward God. Be in his presence and
treasure the time with him. Turn to God every day. He honors our
faithfulness. God sees our devotion when serving and loving others
and when we pray. Be faithful in thought, word, and deed. Give
thanks to God whose love endures forever.

Proverbs 21:3; Matthew 11:25-27
Point to Ponder: Give thanks to God for all his blessings.

Pray: Lord, lead me. Keep me focused on what is right. Thank you
for loving me.

 July 31

Rich and poor have a common bond;
the LORD is the maker of them all.

— Proverbs 22:2

Many people have a great deal of difficulty being around poor people and the homeless; they actually fear for their livelihood. Likewise, some feel out of place and awkward in the presence of extremely wealthy people; they feel inadequate and have limited common interests.

The way we react to others is a choice. If we have built a strong foundation of faith, we realize God places us in situations for reasons sometimes beyond our understanding. God puts people around us who need our ministry.

Our interactions are directly related to our understanding of Christ. Those who do not know his teachings may be weak, turn the other way, and be unkind or harsh. They avoid people who look different, live on the margins of society, or dwell in poverty.

God deeply desires that we have unity with him and our neighbors. Salvation from God is for everyone. The Lord made each of us in his likeness. We should not fear those who are different.

When we meet new people, whether rich or poor, we make a choice to avoid them or approach them as brothers or sisters. Pray for God to guide our decision. He sends us strength to do his will, wisdom to learn from others, and patience to meet and help all people in the way he desires. God gives us the grace we need in every new encounter.

Increase our love for God by accepting all people. Look for commonalities. We are all made in God's image.

Matthew 19:23-30; 2 Chronicles 16:9
Point to Ponder: We are all God's children, rich and poor.

Pray: Lord, keep my eyes focused on doing your will. Teach me to be open and welcoming.

August 1

As you go make this proclamation: "The kingdom of heaven is at hand. Cure the sick, raise the dead, cleanse lepers, drive out demons. Without cost you have received; without cost you are to give."

— Matthew 10:7-8

Freely receive blessings from God, but as joyfully give them away to others. God gives each of us special gifts. Perhaps an artist comes to mind who captures details of a moment in time, or a favorite teacher who shares knowledge, or a doctor who treats us with favorable results. These people give of their talents willingly and in ways pleasing to God.

Some people forget from whom we receive our uniqueness and gifts. Scripture tells us, "Do not be deceived, my beloved brothers: all good giving and every perfect gift is from above, coming down from the Father of lights, with whom there is no alteration or shadow caused by change" (Jas. 1:16-17).

Giving of our time, talents, and treasure is productive and joyful. The saying, "The more you give, the more you receive," is true. God knows our willingness to give freely. Be alert to how much more we receive when we give to others. God's resources are endless.

Do not become attached to worldly treasures. When God calls us to heaven, we leave everything behind. Material wealth does not matter to God. What matters most, is how we shared love and the gifts and wealth given to us. For those who give generously, God responds in a like manner. Resolve to show gratitude to the Lord through giving.

Proverbs 22:22-23; Psalm 37:27-28
Point to Ponder: Everything you have is from God. Share with others.

Pray: Lord, give us the grace of a generous heart and a pleasing attitude.

August 2

*Every command that I enjoin on you, you shall
be careful to observe, neither adding to it nor
subtracting from it ... The Lord, your God, shall you
follow, and him shall you fear; his commandment
shall you observe, and his voice shall you heed,
serving him and holding fast to him alone.*

— Deuteronomy 13:1, 5

Every day we face choices. Sometimes when the choice is difficult, we stumble and fail to focus on the Lord and his commandments. We please ourselves with little thought of the outcomes and ramifications to others.

Instead of making snap decisions, pause to reflect on why God has given us the situation. Discern what God intends to do through our circumstances. When we are firmly grounded and have a relationship with Christ, we understand he directs our actions. Pray for his guidance.

God has given us a roadmap to follow — the Ten Commandments. Listen for the Holy Spirit within. The Spirit urges us to live a life of goodness, be in control of our actions, exhibit kindness, and let others see joy and peace in our hearts. These habits are aligned with God's ways, and ultimately lead us to righteous living.

Serve the Lord and have faith that God wants us to do good works. He places us in situations where we practice and demonstrate our beliefs and righteous acts. Our success depends on how we serve the Lord and obey the promptings of the Spirit.

Psalm 40:8-11; Philippians 1:9-11
Point to Ponder: Obey God's commandments. Follow his will.

Pray: Lord, thank you for showing me how to be generous and discern your will. I want to serve.

August 3

The LORD is gracious and merciful, slow to anger and abounding in love. The LORD is good to all, compassionate to every creature.

– Psalm 145:8-9

Convey love to those around us. Many people love naturally because they have seen the emotion modeled. Others struggle to express love in words or actions because they live in homes where love is not valued or minimally practiced.

We cannot be close to God without being affected by his love. God's unconditional love is difficult for us to understand. No ordinary love, Christ's love is endless. He loves us even when we have rejected and ignored him. He never abandons us even in the depths of our sinfulness. We are never separated from the love of God.

St. Augustine wrote, "What does love look like? It has the hands to help others. It has the feet to hasten to the poor and needy. It has the eyes to see misery and want. It has the ears to hear the sighs and sorrows of men. That is what love looks like."

Watch how our love for Christ grows as we spend time with him through prayer, reading scripture, and serving others. There are answers within the pages of the Bible. We learn that Jesus is the way and the truth and the life (Jn. 14:6). God places us in situations where we see love and experience love for ourselves. Our lives change forever when we give love away. Make a point to share a little extra love today. See how people respond.

Matthew 22:36-39; Colossians 2:5-8
Point to Ponder: God is compassionate and merciful and filled with love.

Pray: Lord, teach me to love. Look into my heart today and strengthen me.

August 4

The Lord supports all who are falling and raises up all who are bowed down. The eyes of all look hopefully to you; you give them their food in due season. You open wide your hand and satisfy the desire of every living thing. You, Lord, are just in all your ways, faithful in all your works.

— Psalm 145:14-17

God has plans for our lives before we are born. The challenge comes when we make plans "doing this or that" without paying attention to the spiritual ramifications. We step out to follow our own plan, not God's plan for us. We sometimes close our eyes, ears, and hearts to God. Our relationship flounders. We have trouble discerning his will. Confusion and unrest abound.

When we encounter God something changes. Our eyes are opened to reveal a new facet of who he is as we yearn for him. God is many things: our savior, teacher, counselor, healer, minister, and judge. He invites us to join him in building his kingdom. But first, we have to know him and trust him to lead the way for us.

Encounter God each day by whispering, "Here I am, Lord. How can I do your will?" In scripture we read, "Be eager to present yourself as acceptable to God, a workman who causes no disgrace, imparting the word of truth without deviation" (2 Tm. 2:15).

Our heavenly Father holds our lives, including our future in his hands. God does not expect perfection but he does ask us to be persistent in building a strong relationship and following him all the way to eternity. He is forever faithful.

Acts 26:12-18; Proverbs 18:10
Point to Ponder: God is faithful and just.

Pray: Lord, open my eyes and ears to your glory. Give me courage to encounter you and change.

August 5

If then you were raised with Christ, seek what is above, where Christ is seated at the right hand of God. Think of what is above, not of what is on earth. For you have died, and your life is hidden with Christ in God. When Christ your life appears, then you too will appear with him in glory.

— Colossians 3:1-4

Christians learn about heaven from their parents, from religious leaders, from reading the Bible, and through personal prayer. We study scripture to learn about God the Father, Jesus Christ, and the Holy Spirit – the Holy Trinity. We practice the Ten Commandments and worship and praise the Lord. Through all of these experiences, we build a relationship with God.

Believers have access to God. He is available at any time. He hears our prayers and answers them. He asks us to serve him and follow his will. For some this is a stumbling block. People get caught up in acquiring material possessions. They want the biggest houses, the best jobs, and the finest cars. Money is their master. They forget about God and his sovereign power over the universe.

God's kingdom rejects the world's measure of wealth. The Lord sees great value and goodness in serving others and loving our neighbor without complaint and without seeking recognition. Look to God as our model and imitate him. Ask him to teach us how to serve with love and generous hearts. Watch what happens next when we entrust our lives to God.

Psalm 117:1-2; Hebrews 12:14, 28
Point to Ponder: Be Christ-like and serve others before yourself.

Pray: Let my service to others be pleasing to you. Keep me on the pathway to heaven.

August 6

*A man named John was sent from God. He came
for testimony, to testify to the light, so that all might
believe through him. He was not the light, but
came to testify to the light. The true light, which
enlightens everyone, was coming into the world.*

– John 1:6-9

God chose to express himself through John the Baptist. This strange man preached to the crowds as he baptized them in the Jordan River. John the Baptist, a great orator and minister, spoke with authority about Jesus; and the people listened. John told everyone that the one coming after him would baptize them with the Holy Spirit and fire.

God uses each of us to carry his message and his word to others. Jesus lives in us. Every Christian has his light within his or her soul. Seek to help friends, coworkers, and family members find Christ, and dispel any sin or darkness from their lives.

We may feel inadequate to tell others about God and his saving grace. Quoting scripture is difficult for many. Verbally expressing his truths is daunting. Never underestimate the knowledge and understanding of how God works in our lives. We may not know all the answers or the best words to use, but we know someone who does. We know God.

Trust the Lord to adjust our lives to better serve. God never stops giving. When he chooses to use us to bring someone to him, we do not fail. We are commissioned by God to do his will. Have faith and let his light shine through.

Mark 16:15-16; Matthew 5:13-16
Point to Ponder: God uses ordinary people to bring others to him.

Pray: Jesus, help me show others what is true, noble, and pure. Shield me from discouragement so I become a visible sign of your love.

August 7

The greatest among you must be your servant.
Whoever exalts himself will be humbled; but
whoever humbles himself will be exalted.
— Matthew 23:11-12

Jesus chose humility over becoming a king. Meek and humble of heart, his purpose while he lived on earth was to follow the will of his Father so man could be free of sin and live abundantly.

Be righteous in God's eyes by demonstrating humility and Christ-like behaviors. True humility means not trying to take credit for all the success and glory when a job is completed and done well. Being humble means sharing the spotlight and blessings with others. We do not judge others critically in hopes of elevating our own worth. Give praise and glory to God.

God's light within us shines as he carries out his work through our lives. Impart his blessings. Let God's grace shape our hearts and minds. When we act on God's behalf and serve others, we respond and trust God to show us the way and give up our futile efforts to do things our way. This humbles us and makes us keenly aware of how much we depend on and owe the Lord.

God sees all we do and how we act. He knows when we place our trust in him. He never stops giving to those who recognize where their strength comes from, God Almighty. Be humble and exalted by God. He sends his grace so we live abundantly. Give God the glory.

2 Chronicles 7:14; Psalm 139:17-18
Point to Ponder: Serve God first. He provides for all your needs.

Pray: Lord, give me the grace to be humble. Teach me to be generous with my gifts from God.

August 8

Do not quench the Spirit.

                         – 1 Thessalonians 5:14-19

Do not neglect the Holy Spirit. The Spirit nudges us to do God's will. We may not always be comfortable with what the Spirit says, but we should not resist the promptings. The Spirit dwells within us to guide and teach us about the Trinity of Divine Persons – God the Father, the Son Jesus Christ, and the Holy Spirit.

Lean on the Spirit and hold fast to what is good. Some may be critical of our steadfast belief in God. It is not important what others think. We spend time with him through worship, prayer, and reading the Bible. Others do not understand our need to hear God's voice, rest in his presence, and give him all the glory.

For those who reject the Spirit's promptings, their hearts grow cold and circumstances change. When the Spirit's voice is muted, people no longer have reminders to hold their tongues. Bitter words may cut and hurt others. They may succumb to Satan's trickery. Those living without the Spirit's promptings become impatient and act pompous and prideful. They forget to be humble and do not reach out to others with kind acts or generous hearts. Life becomes confusing and filled with indecision. They have grown insensitive to God's teachings.

God holds us accountable for our actions. Pray for our ears to be open to understand and our eyes able to perceive good so we live abundantly. Listen and follow the Spirit's promptings to do God's will. Treat others with love, respect, and mercy.

Proverbs 22:24-25; Psalm 139:7-12
Point to Ponder: Believe in the Holy Trinity – the Father, the Son, and the Holy Spirit.

Pray: Lord, guide me to do your will.

August 9

He who finds a wife finds happiness; it is
a favor he receives from the Lord.

– Proverbs 18:22

Marriage is not an invention of man. God instituted marriage when he created Adam and Eve. God felt man should not be alone, and so he made a suitable partner for him. The Lord created a woman from the rib he had taken from man (Gn. 2:18, 22).

Divorce rates across the globe have been rising rapidly owing to problems like incompatibility between couples, infidelity issues, lack of trust and understanding, and financial pressures. Some couples view marriage as a contract. There is little mention of God and the promises they made before him and others. Happiness and love may have disappeared from these unions.

During times of strife, some couples quit going to church and cease all activities necessary to sustain their faith in God. Often this happens out of shame and depression. When problems in a marriage come, seek help from God through prayer and participation in a faith community. Digging deep to sustain faith in God eventually helps unhappy couples through the rough times. Learn to compromise with God as the mediator.

The sacrament of marriage brings great satisfaction and enduring love. A marriage based on love takes lots of work and commitment. Lean on God, lead the life he has given us, and pray for his blessings. Glorify God by sharing his blessings of love through a strong and faithful marriage.

Genesis 2:24; 1 Corinthians 7:1-7
Point to Ponder: Believe in the sacrament of marriage.

Pray: Lord, help us find love and happiness in marriage.

August 10

Whoever preaches, let it be with the words of
God; whoever serves, let it be with the strength
that God supplies, so that in all things God may
be glorified through Jesus Christ, to whom belong
glory and dominion forever and ever. Amen.

– 1 Peter 4:11

God gives each person gifts to carry out his mission on earth. Our gifts are used daily at work and when we interact with others. Many use their God-given talents in the service of others and for the glory of God. Some give money and time to charity to help the needy while others befriend and visit the sick and lonely. Still others recognize God's gifts in careers as CEO's, teachers, doctors, lawyers, ministers, and more.

Some people get caught up with life and their work. They believe their skills and knowledge are due to their own dedication, persistence, and intellect. Since they experience success most of the time, their prosperity persuades them they no longer need to give thanks to God.

Beware of this mentality. Being thankful to God brings meaning to life in a way wealth, power, possessions, and self-centered pursuits never match. As Jesus said, "Give and gifts will be given to you … For the measure with which you measure will in return be measured out to you" (Lk. 6:38). It does not matter whether we have been given great talents, abilities, wealth, or very little. What matters is that we use what we have been given for the glory of God. Build his kingdom on earth.

Proverbs 6:6-11; Matthew 25:14-30
Point to Ponder: Glorify God in all things. He gives meaning to your life.

Pray: God, thank you for blessing me. Teach me to use my gifts to serve you and others.

August 11

But when you pray, go to your inner room, close
the door, and pray to your Father in secret. And
your Father who sees in secret will repay you.
                                    – Matthew 6:6

We Christians pray continuously. We find ourselves lifting up quick thoughts and prayers to God throughout the day. Our whispered words bring us closer to God. Do we actually take time to quiet our minds and bodies, close out distractions, and pray from the heart? Do we listen for God's response?

How does someone have fervent prayer? Scripture says, "Therefore, confess your sins to one another and pray for one another, that you may be healed. The fervent prayer of a righteous person is very powerful" (Jas. 5:16). *Webster's Dictionary* defines *fervent* as "exhibiting or marked by great intensity of feeling." Do you cry out to God with your heart and soul? Fervent prayer means heartfelt intense prayer with thanksgiving.

God answers our prayers. He never abandons us. He looks beyond our actions and directly into our hearts. If we feel our prayers are not answered, do not blame God. The problem lies within us. We are not walking closely enough with him to see his activity. Prayers, short or fervent, are answered aligned to God's purposes and will. The response to our prayers may not be what we expect or want, but count on God to guard our hearts and minds, and answer our prayers for good and according to our needs.

James 5:16; Colossians 4:1-4
Point to Ponder: Pray fervently every day.

Pray: Lord, open my eyes and ears so I see you in all things.
Answer my prayers according to your will.

August 12

*For a sun and shield is the L*ORD *God, bestowing
all grace and glory. The L*ORD *withholds no good
thing from those who walk without reproach. O
L*ORD *of host, happy are those who trust in you!*
— Psalm 84:12-13

Those who walk with the Lord feel his presence. We hear his gentle whisper and see his majesty at different times: through the voice of a neighbor, during church services, as the wind blows or lightning strikes, or when waves crash on shore, or as a delicate flower blooms in nature, or as we sit quietly to read scripture. We are content to be in God's presence.

But at times, life gets hectic and our decisions are rushed. We see problems and limitations no matter which way we turn. Our vision is limited and God's voice is muted. During times of uncertainty, the Holy Spirit prompts and guides us step-by-step to follow God's will. We trust God to place us in situations where we demonstrate his goodness and mercy. God sends his grace. He never gives us too much to endure.

When we become disoriented and confused, take time to pray. God is close and listens attentively. Talk to him about problems and concerns. Ask him to send wisdom. Be patient. God does not ask us to understand, comprehend, or figure it out. He asks us to pray, seek, and trust. He shows us the way step-by-step to eternity.

Proverbs 8:10-14; John 14:6
Point to Ponder: God bestows grace on those who love him.

Pray: God, send me what I need to fulfil your plan for me. I trust you to show me the way.

August 13

I command you: be firm and steadfast! Do not fear nor be dismayed, for the LORD, your God, is with you wherever you go.

— Joshua 1:9

When we face challenges, sometimes we feel weak and weary. We doubt our skills and abilities. We ponder our choices. When doubt overwhelms us and we do not know which way to turn, be still, pray, and wait for God.

Stop worrying. God listens as we sift through the contents of our hearts, our feelings of doubt, our fears and frustrations. Scripture tells us to, "Trust in the LORD with all your heart, on your own intelligence rely not; In all your ways be mindful of him, and he will make straight your paths" (Prv. 3:5-6). God watches over us wherever we go and whatever decisions we make. He wants to be a part of our lives and direct our paths.

He is the same God who performed miracles through men and women in the Bible. He walked with Moses, Peter, James, John, Thomas, and Paul. Nothing is too difficult for the Lord. Through him, all things are possible. He wants to work with us as we follow his will.

We have no power on our own. God blesses us with his faithfulness and wisdom. Trust him to guide us. Remain firm and steadfast in his presence. Follow Christ and experience a blessed way to live.

Psalm 104:33-34; John 12:25-26
Point to Ponder: Do not fear. God walks with you. He is everywhere.

Pray: Lord, help me in all things. Teach me each day so you use me to complete your work.

August 14

God indeed is my savior; I am confident
and unafraid. My strength and courage is
the LORD, and he has been my savior.

— Isaiah 12:2

We sometimes feel impatient and frustrated when we expect to see immediate change or answers to our prayers, and nothing happens. Our minds go into overdrive, searching for solutions and security. Even when the Lord answers our prayers, and we do not see or understand, we try a different tack. We give thanks and praise hoping to please God with our additional prayer time. We think if we pray enough, he will answer more clearly.

God works in mysterious ways. Often yes or no answers do not come. We have to practice patience. Inherent in this idea of patience is trust. The essence of wisdom is trust. We have to trust God is working through us for good. He is our Savior today, yesterday, and all the days to come.

Our heavenly Father wants only the best for his children. His love is boundless; and his timing is perfect. Our lives change when we dwell on his promises and love. We have a personal connection to him as we live in his presence. Our hearts are soothed as we experience comfort and peace from him. God transforms us. Trust him to send what we need in his time. Pray he brings us all into his promised land!

Psalm 72:18-19; Proverbs 3:9-12
Point to Ponder: God is my strength.

Pray: Lord, teach me your ways on my journey to heaven.

August 15

But he bestows a greater grace; therefore,
it says: "God resists the proud, but
gives grace to the humble."

– James 4:6

If God seems distant and we have difficulty hearing him, we need to slow down and reflect on our priorities. When we direct our own paths without God as our focal point, we make decisions which may lead us away from him. We spend less time praying, reading the Bible, and worshiping him. We become complacent spiritually. Our tendency is to be prideful and step out on our own.

Then one day we realize God is not our focal point. Material riches have taken his place. We keep searching for happiness but those feelings are elusive. When we realize sin has taken over and our habits seem compulsive, seek God's intervention. Be humble and pray. Ask God for forgiveness and cleansing of our hearts. Let him guide our steps and place us in situations that require us to be humble, kind, and generous. Seek his grace and mercy to rectify offensive acts and make things right.

Be in harmony with God. He promises to lift us up and relieve our worry and suffering, in his perfect time. Vow to serve God in humble obedience. Develop an attitude for grateful service. Do everything for the glory of God.

Luke 14:7-14; 1 Peter 5:6
Point to Ponder: God gives you grace to do his will.

Pray: Bestow your grace on my humble heart. Guide and teach me your ways, Lord.

 August 16

Blessed be the God and Father of our Lord Jesus
Christ, who has blessed us in Christ with every
spiritual blessing in the heavens, as he chose us in
him, before the foundation of the world, to be holy
and without blemish before him. In love he destined
us for adoption to himself through Jesus Christ, in
accord with the favor of his will, for the praise and
glory of his grace that he granted us in the beloved.
— Ephesians 1:3-6

Blessed are we to be included in God's plan of salvation. Do we dare believe he directs each step we take and gives us an advocate through the Holy Spirit? Have we thought about our lives on earth and why God gives us blessings of our family and friends, our work, beliefs, and values?

God knows the master plan for our lives before we are born. We belong to him. He works through us to carry out his plan. God gives each of us talents and gifts and molds us into whatever kind of instrument he requires to build his kingdom.

The Lord is merciful. We are holy and blameless in his sight. In the presence of God, we receive his grace. Be obedient to the Lord. Trust him to bring about his perfect will for each of us which surpasses our knowledge and understanding. Thank God every day for his love, mercy, and forgiveness. He is faithful and never gives up on us.

Psalm 27:11-14; Ephesians 2:13-22
Point to Ponder: God blesses you every day.

Pray: Lord, thank you for the gifts you have given me. Guide me to use them to do your will.

August 17

And be kind to one another, compassionate, forgiving
one another as God has forgiven you in Christ.
— Ephesians 4:32

Some people are naturally tenderhearted. They do not have to think
of ways to be kind because it comes instinctively. On the contrary,
others would rather grumble than find anything good in a person
or situation; they tend to frown and appear troubled. Most of us fall
somewhere in-between in our character.

Kindness is a way of expressing ourselves to others in a
practical sense. We focus on thoughtful and considerate acts and
do little things for others. We put their needs before our own. For
example, if someone grieves, a kind person listens and grieves.
They are sensitive and compassionate to the feelings of others.
Kind people learn to say the right words guided by Christ to give
comfort. These actions are noted by God.

With kindness and compassion we also have to forgive those
who hurt us. We all fall short of God's ideal and are thankful to
be forgiven by God when we do something offensive or succumb
to sin. Most of us find forgiving someone difficult, especially if
the hurt runs deep. Try to set aside judgment and self-centered
attitudes. Show compassion and pray for those who do wrong
and sin against Christ. Practice forgiving others as God forgives
us. Ask Christ for a kind and forgiving spirit. As he builds these
qualities in our hearts and we demonstrate them to others, we are
filled with joy and peace.

Romans 15:5; Hebrews 10:24-25
Point to Ponder: Forgive others. Strive to be positive and kind.

Pray: Lord, help me encourage others. Bless me with a kind and
forgiving spirit.

 August 18

Rejoice in hope, endure in affliction,
persevere in prayer.

– Romans 12:12

When we are afflicted with troubles – whether they are with our health, our relationships and family, or with finances or other worldly issues – we should seek God through prayer. We may be holding on with a thin thread, but we still believe in his love and almighty power. Have faith and know God answers our prayers and watches over us continually.

In scripture we learn, "The God of all grace who called you to his eternal glory through Christ Jesus will himself restore, confirm, strengthen, and establish you after you have suffered a little" (1 Pt. 5:10). Hold fast to hope and remember God is sovereign over all creation and over every circumstance we experience.

Hope is not just wishful thinking that God will intervene and fix things. When we hope and pray for God to guide us, we are not speculating on things he might do. Have confidence in him to direct our steps.

Wait in hopeful anticipation. Waiting forces us to pray often. Fervent prayer keeps us in close communication with God throughout the day. Let us be joyful in hope as we pray and wait for him to fulfill his promises. Our attitude and perseverance lifts us up to God. Be alert, ready, and thankful for blessings and new opportunities to serve each day.

Colossians 1:3-8; Isaiah 30:15, 18
Point to Ponder: Live with hope, endure hurt, and pray daily. God responds.

Pray: Lord, help me be joyful in hope. Remind me to look for opportunities to share your love.

August 19

"Give and gifts will be given to you; a good
measure, packed together, shaken down, and
overflowing, will be poured into your lap.
For the measure with which you measure
will in return be measured out to you."

— Luke 6:38

This scripture reminds us God treats us as we have treated others. Ask, what can we give that does not cost money, is available daily, and may bring happiness to others?

Receive and share God's **BLESSINGS**:

Befriend someone and allow God to demonstrate his goodness.

Learn to smile and love life today. Love our enemies.

Embrace scripture and meditate on God's Word.

Select quiet times to talk about God to others.

Show others how to pray and build a relationship with the Lord.

Invite a neighbor for coffee and trust God to do the rest.

Note Christ-like traits in others. Encourage them.

Grow in confidence. Spread the gospel.

Seek God always and pursue his will.

Give and receive blessings. Pleased when we imitate him, God fills our hearts with joy.

Colossians 1:9-14; Psalm 28:6-9

Point to Ponder: Give and you will receive blessings from God.

Pray: Lord, I want to imitate your love and kindness. Teach me.

August 20

> *And do not grieve the holy Spirit of God, with*
> *which you were sealed for the day of redemption ...*
> *Therefore, do not continue in ignorance, but*
> *try to understand what is the will of the Lord.*
>
> — Ephesians 4:30, 5:17

The Holy Spirit lives in our hearts. The Spirit prompts us to follow God's will. He urges us to be loving, kind, caring, and generous. We grieve the Holy Spirit when we turn a blind eye to his promptings to do the right thing. When we ignore, disobey, or reject what the Spirit tells us, we squelch his activities. When we succumb to the temptations of Satan and live with sinful behaviors and attitudes, the Spirit's promptings are muted. Satan's evil powers have caused us to move away from God.

Do not fear. The Holy Spirit does not leave us when we stumble but instead, continues to love us even though his promptings are limited. We have only to ask the Spirit for help. He devises ways to draw us closer to God. He sends us messages sometimes through our friends, as we read the Bible, by an angel, or through situations that occur in life. Listen and learn from the Spirit. Be alert to his promptings and do not remain in ignorance. Press on and obey the Spirit of God. He sends guidance and peace.

1 Corinthians 2:9-12; John 14:15, 26
Point to Ponder: Turn to the Holy Spirit. Act on his promptings.

Pray: Lord, keep my ear tuned to the Holy Spirit. Never let me forget you love me unconditionally.

August 21

*Give thanks to the L*ord*, invoke his name;*
make known among the people his deeds!
Sing praise, play music; proclaim all his
wondrous deeds! Glory in his holy name;
*rejoice, O hearts that seek the L*ord*! Rely on*
*the mighty L*ord*; constantly seek his face.*

– Psalm 105:1-4

Before we get out of bed, remember to pray and give thanks to God for giving us another day to serve him. Seek to live a righteous life and find security, hope, love, and peace from God, who is the source of our strength and joy.

He sends blessings to those who follow his ways and believe; he sends them in unexpected ways. We may receive a phone call from a doctor with good news. A friend may help when time is limited to prepare for a big event. Someone may stop to change our flat tire. We may receive financial aid from an unexpected source. God's blessings may not be spectacular but they come at the right time and in the ordinary busyness of our lives.

The Lord does not expect much from us in return. His love is unconditional. "Have no anxiety at all, but in everything, by prayer and petition, with thanksgiving, make your requests known to God. Then the peace of God that surpasses all understanding will guard your hearts and minds in Christ Jesus" (Phil. 4:6-7). The next time we receive unexpected blessings, thank God by whispering, "Thank you, Lord. I love you." Rely on his love, sing his praises, and glorify his name.

Psalm 54:3-9; John 10:30-42
Point to Ponder: Saturate my life with blessings.

Pray: Thank you, Lord, for loving me. You are my strength and my salvation.

August 22

Teach us to count our days aright, that we may
gain wisdom of heart ... Fill us at daybreak with
your love, that all our days we may sing for joy.
— Psalm 90:12, 14

The kind of love God has for us is beyond our understanding. His love is unconditional and has no limits. There is no on-again, off-again kind of love from God. He knows our hearts and when we pull away and reject his teachings. God sees us return to sinful ways without fighting Satan's temptations because his ways seem easier and feel good initially. Yet, God's love follows us to the depths of our sinfulness. He knows when we seek forgiveness for our sins, how often we pray, and when we ignore him. He knows us personally. His love flows undaunted as he pursues us until we have nowhere else to turn. The only way God relates to us is through love-filled moments.

Let God's **L**OVE stir in us as we learn to trust him.
Lean on the hand of God to wipe away our tears.
Open our hearts to God and trust him to lead us out of darkness.
View God's love as a divine gift that never ends.
Evolve into the person God wants us to be. Have God as our redeemer.

Focus on God. Trust in his unconditional love.

Proverbs 24:1-6; Wisdom 9:13-18
Point to Ponder: You are God's great treasure. Praise him every day.

Pray: Lord, thank you for your unconditional love. Teach me to turn to you and seek your love and guidance.

August 23

*Do not let your hearts be troubled. You
have faith in God; have faith also in me.*

— John 14:1

When the disciples followed Jesus, they did not have to ask him
where to go next. They looked to him and followed as obedient and
faithful believers. Seek the same feelings of obedience and trust as
we follow God every day and do his will.

Some may say they do not hear God and feel confusion about
his will for them. When we have difficulty hearing God, try
reading scripture and ponder how the passages apply to life. Pray
throughout the day and give thanks to God for his blessings. Look
for his activities everywhere. There is nothing we can do to anger
God to the point of rejecting us. He watches over us and intervenes
at the perfect time.

Sometimes we stray from God when tempted by Satan. We
succumb to sinful ways and expose ourselves to danger. Satan
removes us from the presence of God. We no longer sense his
grace or hear the promptings of the Holy Spirit. When peace and
joy have left our being and our hearts are troubled, turn back to
God. He is waiting for us. Pray.

Our faithfulness to God is vital. He does not want us to worry,
be fearful, or filled with anxiety. When we praise him, he graces
us with blessings. Have complete faith in God. Feel the abundant
peace and joy that only he sends and no circumstance of life
dispels.

Psalm 147:1-6; John 10:7-18
Point to Ponder: God heals the troubled heart.

Pray: Lord, guide and protect me. Build my faith so I stand firm
and follow you more closely.

August 24

*Turn from evil and do good, that you may inhibit
the land forever. For the* Lord *loves justice and
does not abandon the faithful. When the unjust are
destroyed, and the children of the wicked cut off,
the just will possess the land and live in it forever.*

— Psalm 37:27-29

God loves those who are obedient and follow his teachings. He
blesses the faithful. Those who say they are turning away from
evil, yet continue to sin, are putting themselves in danger. They
distance themselves from the Lord. He is not satisfied with
occasional obedience and love.

Our thoughts and actions are controlled by our hearts.
Scientists have found we use only ten percent of our brains. God
knows each of us by name, and looks beyond our intellect, beyond
our lifestyle, and beyond our church attendance to focus his gaze
upon our hearts.

Christ is moved with compassion for us and is willing to
forgive us over and over again. In turn, he expects us to forgive our
neighbors. Many people do not take time to know their neighbors;
they find this type of interaction difficult. Some do not know how
to develop friendships and reach out in kindness. When we take a
step out of our comfort zone and demonstrate Christ-like kindness,
we honor God. He sees all we say and do in his name.

Embrace God's love and do good works. Listen to him in the
quiet of our hearts. Believe and experience a new level of intimacy
through divine grace.

Proverbs 20:22; John 14:23-27
Point to Ponder: God knows what we need before we ask.

Pray: Lord, strengthen my belief and faith in you.

August 25

*Do not repay anyone evil for evil; be concerned
for what is noble in the sight of all.*

— Romans 12:17

When someone is evil and intentionally hurts another person, we cry out for the guilty party to be punished. If we take matters into our own hands and seek revenge, we become bitter and angry. There is a deep yearning in our hearts for revenge, but we must reframe these thoughts and actions to be more aligned with God's teachings. If we do not forgive our enemies, we presume we are wiser than God.

Scripture says, "But to you who hear I say, love your enemies, do good to those who hate you, bless those who curse you, pray for those who mistreat you" (Lk. 6:27-28). For most of us, these acts do not come easy. Though it may be difficult, follow God's ways and demonstrate kindness and love. If we ask God through prayer to send us grace to forgive those who trespass against us, trust he will. Always seek his guidance.

Only God removes the bitterness in our hearts for those who have committed evil and hurt. If we do not trust God's justice, we live in a state of anger and stress. Give the vengeful and negative thoughts to him. Allow his grace to lighten our load and send peace to our troubled hearts. Seek to live with God as our source of strength. There is a tremendous sense of peace in living life where we walk hand in hand with God. He will raise us up!

Luke 6:27-30; Proverbs 29:22
Point to Ponder: Live in the presence of God. Do no harm.

Pray: Lord, I trust in your justice. Help me forgive my enemies.

August 26

*Beloved, let us love one another, because love
is of God; everyone who loves is begotten
by God and knows God. Whoever is without
love does not know God, for God is love.*

— 1 John 4:7-8

Why do believers find it difficult to love their neighbors? God made everyone in his image; we are all his children. Why not follow the Lord's commandment? "The second is this: 'You shall love your neighbor as yourself.' There is no other commandment greater than these" (Mk. 12:31).

How might we express love for our neighbors? First, we need to purify and acquire a compassionate heart. Often what we say and do is directly related to what is in our hearts. For example, do we praise God so that others hear? Do we strive to bring those who do not know God back to the safety of his love? For those burdened and depressed with the challenges of life, do we encourage them to find peace and comfort through reading the Bible and praying? All these behaviors indicate a pure heart. It takes love and a pure heart to reach out to others.

People who have minimal love in their hearts grumble and complain. They seldom find anything that makes them happy. They love to gossip and find fault in others. They do not care if their words hurt. Anger and disapproval appear commonplace. They do not know God.

God commands us to love our neighbors. Only God changes hearts. Do not accept negativity from others. Instead react with love, kindness, and a forgiving attitude. Do this and honor God.

Colossians 3:16-17; Psalm 150:1-6
Point to Ponder: Live a love-filled life. Be happy. Reach out to neighbors.

Pray: Lord, teach me to imitate your unending love and compassion.

August 27

You will show me the path to life,
abounding joy in your presence, the
delights at your right hand forever.

– Psalm 16:11

The Lord has promised to be faithful. He wants us to build a relationship that places him as the focal point of our lives. Every new situation we encounter, he asks us to communicate with him.

Stay connected to God daily. If we focus on problems without prayer, we allow the issues to consume our time and energy, and they determine the direction of our lives. When we fail to pray and seek God's presence, his voice within us is muted. We lose self-control and flounder with indecision.

Allow God to intervene in all decisions. Pray for his guidance and support, letting biblical principles and his promises guide us. Trust him to become our chief advisor. He sends his grace so our decisions have his strength and interpretation. Be alert because God always sends answers to our prayers. Sometimes he responds in unexpected ways. His ways are always best and for our good. Our plans are made perfect when we trust him.

Keep God at our right hand and go to him in prayer every time we face a new experience. Keep our eyes fixed on him. We have nothing to fear with God by our side. We go about our days with joy in our hearts.

Luke 6:43-45; Ephesians 2:10
Point to Ponder: Never reject God's good gifts and blessings.

Pray: Lord, help me turn to you with every new experience. Fill me with your strength.

August 28

*LORD, you have been our refuge through all
generations. Before the mountains were
born, the earth and the world brought forth,
from eternity to eternity you are God.*

– Psalm 90:1-2

Every time we seek Christ, he draws us closer. We sense his
activity within us. God honors our response by teaching us more.
He knows our situation before we pray, and is eager for us to
experience his guiding hand.

The Lord adopted us as his children and loves us unconditionally.
"For those who are led by the Spirit of God are children of God"
(Rom. 8:14).When we read the Bible, we see God as a perfect Father.
He gently disciplines us so we grow spiritually and do not continue
to make the same mistakes. He protects us from Satan and things
that could harm us. Scripture tells us, "The discipline of the LORD,
my son, disdain not; spurn not his reproof; For whom the LORD loves
he reproves, and he chastises the son he favors" (Prv. 3:11-12).

Our faithfulness to God assures us of abundant lives. By
following God's will, we inherit a place in heaven with him and
have eternal life.

If sin and temptation enter our being, God does not leave us.
Sin lures us away from him, deceives us, and leaves us empty. If
we turn away from God and have no time for prayer, he pursues us
until we are ready to turn back to him. God is more powerful than
Satan. The Lord is our refuge and satisfied with us only when our
love for him totally consumes us.

John 1:12-18; 1 Timothy 6:14-16
Point to Ponder: God gently disciplines you because he loves you.

Pray: Lord, direct my path so I do your will. You are my refuge.

August 29

> *Whoever does accept his testimony certifies that
> God is trustworthy. For the one whom God sent
> speaks the words of God. He does not ration his gift
> of the Spirit. The Father loves the Son and has given
> everything over to him. Whoever believes in the Son
> has eternal life, but whoever disobeys the Son will
> not see life, but the wrath of God remains upon him.*
>   – John 3:33-36

As Christians, we know from reading the Bible that God sent his only Son to earth so the world might be saved through him. God told us to believe in him so we might have eternal life (Jn. 3:16-17). When Jesus walked on earth with his disciples, he taught in parables. Often the disciples could not understand Jesus's strange ways and his storytelling. Jesus explained to his disciples that they were gifted with remarkable wisdom to understand the kingdom of heaven and his divine message. He had to open their hearts, and did so as a great storyteller.

Jesus opened their ears to hear, minds to understand, and their eyes to see his goodness and mercy. He employed many graphic analogies using common things familiar to everyone: salt, bread, water, and sheep.

Jesus used parables to get his message out. The parable is an effective and memorable vehicle for the conveyance of divine truths. Here are two parables to ponder: The Parable of the Lost Sheep – Luke15:1-7 and Judging Others – Luke 6:37-42.

Psalm 78:1-4; Philippians 2:5-1
Point to Ponder: Jesus is the master teacher.

Pray: Teach me, Jesus. Let me rejoice in you and follow your ways.

August 30

*Blessed be the L*ORD*, who has shown me wondrous*
love, and been for me a city most secure. Once
I said in my anguish, "I am shut out from your
sight." Yet you heard my pleas, when I cried out
*to you. Love the L*ORD *all you faithful. The L*ORD
protects the loyal, but repays the arrogant in full.
                                    – Psalm 31:22-24

God's mercy is as great as his unconditional love. We experience God's activities in our lives every day. He fills us with good things. Some get so secure with the blessings God sends, they go about their day without giving thanks or without praying. They are content to know God from the peripheral and receive his blessings. They do not really know God or have a relationship with him.

When adverse circumstances come, some people do not seek God, but instead deal with the situation using their own intuitions. They feel helpless and out of control. They dwell in the depths of doubt and anguish. They do not realize God provides opportunities for us to affirm our trust and receive his grace every day. They forget to trust God in all things.

Remember to turn to God in heartfelt prayer and acknowledge how needy we are. Trust him to hear our pleas. The Lord protects us. He leads us out of darkness and satisfies the longings in our hearts. He crowns us with his love and sends us peace in the midst of our struggles. God is faithful. Nothing is impossible for God.

Psalm 103:1-5; Isaiah 40:10-11
Point to Ponder: Be faithful to God as he is to you.

Pray: Lord, have mercy on me. I give you thanks and praise.

August 31

And Jesus went with them, but when he was only a short distance from the house, the centurion sent friends to tell him, "Lord, do not trouble yourself, for I am not worthy to have you enter under my roof. Therefore, I did not consider myself worthy to come to you; but say the word and let my servant be healed."

– Luke 7:6-7

At times in life, we let down our guard, and sin enters our souls. Nothing seems right. The heart hardens, revenge threatens, and anger prevails. We flounder in darkness. We feel unworthy and have no hope.

Call out to God. He knows each of us by name. His love for us is steadfast. He is overflowing with patience and mercy. He waits for those who have sinned to seek him. Reach out for the security and safety of his open arms.

Pray to God often for his strength and wisdom. Even when someone hurts us and bitterness deepens, stand firm and be like Christ. Remember Jesus's dying words on the cross and pray as he did, "Father, forgive them, they know not what they do" (Lk. 23:34).

Draw closer to God. He is extremely patient and never stops loving us. Every person, at different times in life, feels unworthy of God's unconditional love and his forgiveness. God desires we give bitterness up and seek forgiveness. God's mercy endures forever.

1 Timothy 2:1-6; Psalm 28:1-2
Point to Ponder: Be merciful and forgive others.

Pray: May I never judge anyone unworthy of your love, Lord.

September 1

*If someone who has worldly means sees a brother
in need and refuses him compassion, how can the
love of God remain in him? Children, let us love
not in word or speech but in deed and truth.*

— 1 John 3:17-18

There is tenderness in the heart of God. He may choose us to help people who have little faith and do not know him, or he may have us befriend a rich man preoccupied with material possessions who worships money. He places people in our lives so we reach out to them using uplifting words and Christ-like actions. Be open to where God leads us. He uses us to accomplish his will.

God has a plan for each of us no matter the circumstance. We do not have to be perfect before we minister God's word. In many situations, we struggle ourselves or have been through past trials. We simply have to do our best to have compassion and kindness in our souls and share our blessings with others. God directs our words and deeds as we help others in his name.

Something else happens when we surrender to Christ and serve others. We draw closer to him and grow more spiritually alert. Those who serve willingly and with pure hearts experience a reward far greater than money. By serving others, we find unity with God who rewards us with love, peace, and joy. This transcends our understanding.

Psalm 117:2; Psalm 100:1-5
Point to Ponder: Love in word, by deed, and in truth. Serve others.

Pray: Thank you, Lord, for taking my heart in your hands. I trust you will direct my work and actions.

 september 2

> *Then the* Lord *will guide you always and give you*
> *plenty even on the parched land. He will renew*
> *your strength and you shall be like a watered*
> *garden, like a spring whose water never fails.*
> — Isaiah 58:11

Humbly receive all God sends our way. Rejoice in his blessings. God is gracious and merciful, slow to anger, and abundant in kindness. He desires good to prevail over evil.

Feel compassion for those who suffer. Trust God hears their cries. He finds mercy and forgiveness for sins. God's mercy extends to all and is freely given to those who repent. Take refuge in his protective presence.

God renews our strength. We draw closer to the Lord through prayer. Trust him when trials come. Communicate with God. Simply say, "Help me, Jesus." His whispered teachings may be soft at first, but gradually we come to know him. He brings comfort to those who seek him. He wants to purify our hearts and remove bitterness and fear. The Lord has the ability to emerge in a life that seems completely unresponsive.

Christ is our deliverer, comforter, and friend. Be patient and wait for him. He sees everything: our apathy, gluttony, arrogance, and pride. On the other hand, God also witnesses acts of kindness, generosity, and love. He is for us. His word is always at work in us. Be free to experience God's goodness; be refreshed through his guiding hands every day.

Psalm 22:28-32; 1 Timothy 4:11
Point to Ponder: Seek God's call and be refreshed.

Pray: Lord, guide me and renew my strength. Send me what I need to help others.

september 3

The works of your hands are right and true,
reliable all your decrees. Established forever
and ever, to be observed with loyalty and care.
You sent deliverance to your people, ratified your
covenant forever; holy and awesome is your name.

– Psalm 111:7-9

Jesus accepts us with great joy. He knows us each by name. Even when we doubt and have little faith, he never abandons us.

Be like the first disciples and proclaim to all that Jesus is the holy one. Be loyal and follow his teachings. Seek his strength through prayer. Be patient for his response. Waiting forces us to trust him.

Hope in the Lord. He refreshes our souls when we pray. He protects us from the evil one who lurks in darkness. God does not want us to succumb to depression and self-pity or utter negative words that pull others down. Instead, pray unceasingly for his grace. This takes great faith. Stand firm. God is never far from us or too preoccupied to care. He hears and answers every prayer. He constantly protects us from known and unknown dangers.

Scripture says, "Before they call, I will answer; while they are yet speaking, I will hearken to them (Is. 65:24). God always begins where our human ability ends. He surprises us with unexpected revelations of his love and mercy. Give him thanks and praise. Glorify his holy name.

Psalm 28:7; 2 Peter 1:3-9
Point to Ponder: Seek wisdom from God. Praise him.

Pray: Guide me and teach me your ways, Lord. I love you.

september 4

> *Those who want to be rich are falling into*
> *temptation and into a trap and into many foolish*
> *and harmful desires, which plunge them into*
> *ruin and destruction. For the love of money is*
> *the root of all evils, and some people in their*
> *desire for it have strayed from the path and*
> *have pierced themselves with many pains.*
>
> — 1 Timothy 6:9-10

Money and riches are not sinful if we use them wisely. But coveting money does not please God. Greed and dishonesty in acquiring wealth leads us into Satan's realm of darkness and despair. When Christ sees money and material possessions turning us away from him, he acts. God wages relentless war against the propensity to love money more than him.

Be obedient to Christ. Do not let success and wealth distract us. Focus on being generous and helping the less fortunate. This honors God.

If questions come and we feel uncertain what God has planned for us, take time to draw closer to him through prayer. Remember our contentment does not come from possessions, activities, or other people. These can be altered or removed. Our contentment comes from knowing and loving God. He sends his grace and blessings to those who follow his will. When we have God as the focal point of our lives, we enjoy happiness and peace. All good things come from God.

Psalm 49:17-21; Proverbs 10:2
Point to Ponder: God is my focal point. I want to be spiritually wealthy.

Pray: Let my heart be set on things above. Help me be generous to those in need and focus on heavenly riches.

September 5

The depraved in heart are an abomination to the
LORD, but those who walk blamelessly are his delight.
— Proverbs 11:20

What does the word *depraved* mean? *Webster's Dictionary* defines
the word as "marked by corruption or evil: perverted." What
does *abomination* mean? The definition is "extreme disgust and
hatred: loathing." When we reread Proverbs above, and insert
those definitions, the passage reads, "The evil or perverted in heart
are disgusting or hated by the Lord." We should fear the Lord if
we ever find ourselves with depraved hearts. Sin and evil would
prevail.

Strive to follow Proverbs 11:20 and walk blamelessly with the
Lord. In addition, focus on following God's ways:

- Keep the Sabbath holy and speak no malice (Is. 58:13-14).
- Be imitators of God and Christ-like in all we do and say
  (Eph. 5:1-4).
- Follow the Ten Commandments to secure God's love (Jn.
  14:15-21).
- Do not sin or walk in the counsel of the wicked (Ps. 1:1-2).
- Serve the Lord, your God (Mt. 22:36-37).
- Pray unceasingly and give thanks to God in all
  circumstances (1 Thes. 5:17-18).

When we put God first and walk step-by-step with him, we
learn what he loves. Our hearts want the same things God's heart
desires. Walk blamelessly with the Lord.

Psalm 37:4; Psalm 40:9
Point to Ponder: Walk hand in hand with God.

Pray: Lord, teach me your ways so I always follow your will. I
want to love you more deeply.

September 6

He said to them, "Go into the whole world
and proclaim the gospel to every creature.
Whoever believes and is baptized will be saved;
whoever does not believe will be condemned.

— Mark 16:15-16

The Lord desires us to tell others about his goodness and about the gospel. In order to help others find God, we need to follow his ways. We do this through reading and pondering the Bible, praying often, worshiping him in church, and listening to his gentle voice.

When we have a close relationship with God, we sense his presence. Sometimes this happens when we rest with our thoughts and prayers. At other times, we feel his presence in church, or in the beauty of a natural setting, or in kind words voiced by a stranger, or as we communicate to those around us. God is with us and shares his thoughts, words, and blessings.

With pure and receptive hearts, we apply his word to help others. Imitate Christ. He directs our path so that we spread love, kindness, peace, and joy. Serve God by proclaiming the gospel. Sometimes we share God's word with our friends and neighbors in quiet conversations. At other times, we serve those living on the peripherals. There is no cause for fear. God leads us. He gives us direction and lights our path. Bring people to Christ; he does the rest.

God stretched out his arms to welcome and comfort all men when he died on the cross. Be a servant and follow Christ. Spread the good news to all. Proclaim the gospel of love.

Psalm 130:2-8; Luke 8:4-15
Point to Ponder: Proclaim the gospel and build God's kingdom on earth.

Pray: Lord, help me to listen for your voice and learn to act on your word.

September 7

I trust in your faithfulness, Grant my heart
joy in your help, that I may sing of the LORD,
"How good our God has been to me!"

— Psalm 13:6

God continually works in our lives. He is faithful. Be vigilant in asking God to increase our faith. He wants us to trust him without seeing him and adjust our lives accordingly. Believers trust God to send us every resource we need to overcome challenges. The Bible says, "My God will fully supply whatever you need, in accord with his glorious riches in Christ Jesus" (Phil. 4:19).

God does not want us to be afraid when circumstances bring difficulties and hardships. Scripture says, "For God did not give us a spirit of cowardice but rather of power and love and self-control. ... but bare your share of hardship for the gospel, with the strength that comes from God" (2 Tm. 1:7-8). No matter what we face on earth, God remains with us every step along the way. "We know that all things work for good for those who love God, who are called according to his purpose" (Rom. 8:28).

Pray for our faith to be strengthened. Fear and doubt occur without provocation, but they should not consume our thoughts. Problems and difficulties will never be fully eliminated while we journey on earth. When troubles abound, go to a quiet place and pray. Cast all worries up to God. Be faithful in prayer for God refreshes us with his grace and sustains us.

Luke 11:9-10; Proverbs 13:21
Point to Ponder: Pray for great faith.

Pray: Lord, fill me with faith so that I draw closer to you every day.

september 8

Yet for us there is one God, the Father, from
whom all things are and for whom we exist,
and one Lord, Jesus Christ, through whom
all things are and through whom we exist.

— 1 Corinthians 8:6

When someone asks, "Who is Jesus? Why do people worship him?" How we respond may have a profound effect. Jesus lives through us and wants to reveal himself to those around us. Our words and actions matter.

For a young child, we may talk about Jesus's birth to Mary and Joseph. We emphasize his majesty as the only Son of God, and how he grew up preaching. He healed the sick and performed other miracles. He never sinned or went against his Father. He died for us. We worship Jesus because he leads us to his Father, and we will live with him in heaven, free of pain, anger, and sin. He fills us with love and joy. We pray and honor him.

When talking to an adult seeking to know Jesus, we go into greater detail. Help the discerning person develop an attitude pleasing to God. Discuss what it looks like to live by faith. Stress the importance of reading scripture and praying. If the person says he is not sure how to pray, tell him to start as if having a discussion with his best friend. Teach him to say the Lord's Prayer. Encourage the person to search for God everywhere.

Strive to develop pure hearts so the words and actions we exhibit are meaningful and filled with love. Our interactions with those searching for God should leave a spiritual blessing.

Matthew 16:16-17; Proverbs 18:10
Point to Ponder: Jesus is Lord. Feel his presence; bring others to him.

Pray: Lord, teach me to spread the gospel. Give me the right words to say.

September 9

When the lot is cast into the lap, its
decision depends entirely on the Lord.

— Proverbs 16:33

We strive to follow God's will, but sometimes the evil one, Satan, disguises himself and tempts us to make choices which look inviting on the outside but are not in our best interests.

When in doubt, be still and communicate with God. Listen for the promptings of the Holy Spirit. Do not make quick decisions. Call God's name out loud. Seek his guidance. Read the Bible which is inspired by God. The word of God helps us make Christ-like decisions, and shows us the way forward.

We sometimes get caught up in instantaneous results and gratification. Satan's temptations intrigue us at first, but once we are caught in his grasp, the situation changes quickly. Be on guard. Do not rush to make a decision without prayer, or select the first action that comes to mine. Be still and think through difficult decisions. Pray for God's grace.

Ultimately, when our lives end on earth, God will judge our actions. We give him an account of our lives. He looks for truth. Being accountable for our actions and deeds bring a sense of responsibility and honesty. God sees all our actions and inactions. Be motivated to follow God's will and his word. Say no to Satan and sin and mean it. God leads us to eternal life.

Matthew 14:22-33; Psalm 62:8-9
Point to Ponder: Step out in faith. Trust God to lead you on the right path.

Pray: Lord, I want to do your will. Teach and guide me to serve you and others.

september 10

If possible, on your part, live at peace with all.
– Romans 12:18

What would it be like to live in peace? There are multiple verses in the Bible that focus on peace. As a guide for all of God's children, we live in peace by:

- Praising God and being glad-hearted always; giving thanks (1 Thes. 5:16, 18).
- Casting our burdens to the Lord through prayer (1 Pt. 5:7).
- Turning away from sin and doing good works; seeking to imitate Christ (1 Pt. 3:11).
- Trusting God so all things work together for good; following his will (Rom. 8:28).
- Applying and loving God's teachings and commandments (Ps. 119:165).
- Building a relationship with God; being faithful at all times (Rom. 5:1).
- Pursuing righteousness, faith, love, and peace with a pure heart (2 Tm. 2:22).
- Demonstrating the fruit of the Spirit – love, joy, patience, kindness, generosity, faithfulness, gentleness, and self-control (Gal. 5:22).

When we cherish our relationship with God and live in his presence, we know and experience his peace. We return day after day to his outstretched arms. God sends his peace when we humble ourselves. We dwell in the comfort of his love.

Psalm 31:15-18; Luke 9:37-43
Point to Ponder: God sends peace to fill your heart.

Pray: Lord, strengthen me to pursue peace and righteousness.

September 11

> *In every way I have shown you that by hard work*
> *of that sort we must help the weak, and keep in*
> *mind the words of the Lord Jesus who himself*
> *said, "It is more blessed to give than to receive."*
>
> — Acts 20:35

God sends generous blessings when he sees us serving others and experiencing the fullness of life. He knows the weak and poor are extremely vulnerable and suffer greatly. When we freely and willingly give of ourselves through work or service, then God responds to us in a like manner.

Scripture states, "The soul of the sluggard craves in vain, but the diligent soul is amply satisfied" (Prv. 13:4). Be a conduit through which the Lord blesses others. Guard against selfishness and grumbling and becoming too attached to money. Instead, face each day with gratitude, diligence, and a generous heart. Our words and actions matter because they affect others. They say a lot about our hearts and our beliefs. Strengthen and encourage others with uplifting comments and positive actions. Feel joy and peace that come through God's grace when we give of ourselves. Our lives change when we encounter God, become more Christ-like, and reflect our Lord and Savior's ways.

Give thanks to God for the ability to secure a job and have meaningful work. He desires us to use every tool he gives us to live productive lives and build his kingdom.

Mark 10:45; Proverbs 19:17
Point to Ponder: Demonstrate simple acts of kindness. Share God's blessings.

Pray: Lord, bless me with a generous heart. Teach me to be kind and loving.

september 12

*Finally, brothers, whatever is true, whatever is
honorable, whatever is just, whatever is pure,
whatever is lovely, whatever is gracious, if there
is any excellence and if there is anything worthy
of praise, think about these things. Keep on doing
what you have learned and received and heard and
seen in me. Then the God of peace will be with you.*
— Philippians 4:8-9

What we think and fill our minds with has a profound effect on our character. No one experiences life without burdens, but how we react and reflect on situations makes the difference. Concentrate and train our minds to focus on the teachings of Christ. Fill our thoughts with truth, love, mercy, kindness, gentleness, and peace.

Build character by reframing negative thoughts. Focus on the word of God by reading scripture to feed and exercise our minds. Choose to concentrate on the Lord's goodness and his unending love. These activities help to develop a righteous character modeled after Christ. We find joy and peace when we imitate him.

Expect a fair amount of troubles and disappointments, but realize God is our strength. Even with the best intentions, we say and do things that hinder God's plan. Work to develop the gift of discernment. God wants to teach us how to identify Satan's ploys and reject his temptations. Pray for God's grace each day and watch the gift of discernment grow. He desires us to live righteous lives.

James 4:7-10; Proverbs 28:25
Point to Ponder: Focus on an upbeat attitude and spread joy.

Pray: Lord, open my eyes and heart to your great gifts and blessings. Help me discern your will.

 September 13

We must consider how to rouse one another
to love and good works. We should not stay
away from our assembly, as is the custom of
some, but encourage one another, and this all
the more as you see the day drawing near.
— Hebrews 10:24-25

When hardships come, we struggle to live by faith. We wonder why God allows bad things to happen to good people. We feel vulnerable. Our faith is tested.

Christ gently disciplines us in order to gain our attention and to bring necessary change to our lives. He wants us to practice persistence and learn to trust him during difficult times. The Bible says we should encourage one another and not withdraw from others. God places people in our lives for reasons we do not understand. He tests us to see if we truly love and accept one another as he commanded.

Trust God's power and wisdom. He is the authority on love. With his guidance, we learn to accept each other and put away intolerant attitudes. He makes each person in his image. God desires us to turn into a reflection of who he is. We learn to accept and encourage our neighbors no matter the color of their skin or nationality.

Give thanks that God expresses his life through us. As we draw closer to him, he teaches us to love one another and work together to carry out his mission to redeem a troubled world. Stand firm and hold fast. Apply scripture and accomplish good works in his name.

1 Peter 1:13-16; 2 Timothy 3:16-17
Point to Ponder: We are all God's children. Encourage one another.

Pray: Lord, teach me to treat all people with love and kindness. Help me share compassion.

september 14

For God commands the angels to
guard you in all your ways.

— Psalm 91:11

Angels sent from God constantly watch over us. They protect us from physical dangers and from Satan's temptations. Many Christians believe we are assigned a guardian angel at birth to serve as a companion through life. Others believe God sends additional angels when the need arises. Angels help us choose righteous lives on earth.

They intercede for us according to God's commands. They are a sign of his presence. When fearful or confused, God asks us to pray. He hears and sends his angels who advise and protect us from spiritual and physical harm. Angels inspire us to do good works.

Most of us go about our day not thinking too much about our guardian angels. How many times have we been tempted by sin, reminded to call someone, or escaped danger, and wondered in amazement how in the world we made it unsheathed?

God never abandons us. Angels serve God by protecting, guiding, and comforting us. They guard against Satan invading our reality. They are older than creation. Listen for the gentle promptings of our guardian angel. Have an open mind and welcome the additional guidance. Angels summoned by Christ are helpful all our days on earth.

Hebrews 13:1-2; 1 John 4:1-6
Point to Ponder: Believe that God sends angels.

Pray: Thank you, Lord, for sending angels to watch over and protect me. Thank you also for giving me so many traveling companions that follow your ways and choose to follow your will.

September 15

But the Lord's kindness is forever, toward the
faithful from age to age. He favors the children's
children of those who keep his covenant.

— Psalm 103:17-18

When we find ourselves in situations beyond our control, step out in faith and call out to God. He waits to guide and protect us in every situation. Allow him to take control. With faith and God's unconditional love, we learn to live in unity with others.

Nothing is too hard to face when we have the fullness of God dwelling within us. He brings every divine resource with him. He treats his children with gentleness and kindness. When he invites us to carry-on his work, he gives us the strength of his Son, Jesus. He wants to reveal himself to others through our lives.

God sanctifies us before he sends us to do his work. He gives us grace and wisdom. Satan may try to convince us that we are unworthy or that the work is too difficult, but we learn to reject these self-defeating thoughts. We call out to God and allow his truth to realign us to his will. Then the power of God is released to us. God is more powerful than Satan.

The Lord's kindness and love sets us free to do his will. He never leaves our side. God restores our souls and works mightily in our lives. Trust him to be our guiding light. Grow strong in awareness of his almighty presence.

Proverbs 26:18-19; John 17:11-26
Point to Ponder: God knows you intimately and loves you unconditionally.

Pray: Lord, allow me to walk in your truth. May I never lose sight of your love and kindness.

september 16

Therefore, confess your sins to one another and pray for one another, that you may be healed. The fervent prayer of a righteous person is very powerful.

– James 5:16

Be persistent in prayer. When we pray, we raise our minds and hearts to God. Prayer is two-way communication. We speak; God listens. He speaks, but we sometimes have trouble hearing him. We rush ahead of God. If he does not answer our prayers immediately, we often lose hope and our faith weakens. Sometimes God chooses to answer our prayers differently than what we expect. He always has our good in the forefront, so trust his will. He sends what we need, not necessarily what we want.

God sees all we do. Before a thought comes to our minds, he listens. He looks for a pure heart and one willing to be shaped. If we adhere to what God requires, he leads us to pray for things aligned to his plan.

If we return to sinful ways, Satan holds evil over us. Our prayers are minimal and muted. We feel anxious and lost. Call out to God. Asking God for forgiveness is not a sign of weakness, but instead a way to rid ourselves from the burdens of evil. God intervenes at just the right time and hears our prayers and responds.

Allow the Holy Spirit to guide us. He gives us sufficient revelation and strength to return to God. When we quiet our souls, pray continually, and obey God, he forgives us. We may not receive what we ask for, but God fills our needs and sends us hope.

Colossians 4:2; Mark 11:24
Point to Ponder: Fervent prayer is powerful.

Pray: Hear my prayers, Lord. Lead me on the path to righteousness.

september 17

When I say, "My foot is slipping," your love,
Lord holds me up. When cares increase
within me, your comfort gives me joy.

– Psalm 94:18-19

When we grow weary and our energy wanes, remember to ask God for help. Let his comforts delight our souls. Scripture tells us, "God is our refuge and our strength, an ever-present help in distress" (Ps. 46:2). His grace is available to us anytime and in any place.

People grow tired from fighting physical illnesses, addictions, and emotional battles. When we feel sick or unworthy, nothing seems to motivate us. Fighting illnesses takes energy and effort. We lose hope in ever regaining our strength. Our lives are a constant battle. There is fatigue deep in our souls that goes beyond physical tiredness. This condition can only be rectified by the Lord.

When we feel tired to the core, seek rest, spiritual renewal, and the grace to follow Christ. Read scripture and meditate on the Word. Pray often every day. Seek the stillness of God and his peaceful presence. He sends grace so we press on. Trust him to give us refreshing rest as nothing else can. God restores our strength and encircles us with his peace.

Never give up on God. Be faithful in prayer and persevere through hardships. His love for us goes beyond human understanding and never ends. Start fresh each day with prayer and quiet praise.

Matthew 11:28-29; Proverbs 3:26
Point to Ponder: God graces you with rest and peace. Ask for his help.

Pray: Lord, renew my soul. I want to be strong to do your will.

September 18

The curse of the LORD is on the house of the
wicked, but the dwelling of the just he blesses.
When he is dealing with the arrogant, he is
stern, but to the humble he shows kindness.
— Proverbs 3:33-34

When we feel successful in our vocation, we sometimes acquire a false sense of security. We think we have sufficient wisdom and skill level to meet any challenge. Thoughts constantly roll in and out of our minds – good, bad, and indifferent. We criticize and readily judge others' abilities, unaware of how much growth is still required in us. Our pride clouds our view of God's part in our daily activities. We forget to be humble and pray for his guidance.

Scripture teaches us God disciplines his children (Heb. 12:5-11). His actions are meant to develop growth and maturity. He chastens because he loves us and wants to keep us on the right path. Never take God for granted or his discipline lightly. Every good thing we have is a gift from God.

He disciplines with love. We may lose rewards or material riches, but we do not lose salvation. When we experience events that surpass our understanding, God is communicating a critical message. Pray for a teachable spirit. Thank him for his faithfulness and return to him often in prayer. Give God the glory.

Luke 10:20; Psalm 32:7
Point to Ponder: Thank God for his love and kindness.

Pray: Lord, thank you for loving me enough to correct my ways. I want to draw closer to you.

September 19

Love never fails ... At present we see indistinctly,
as in a mirror, but then face to face. At present
I know partially; then I shall know fully, as I
am fully known. So faith, hope, love remain,
these three; but the greatest of these is love.

— 1 Corinthians 13:8, 12-13

God's love for us never ends. We might turn away, reject his teachings, and ignore or disobey him, but he never gives up on us. He follows us to the depths of our sinfulness until he reclaims us. He pursues us until we return to the safety and comfort of his love. We cannot understand God's unconditional love. It is different then what we experience with human love.

God asks us to love others because we are made in his image. He sends angels to guide us along the way. We are never without help. He dwells deep within our souls. When we love our neighbors, God makes us a vessel of grace to signal love.

As people of faith, strive to always imitate Christ and love others. Part of our calling requires us to urge those around us who have more, to help those who have less. Through these actions, we draw closer to God and deepen our relationship with him. We rest in his love.

Colossians 3:14; Psalm 56:13-14
Point to Ponder: Reveal God's love and mercy to the world.

Pray: Lord, may others find in me a reason to love. Give me the courage to speak to others about your saving grace and love.

september 20

Come, let us sing joyfully to the Lord; cry out to the
rock of our salvation. Let us greet him with a song
of praise, joyfully sing out our psalms. For the Lord
is the great God, the great king over all gods.

— Psalm 95:1-3

Be filled with joy knowing we have been chosen by God to be his children and joint heirs to his kingdom. Do not fear death; instead look to heaven as our final resting place where there is no hurt or pain. Our presence there with God will be filled with peace, joy, and love. He has prepared a place for us to spend eternity with him.

Never be satisfied with a joyless life. Deep within our souls, there should be the joy of Christ that no circumstance dispels. Feel the joy of God's love daily. Look for joy in the small things. It should permeate our lives and everything we do. True joy comes from knowing Christ is within each of us. God is there for us, never letting go.

Sometimes bad things happen to us or our neighbors. Do not blame God. Use trials and troubles to draw closer to him. Repeat familiar prayers until we feel God working in our midst. He heals the brokenhearted and graces us with his comforting arms.

Strive to experience life as a succession of little miracles with blessings too many to count. Sing songs of joy and experience a grateful heart. Enjoy God's blessings.

James 1:2-5; Romans 8:28-30
Point to Ponder: Sing joyfully to God. Feel his love and share it with others.

Pray: Lord, help me be joyful in all circumstances, and persevere as I grow closer to you.

September 21

*Lord, my heart is not proud; nor are my eyes
haughty. I do not busy myself with great
matters, with things too sublime for me.
Rather, I have stilled my soul, hushed it like
a weaned child. Like a weaned child on its
mother's lap, so is my soul within me.*

— Psalm 131:1-2

In our daily routines, we often get so busy that we forget to pause and enjoy the day and God's blessings. We tend to rush from one thing to another and never seem to finish tasks. Some people are extremely successful in their busyness and their endeavors. They tend to have an endless supply of money, energy, and knowledge. For some, money is their God, and it buys happiness. Riches persuade many they no longer need God.

When earthly riches no longer fill the void in our hearts, we become stressed and disoriented, and we may find sinful ways the norm. If God is not in our lives and we fail to pray, we feel loneliness and despair more. We realize money cannot buy happiness or cure illness.

We take nothing with us to heaven. True wealth does not hinge on the amount of money we have or our material riches. God's desire for us is to have spiritual wealth and build his kingdom on earth.

We are instruments in the hands of God and need his guidance, grace, and strength. Be thankful for all the blessings he sends our way. Be rich in the things that matter to him. Acquire spiritual wealth through prayer and reading scripture. Share so we build God's kingdom.

Psalm 18:31; Proverbs 4:20-22
Point to Ponder: Spiritual wealth comes from God.

Pray: Lord, send me peace. Quiet my soul so I sense true wealth from you.

265

September 22

*Then he told them a parable about the necessity
for them to pray always without becoming weary.*
— Luke 18:1

Jesus told parables to his followers because they could understand him better through his stories and familiar images. In the Parable of the Persistent Widow (Lk. 18:1-8), the focus remains on the power of praying every day and the importance of fervent prayer.

Prayers, short or long, bring us closer to our heavenly Father. Prayer does not have to be complex or difficult. Conversations from the heart with Jesus are the best kind. Even before we call on him, he knows our needs. He continually works in our lives.

Some people doubt that Jesus knows our situation. They wonder if prayer is necessary. Sometimes we may feel Christ is far away and our prayers go unanswered. Jesus Christ never changes. Satan may have us in his grasp. We become prideful and feel we can make decisions without help from anyone. We choose our own direction and spend less time in prayer. We have moved away from Jesus.

When we feel distant from Christ, pray and seek him. Ask for forgiveness. He works through us and welcomes us back to his presence. Prayer enables us to draw closer to him.

Today experience God in the midst of our lives as he provides for us. His healing light shines brightly upon us, and we no longer walk in darkness. Feel God's peace calm our hearts.

Psalm 92:2-5; Matthew 6:7-8
Point to Ponder: Never stop praying. Jesus listens and responds.

Pray: Lord, teach me to pray faithfully so I draw closer to you.

september 23

Jesus spoke to them again saying, "I am the light
of the world. Whoever follows me will not walk
in darkness, but will have the light of life."

– John 8:12

Strive to walk in the light of God. When the light becomes hazy, pause and refocus. There are two blockages to the light of God: clutter and dust. Clutter happens when our material riches take priority. We form habits that require us to rush around from one activity to the next with little time for prayer or church attendance. Our hopes and dreams focus on the next fabulous vacation, second home, new cars, or other material possessions. Our minds become cluttered with earthly riches.

Dust is sin that eats away at our souls, keeping us in darkness and shadows. We get addicted to sinful habits, and they become the norm. A film forms over our hearts as God's image fades. We live in a world made of shades of gray.

God watches all we do and say. When we turn away and have little time for him, he allows us to endure the consequences of living in sin and darkness. Christ gently disciplines us. He wants us to have order in our lives with little clutter and dust, and live in harmony with him.

Turning to God is like spring cleaning: we spruce up our spiritual lives and put away our lack of faith and hope. We seek forgiveness and live in a world filled with the blessings from God.

Matthew 5:14-16; Ephesians 5:8
Point to Ponder: Walk in the light of life with God.

Pray: Lord, I trust you. Help me see your light and discern when my world is cluttered.

september 24

Finally, draw your strength from the Lord
and from his mighty power. Put on the armor
of God so that you may be able to stand
firm against the tactics of the devil.

— Ephesians 6:10-11

Our responsibility as Christians is to turn away from Satan and not become entrapped in his evil ways. He lurks around, waiting for a weakness to appear, and then silently invades and overtakes our souls.

When we feel trapped and guilty, and evil is the norm, turn to God. Flee from Satan, the master of lies and deceit. If we allow ourselves to remain in sin or repeat sinful acts as our lifestyle, we move away from God.

Allow the Holy Spirit to eradicate every trace of sin. Strive never to repeat sinful acts. Know the enemy, Satan. Learn from mistakes. God is more powerful than Satan, and has already defeated the evil one when he sent his only Son, Jesus, to die on the cross. His resurrection leads us to glory. Abide in Christ and seek forgiveness.

Take refuge in the Lord who has already defeated the enemy. When we trust in God, Satan flees from us. Feel God's presence as he blesses us with peace and love. God's love for us never wavers. He wants only good for his children. He loves and supports us without tiring. Praise and thank God for his faithfulness.

1 John 3:8-10; 1 Peter 5:8-11
Point to Ponder: Never remain in sin and darkness. Say no to Satan and yes to God.

Pray: Lord, protect me from all evil. Help me to rest in your presence.

september 25

You shall not fear the terror of the night nor
the arrow that flies by day ... You have the
Lord for your refuge; you have made the Most
High your stronghold. No evil shall befall
you, no affliction come near your tent.

– Psalm 91:5, 9-10

When we seek God daily and have a relationship with him, we need not fear anything. He watches over us and keeps us safe. His love never ends, like a father's love for his children. God is unfailingly good and changeless in his commitment to us. We have been chosen and sealed with his Spirit to start fresh every day, spread the gospel, and do his will.

The Holy Spirit prompts us to do an about-face from self-centeredness to God-centeredness. The Spirit guides us back to Christ. Even though we may experience some level of happiness as we live self-centered lives, giving our time and effort to this world, it is nothing like the peace and joy we feel when we have God leading the activities in our lives. Trust God in all things. Feel the confidence that comes from knowing we are doing his will.

Resist the temptation to invest in earthly things. Instead, take refuge in God. Let him lead us. Follow him, pray continually, and fear nothing. Allow Christ to live out his divine life through us. No one removes Christ, our stronghold, from us. His way, though mysterious and beyond our understanding, is perfect. God reassures and strengthens those he loves.

Psalm 117:13-14; Isaiah 25:3-4
Point to Ponder: When we are with God, no evil befalls us.

Pray: Lord, watch over me and fill me with kindness and love. I praise your holy name.

september 26

Everything that the Father gives me will come
to me, and I will not reject anyone who comes
to me, because I came down from heaven not to
do my will but the will of the one who sent me.
— John 6:37-38

God sent his only Son to earth so we could be saved and have eternal life. As we mature, we see people marked by physical deformity, social isolation, and despair. These people are modern day lepers, sometimes shunned by their families and community.

Jesus wants us to put away our pride and remember these needy people are often ill, with questionable lifestyles, habits, and addictions, but they are still children of God. Many people find discomfort when we take a step into a world so different than our world. Remember that God is in us and controls how we react. Ask God for guidance. He sends us the strength we need.

When we sacrifice our time, possessions, money, and energy to serve others, we demonstrate to God how much we love him. We open our hearts to him and imitate his gentleness, kindness, and love.

The Lord created all his children in his image. He wants us to treat all people, even those who look and act differently and live on the margins, with dignity and kindness. Meaning in our lives comes from how God sees us, not how others judge us. Allow him to shape us so that we go forth to spread the gospel and tell others of his love.

James 4:11-12; Luke 17:11-19
Point to Ponder: We are created in the image of God. Imitate his ways.

Pray: Lord, help me have the courage to reach out to others who are less fortunate.

September 27

A brother is a better defense than a strong
city, and a friend is like the bars of a
castle ... Some friends bring ruin on us, but
a true friend is more loyal than a brother.

— Proverbs 18:19, 24

We do not choose to be a friend of God. By his nature, he chooses us. He wants us to draw close and share our lives with him even though we have nothing to offer in return except our gifts of song, thanksgiving, and praise.

When we share our blessings with others, we honor God. We impart our beliefs in regard to the uniqueness and dignity of every person. People hunger for an expression of Christ as he really is, living out his life through his people.

Sense God's presence. Do not envy what God has given others. There is a great temptation to compare our situation to the life of others. "Why did God give my neighbor a bigger home in a more luxurious neighborhood? Did God heal my neighbor of cancer and not my mother? Why did my friend get the promotion when I work as hard as he does?" Only God knows these answers.

Welcome friendship and love for our neighbors. God has a perfect plan for us. He leads and places us where we need to be. Never doubt God's love because he brings his promises to fruition in our lives and the lives of our friends. God's plan is best. Consider him to be our best true friend.

John 15:13; 1 Thessalonians 5:11
Point to Ponder: Pray for true friendships.

Pray: Lord, I love you. I need wisdom to be a better friend to my neighbor. Help me be filled with your love and grace, and share these blessings with others.

If there is any encouragement in Christ, any
solace in love, any participation in the Spirit,
any compassion and mercy, complete my joy
by being of the same mind, with the same
love, united in heart, thinking one thing.

— Philippians 2:1-2

The Lord gives us what we need to follow his will. He adjusts our lives so that we become aligned to his plan. When this happens, we sometimes feel unsettled. Change causes fear. Unfamiliar feelings and doubts creep into our being. We do not understand clearly.

People have a human tendency to resist change. Our attitude is typically positive when things go according to our plans, but when changes occur, we become unsettled, or we marginally accept the new order. God may have us sacrifice some of our treasures and material riches. This may prove difficult.

If we find ourselves resisting and turning negative every time God adjusts our lives, ask the Holy Spirit to give us an attitude adjustment, and pour humility into our lives. Ask for the gift of a generous heart and let go of material possessions trusting God to provide. He teaches us to be careful with our resources and not waste what we have been given. He sees to our needs.

Live to please God. Take a step back and give thanks for the blessings he sends, and for the lives we have been given. God's approval of our actions matters. Run as to win the prize of eternal life with God. Reach the ultimate goal.

Luke 11:37-41; Colossians 3:2
Point to Ponder: Be united with Christ. Make changes to be more like him.

Pray: Thank you for allowing me to be in your presence, Lord. Teach me to trust your will.

September 29

My soul rests in God alone, from whom comes
my salvation. God alone is my rock and
salvation, my secure height; I shall never fall.

— Psalm 62:2-3

When Jesus walked the earth and ministered to the people, he was different from other men. He went days without eating. He told his disciples God would provide for them but they still hungered for earthly food. We read scripture that tells us about Jesus feeding five thousand people. He ordered the crowds to sit. Then his disciples fed everyone with five loaves of bread and two fish (Mt. 14:13-21).

While the disciples sought earthly nourishment, Jesus followed the will of his Father who sent him. Spiritual food remained most important to Jesus. The disciples had problems understanding Jesus's ways. He told them the kingdom of God was not about providing food, but rather, about feeding the spirit things like joy, peace, and love. Jesus taught his disciples that God provides everything we need to live abundantly.

The key to living with God and following his will is to believe completely. He alone is our Lord and Savior. Great faith in Christ is critical for spiritual growth. He rewards faithfulness.

Sometimes we need to specifically ask him to forgive and heal us. There are no sinful habits or past hurts God cannot heal. Remember when he said, "Ask and it will be given to you, seek and you will find; knock and the door will be opened to you" (Mt. 7:7). Go ahead and ask. Be a generous, open-hearted receiver of blessings from God. Give him thanks and praise.

Romans 2:1-11; Luke 11:42-46
Point to Ponder: Rest in the presence of God. He sends comfort.

Pray: Lord, I trust you. Send me grace to do your will.

september 30

The sayings of the wise: Incline your ear, and
hear my words, and apply your heart to my
doctrine; For it will be well if you keep them in
your bosom, if they all are ready on your lips.
— Proverbs 22:17-18

We are born to worship and serve the Lord. Worship is not just church attendance and rituals. True worship includes intimate and vital encounters with God the Father, Jesus Christ, and the Holy Spirit – one and the same through the blessed Trinity. We read passages in scripture about the Holy Trinity. "The grace of the Lord Jesus Christ and the love of God and the fellowship of the holy Spirit be with all of you" (2 Cor. 13:13). True worship includes the full recognition of who God is: our heavenly Father, our almighty Creator, our Savior, and our merciful Lord.

When we worship God, we draw closer to him. We avoid sin and strive to be obedient. He blesses us with the fruit of the Spirit. Through his grace we receive love, joy, peace, patience, generosity, gentleness, and self-control. Our faithfulness to God increases as we follow his will. We change from the inside out as we grow in holiness. Others observe our actions and hear us speak of God's love. They see his light in our souls and reflected in our actions. We have a sense of peace and confidence.

Join those who worship and love the Lord. Let our actions and words reflect the one who has been worshiped for thousands of years. Praise his holy name.

John 4:1-42; Romans 2:12-16
Point to Ponder: Worship God always.

Pray: Lord, I praise you and thank you for the many blessings you send. I trust you will guide me.

October 1

He who is a friend is always a friend, and
a brother is born for the time of stress.

– Proverbs 17:17

God sends us friends so that we do not become discouraged. Friends comfort and remain steadfast during times of despair as well as in times of great joy. *Webster's Dictionary* defines a friend as "one attached to another by affection or esteem." Is friendship about companionship, faithfulness, and loyalty? Yes, but there is more. A friend listens, shares hardships and triumphs, and offers encouragement at the right time.

Think of friends we have counted on in the past to be there at important times. Friends sharpen us and make us better than we ever dreamed, and they motivate us to do the right thing. Strive to be sensitive to those whom we call friends. Look for them to be kind, concerned, and aware of our needs. Thank God for those friends who remain true and trustworthy over the years. They help us mature spiritually and become more Christ-like.

God is our best friend. When we seek harmony with him, we enjoy life more. But be alert, and do not assume everyone who comes along is a friend. Satan disguises himself to be a good friend until he has a stronghold in our souls. Then he leads us away from God and into sin.

Choose friends wisely. Pray for God's help in guiding us toward trustworthy and righteous friends. True friends are blessings from God.

1 Thessalonians 5:11-13; 1 Corinthians 15:33
Point to Ponder: God sends you special friends to treasure.

Pray: Thank you for giving me friends to love, Lord.

october 2

> *Quarrel not with a man without cause, with*
> *one who has done you no harm. Envy not the*
> *lawless man and choose none of his ways. To*
> *the* LORD *the perverse man is an abomination,*
> *but with the upright is his friendship.*
>
> — Proverbs 3:30-32

God's will for us is not hard to discern, yet we find his ways challenging at times. We fool ourselves into thinking God's ways are too difficult. Confusing and unsettling challenges turn us away. We hang our heads in defeat without turning to God for support.

God has prepared the way for us. He gives us scripture that reveals what we should do and how we should act toward others. He has placed the Holy Spirit within our souls to guide us. So why do we fail and find ourselves losing patience and walking away without trying?

We are human and lack confidence and faith. God gives us free will to make choices. He expects us to be obedient and follow his commandments, but sometimes we forget to turn to him. We make poor choices, flounder, and lose hope. Those who knowingly disobey the Lord face his wrath. Our merciful God forgives us when we call out for help. He is a whisper away and has power over all the earth.

It is challenging at times, but always say yes to God. Pray often so that no obstacles separate us from him. He gives us everything we need to cope. Have faith that he directs our steps. He knows what lies ahead.

Luke 12:8-12; Deuteronomy 30:1-10
Point to Ponder: Be persistent. Follow the will of God.

Pray: Lord, I embrace your teachings. Teach me to be obedient.

october 3

God will not allow your foot to slip; your guardian
does not sleep. Truly, the guardian of Israel never
slumbers nor sleeps. The Lord is your guardian;
the Lord is your shade at your right hand. By
day the sun cannot harm you, nor the moon by
night. The Lord will guard you from all evil,
will always guard your life. The Lord will guard
your coming and going both now and forever.

— Psalm 121:3-8

Strive to follow Christ and his teachings at all times. He walks with us as we journey toward eternal life. This does not mean our lives will be without hardships. Jesus suffered. Do we expect less?

In today's world, many people increasingly tolerate ungodliness. Some are impatient and feel they can control situations without heavenly intervention. They see no need for God and do not believe in his sovereignty.

When we seek God in every situation and strive to live righteously, we should expect some hostility from nonbelievers. The Lord has promised to be our guardian. Fear not, because he guards us with perfect love. Turn to God often in prayer and seek his guidance and grace. When we experience God's love, we want to shout out and tell others about him. Our responsibility is not to convince others of the reality of God, but simply to bear witness to what the Lord has said and done for us. Demonstrate to others that with his love, we are able to do anything in his name.

1 John 1:5-9; 2 Timothy 3:10-15
Point to Ponder: God is the answer. He guards you from evil.

Pray: God, help me be patient and free me from worry. Thank you for being my guardian.

october 4

Better a poor man who walks in his integrity
than he who is crooked in his ways and rich.
— Proverbs 28:6

The condition of our hearts determines how much we tell others of God's teachings. If we are hardened by challenges and worn down by bitterness, we find it difficult to serve our neighbors and reach out. We tend to hold tight to our possessions and earthly comforts, limiting our outreach. As Christians, we know God wants us to love and serve others. We accept this in our minds, but the truth does not penetrate our hearts to make a difference in our actions.

Believers must examine their hearts. God cannot be deceived. He blesses each of us with different skill sets. If we share our talents with others and do not allow earthly possessions and material riches to prevent God's word from taking hold, we experience his loving presence.

God walks with us as we step out in faith and integrity. Scripture says, "Do not neglect to do good and to share what you have; God is pleased by sacrifices of that kind" (Heb. 13:16). Develop a strong relationship with God so that our hearts are filled with his love and joy. Feel compassion for others and reach out and share God's blessings.

Spend time with the Lord. Make him a constant companion. Focus on today. Pray often and trust him to show us real wealth. Realize that having lots of money does not guarantee happiness or a place in heaven. Only God clothes us with grace, integrity, and true wealth.

Luke 12:15-21; 2 Corinthians 4:16-18
Point to Ponder: God never changes. Become spiritually wealthy.

Pray: God, fill me with generosity and kindness. Prompt me to share what I have with others.

october 5

> *"Blessed are those servants whom the master finds*
> *vigilant on his arrival. Amen, I say to you, he will gird*
> *himself, have them recline at table, and proceed to wait*
> *on them. And should he come in the second or third*
> *watch and find them prepared in this way, blessed are*
> *those servants ... You also must be prepared, for at an*
> *hour you do not expect, the Son of Man will come."*
>
> – Luke 12:37-40

Are we ready to meet the Lord? Have we served our neighbors, given love away, and been kind and generous with our material possessions? If we cannot say yes, pause and reflect and then refresh our priorities so the master finds us vigilant. Strive every day to please God.

Expect the unexpected in life. God works through us. We become his voice, hands, and feet on earth. He sends opportunities to us to make known our faith. God may call our attention to someone who struggles and needs discipline, comfort, or prayers. Whatever occurs in life, do not limit what God does in us and through us. We need to be fed each day with spiritual food so we can share the gospel with others.

When we have God leading the way, we are prepared for him to come at any time. Strive to please Christ through our words and actions. Hear him say, "Well done, my good and faithful servant. Since you were faithful in small matters, I will give you great responsibilities. Come, share your master's joy" (Mt. 25:23). Be vigilant and prepared to meet God at any time. Praise him forever.

Psalm 40:12-18; Proverbs 3:33-34
Point to Ponder: Serve God. Be ready for the journey to heaven.

Pray: God, give me the grace to serve others so that my actions please you.

October 6

> *None of us lives for oneself, and no one dies*
> *for oneself. For if we live, we live for the Lord,*
> *and if we die, we die for the Lord; so then,*
> *whether we live or die, we are the Lord's.*
> — Romans 14:7-8

As we grow in faith, we may feel God leading us down a certain path. Know that he travels each step with us. He guides and protects us. Hold tight to the hand of God, and step out in faith.

Along the way, difficulties may evolve. Fear not, for God does not place any obstacle before us we cannot overcome. Remember, we can do anything with his help. Look at the challenges as opportunities to draw closer to him. Engage our hearts a bit more when we pray. Be steadfast in faith. We may not always receive what we pray for, but God does send what we need.

Be thankful for gifts from the Lord. Use them wisely so others see his presence in our lives. Allow God to influence us in every area: how we treat our neighbors, how we influence our children and teach them about the Lord, and how we serve others through our work.

Whatever we choose as a career, persevere and commit to our calling to use our God-given skills and talents to make the world a better place. Let our paths in life lead us to a deeper relationship with the Lord. His way is always best.

Psalm 125:1-5; Proverbs 3:29
Point to Ponder: Encounter God every day. Seek his guidance.

Pray: God, teach me your ways so that I help others see your goodness, mercy, and love.

October 7

*For you were called for freedom, brothers. But
do not use this freedom as an opportunity for the
flesh; rather, serve one another through love.*

– Galatians 5:13

Christ has given us the grace to make choices and use free will.
Unfortunately, Satan gets in our path if we let down our guard.
Satan's choices appear enchanting and harmless and maybe even
good for us. We fall for the temptation and find ourselves bound in
the grip of the devil. We take detours and step out on our own with
little thought of what God wants for us. We turn away from him.
Nothing seems to go right. We feel frustrated and overwhelmed as
darkness prevails.

When we are far from God and cannot feel the promptings
of the Holy Spirit, pause and pray. Find a quiet place and spend
time communicating with him. Listen for the quiet voice within
our souls. The Lord waits for us to turn back to him. He forgives
our transgressions when we repent. Satan's power is nil. God is
almighty.

Our free will is a gift to use to choose how best to serve the
Lord. Free will gives us the freedom to choose righteousness and
not succumb to the bondage of sin. Before making major decisions,
pray for guidance. Receive the life-giving grace of God and live in
righteous harmony with him.

Matthew 7:13-14; Galatians 6:7-10
Point to Ponder: Pray for God's guidance. He gives you freedom to
make righteous choices.

Pray: Lord, help me make choices to glorify you. Teach me to say
no immediately to the temptations of Satan and remain free of sin.

october 8

For whatever was written previously was written
for our instruction, that by endurance and by
encouragement of the scriptures we may have hope.
— Romans 15:4

Accepting God's teachings and practicing his truths as written in the Bible is life - changing. When we read scripture, we encounter God. We seek his presence. Our confidence in him gives us hope.

The Bible says, "All scripture is inspired by God and is useful for teaching, for refutation, for correction, and for training in righteousness so that one who belongs to God may be competent, equipped for every good work" (2 Tm. 3:16-17). The same God, who walked with Moses and then became man in Jesus Christ, lives within each of us. No power defeats him. When we read and follow Christ's teachings, he guides and protects us. We have no power of our own.

Some people go through life without knowing God. They have little to no relationship with him. God sees his influence on some as negligible but he still loves them.

Times may change, but God does not. Scripture says, "Jesus Christ is the same yesterday, today, and forever" (Heb. 13:8). Turn to God and build a relationship with him. Invite him to search our souls and remove negative attitudes, unhealthy relationships, and questionable activities. Pray often and read scripture to nourish our souls. He rewards those who seek him. Rejoice in God's love and experience the blessings he sends to those who follow his teachings.

Psalm 119:113-120; Joshua 1:6-8
Point to Ponder: God's grace is a blessing. He never denies his love.

Pray: Lord, be with me wherever I go. I trust you. Teach me to follow your plans for my life.

october 9

Everyone who has this hope based on him
makes himself pure, as he is pure.

— 1 John 3:3

Build a strong relationship with the Lord. Ask him to cleanse us of our sins, and then make our hearts pure. Pray often for his grace. Believers rejoice with others in God's goodness. We feel empowered when we trust God. His way for us is always best.

People who have little or no hope in God need to see the changes he makes in our lives. Those who encounter God are calmer and able to speak and bear witness to his goodness and mercy without hesitation. They are generous with God's blessings of time, talents, and treasures. Changes in our lives are our greatest testimony to God working through us.

Believers provide hope and knowledge of God's ways and bring others to him. There is nothing more appealing than to see someone living God's word. Followers place hope in the one who is faithful and stands by his word. Be a believer and marvel and bask in God's love and joy.

For those who want to grow closer to God, take the first step and pray. Reach out with hope and wait for him. The more we pray and wait for God to respond, the stronger our faith grows. Trust him to hear our prayers and answer them. He blesses us in many ways and strengthens our hearts. Remain steadfast in hope and have the peace of God in our hearts.

Romans 15:13; Psalm 31:24
Point to Ponder: Hope in God. Seek his blessings.

Pray: Make my heart pure, Lord. Increase my faith and hope in your love.

October 10

Let mutual love continue. Do not neglect hospitality, for through it some have unknowingly entertained angels.

– Hebrews 13:1-2

Some people believe angels take on human characteristics for a short period of time (Gn. 19:1). Christians look at spiritual angels as a gift from God. Angels are a totally separate kind of creation than human creation. They are considered virtuous messengers sent to lead, support, and guard us from harm.

Throughout scripture, we find angels given different unique attributes. Michael, the angel of mercy, has been fighting wars on behalf of God since the fall of Satan (Rev. 12:7-9). The evil one and other angels were cast out of heaven when Satan became too pompous and believed he was more powerful than God.

Two other angels mentioned in scripture passages are Gabriel and Raphael. John 1:26-38, describes Gabriel as the angel of justice and messages, announcing to Mary the birth of Jesus. In addition, Raphael, the angel of healing, is known to heal emotions and the sick, heal the heart, heal our connection to God, and heal messed up areas of our lives. Raphael is said to bring wholeness and helps us be observers of truth.

God's angels are sent to guide us on our journey on earth in a gentle manner, spreading love and harmony in a graceful balance. When we get to heaven, we will understand the full truth about what angels have done in our lives and how they have protected us.

Psalm 91:11-12; Psalm 43:1-5
Point to Ponder: Welcome angels sent from God.

Pray: Lord, send your angels to guide, support, and protect me from all harm.

October 11

Those whose steps are guided by the Lord; whose
way God approves, may stumble, but they will
never fall, for the Lord holds their hand.

– Psalm 37:23-24

We may have times in our lives when we do not imitate what God
would do. We find our focus shifting away from him. The Lord
knows there are times when we grow weary on our journey and our
walk with him, but we never have to fear evil. God has overcome
Satan and his evil angels. The Lord our God has soundly defeated
every form of wickedness. Trust him to guide us away from evil.

When difficult times occur, and we need rest and reassurance,
remember to pause and go to a quiet place to pray. Return to God
and ask him to restore us. Even though we cannot see God, he sees
all we do and hears our prayers. When troubled and exhausted
from carrying a heavy burden or resisting temptations, draw closer
to God and rest in his presence. His love reaches our brokenness
and heals us.

The Lord works through us in mysterious ways. Trust him to
provide all we need. Even in the worst case scenario in the midst
of a hostile and menacing world, God's love for us never falters.
His love fills our hearts. His incomprehensible peace surrounds
us. Choose to relate everything we encounter to him. Focus on the
Lord, our comforter and protector. He has prepared a place for us
in his heavenly kingdom.

1 Peter 5:6-7; Acts 11:19-26
Point to Ponder: Trust God. Follow him.

Pray: Lord, guide me and teach me your ways. I trust you.

october 12

*See, upon the palms of my hands, I have written
your name; your walls are ever before me.*
— Isaiah 49:16

God knows us by name and has a unique plan for each person. He constantly renews us to be his eyes, ears, hands, voice, and feet on earth. God knows all of his children and has promised to never abandon us. We are his.

God anticipates our cries. He asks us to come to him throughout the day and trust in his unfailing love. Call his name as a whispered prayer, as praise, or as a call for help. Christ invites us to have a relationship with him so that we better understand the importance of living in his presence and being close to him. He looks at each person – young and old, rich and poor, spiritual and non-spiritual – with the same love and interest. God has a pure and generous heart.

Every time we encounter an unfamiliar situation, pray for strength to meet the challenge head-on. If mistreated, faulted, or embarrassed without cause, seek direction from Christ, and ask for guidance on how to respond. If someone writes hateful remarks or speaks with an evil tongue, do not lash back in-kind. Instead, turn the other cheek and wait. God sends us strength to deal with hateful situations. Everything we do, all our actions and reactions, should be in the context of our relationship to Christ.

Our Lord is an incredible teacher. He sends grace to guide, protect, and counsel us. Honor him with praise and adoration.

Matthew 1:21-23; Philippians 2:10-11
Point to Ponder: God knows you by name before you are born.

Pray: God, let me draw closer to you. Teach me, guide me, and most of all love me.

october 13

*If I speak in human and angelic tongues, but do not
have love, I am a resounding gong or a clashing
cymbal. And if I have the gift of prophecy and
comprehend all mysteries and all knowledge; if I
have all faith so as to move mountains, but do not
have love, I am nothing. If I give away everything
I own, and if I hand my body over so that I may
boast but do not have love, I gain nothing.*
— 1 Corinthians 13:1-3

God is love. We cannot be close to God without being affected by
his love. The depth of his love is incomprehensible to man. We
have only our human experiences of love to ponder.

God has commanded us to love. "Owe nothing to anyone,
except to love one another; for the one who loves another has
fulfilled the law" (Rom. 13:8). God treats us with patience,
kindness, and understanding. We desire to imitate his ways and
learn to love our neighbors.

The Holy Spirit nudges us to extend a helping hand and
speak words that are uplifting and kind. If we have elderly people
living near us, be kind and offer them a ride to the grocery or to
church. Do not shun homeless people; instead give them a care
package of food or clothing. Compliment those who demonstrate
kind acts rooted in love. Do not let negativity or sin deny us from
experiencing love. The Spirit guides us even when we find it
difficult. He sends us grace so his love overflows through us. We
can change the world simply by loving others.

1 Corinthians 13:12-13; Proverbs 22:11
Point to Ponder: Help me see the opportunities to share love.

Pray: Lord, give me a fresh outlook so I love everyone.

october 14

Jesus said to him, "Have I been with you for
so long a time and you still do not know me,
Philip? Whoever has seen me has seen the
Father. How can you say, show us the Father?
Do you not believe that I am in the Father and
the Father is in me? The words that I speak to
you I do not speak on my own. The father who
dwells in me is doing his works. Believe me that
I am in the Father and the Father is in me, or
else, believe because of the works themselves.

— John 14:9-11

How often do we have doubts? They seem to crop up during
the day without provocation. Sometimes we doubt our ability,
worthiness, and faith. As we pray and walk daily with the Lord,
our path is not distinct. We often get confused, question God, and
have doubts.

The first disciples were often confused and fearful, and they
had doubts about Jesus. He taught them to listen to his parables,
and then explained things in private to them. Jesus established a
relationship with the disciples where they felt free to ask questions.
They came to know his voice and understand his words.

God wants to have a relationship with us. Draw closer to him.
Read scripture, worship at church, and pray daily. Keep his image
in the forefront of our minds. He wants to steady us. Allow him to
direct our steps as we journey to eternal life.

Proverbs 22:2; 1 Peter 5:9-11
Point to Ponder: God loves you unconditionally. Trust him.

Pray: Jesus, keep me close. Increase my understanding.

october 15

A mild answer calms wrath, but a harsh word
stirs up anger. The tongue of the wise pours out
knowledge, but the mouth of fools spurts forth folly.
– Proverbs 15:1-2

Words affect how we perceive things. Throughout scripture we read verses about the importance of controlling our tongues and our speech. How do we react when someone challenges our Christian beliefs and values? Do we respond by making harsh or sarcastic statements? Do we quote well known Bible verses? Or do we simply clam-up or walk away, choosing to have limited interaction with the naysayer?

Many people have difficulty talking about God. Most of us have been in uncomfortable situations when we disagree wholeheartedly with someone and feel temporarily caught off-guard and tongue-tied; or we have said things in haste we wish we could take back. Be alert to guard our thoughts and especially our tongues. Stop and think before responding. Pray for the individual causing the stir and babbling untruths or misinformation. Scripture says, "All bitterness, fury, anger, shouting, and reviling must be removed from you, along with all malice" (Eph. 4:31).

When we believe in God's almighty power, his word does not change. This gives us stability and self-control. As his life flows into ours, he sends us the grace we need to deal with negative people and those who stir up strife. Use kind and uplifting words to counter balance the negativity. Follow God's ways.

James 3:1-12; 2 Corinthians 12:9-10
Point to Ponder: Use uplifting words to please God.

Pray: Lord, control my thoughts and words. Help me be patient with naysayers.

october 16

> *"This is my commandment: love one another as I love you. No one has greater love than this, to lay down one's life for one's friends. You are my friends if you do what I command you ... It was not you who chose me, but I who chose you and appointed you to go and bear fruit that will remain, so that whatever you ask the Father in my name he may give you. This I command you: love one another."*
> — John 15:12-17

Jesus called his disciples friends because he felt a special bond with them. He knew their hearts. Jesus told them and others who followed him, to love one another.

Today, God patiently teaches us how to love and what loving our neighbor means. He desires to work through us to draw others to him. By his nature, he is patient, kind, and merciful. The closer we grow to the Lord through prayer and praise, the more we learn to love. God sends us the strength we need to love others. He sees the difficulties we have in loving those who look different or live on the margins. Yet, he is patient with us and shows us not to be fearful of the unknown for he is with us.

Enjoy the sense of security knowing we are loved by God. Pass his love on to others who are searching. Bring them to see his goodness and mercy. He dwells within each of us. Give glory to God.

Psalm 57:8-12; 1 John 4:7-21
Point to Ponder: Love with a pure heart.

Pray: God, send me blessings of strength and love for my neighbor. Help me reach out to others.

october 17

*My brothers, show no partiality as you adhere
to the faith in our glorious Lord Jesus Christ.
For if a man with gold rings on his fingers and
in fine clothes comes into your assembly, and
a poor person in shabby clothes also comes in,
and you pay attention to the one wearing the fine
clothes and say, "Sit here, please," while you
say to the poor one, "Stand there," or "Sit at
my feet," have you not made distinctions among
yourselves and become judges with evil designs?*
                                    – James 2:1-4

The Lord cautions us not to judge others by what they wear or how they look. Instead be gracious and merciful to all people. If patient and nonjudgmental, we see Christ in others. Pause and look for his reflection to shine through.

God allowed his only Son, Jesus, to die a painful death for us so our sins would be forgiven. He demonstrated mercy to the men who nailed his Son to the cross. Make a concerted effort to be merciful to others as God is to us.

Repent and ask for forgiveness when we disobey God and judge others. We do not have to quote scripture or be perfectly clear on every theological truth before we tell others about God and his mercy. He blesses us with the strength we need to lead and speak his truths. Be a laborer for God. Bring others to him and do not judge their worthiness. God will do the rest.

2 Peter 3:9, 17-18; Luke 10:25-28
Point to Ponder: Find the good in every person.

Pray: Jesus, help me see you in everyone I meet. Teach me to be merciful.

october 18

*Happy those who do not follow the counsel of
the wicked, nor go the way of sinners, nor sit in
company with scoffers. Rather, the law of the L*ORD
is their joy; God's law they study day and night.
— Psalm 1:1-2

We know people who are happy all the time. God's love shines through their eyes as they smile and appear content with their lives. These people have a special relationship with the Lord. They have encountered him, and have been transformed by his love. For them, truths come off the pages of the Bible, and the word has touched the deepest corners of their hearts. The mystery of God is revealed to them through scripture. They remain in the presence of God throughout the day. In everything they do, God is first.

Christians, who live the word of God, do not seek those who sin. They shy away from ungodly people because they do not want to acquire cynical ways and be led down a path away from God. They trust God, who is a whisper away, and have faith that he leads them on the path of righteousness.

Believe in Christ. He transforms us. Embrace and meditate on scripture until the Word becomes an integral part of our being. By studying the Bible, we encounter Jesus Christ. Others notice and seek our encouragement and peaceful ways. Become an instrument of God's love. Bask in his joyful presence as he guides us on our way to eternity.

Sirach 14:1-2; Psalm 37:3-4
Point to Ponder: Be happy and kind to everyone. Share the joy of God.

Pray: Lord, let your peace be with me so I encourage others to abide in your ways.

October 19

*Jesus answered them, "I told you and you do not
believe. The works I do in my Father's name testify
to me. But you do not believe, because you are not
among my sheep. My sheep hear my voice; I know
them, and they follow me. I give them eternal life,
and they shall never perish. No one can take them
out of my hand. My Father, who has given them to
me, is greater than all, and no one can take them
out of the Father's hand. The Father and I are one."*

— John 10:25-30

Jesus used parables to teach his followers. Parables with familiar
images, made it easier for many to understand. He used sheep in
several parables. Sheep are known to follow the shepherd and come
when he calls. They hear his voice and follow him. Jesus was the
greatest shepherd of all (Jn. 10:14).

Many did not believe or understand Jesus's ways and turned
against him. They thought him too severe and demanding. He
did not fit their image of what the Messiah should look like.
These people dismissed Jesus on the basis of their prejudices and
mistaken judgments. As a result of their closed mindedness, they
missed out on knowing him.

Those who heard Jesus's call and followed him were not
perfect. He did not expect perfection. The same holds true today.
Jesus gives us the strength we need to follow him. Be alert.
Nothing separates us from his love. Follow Jesus all the way to
heaven.

Ephesians 4:1-7; John 10:1-10
Point to Ponder: Follow the Good Shepherd.

Pray: Jesus, call me so I can serve you.

october 20

> *Be doers of the word and not hearers only,*
> *deluding yourselves. For if anyone is a hearer*
> *of the word and not a doer, he is like a man*
> *who looks at his own face in a mirror. He sees*
> *himself, then goes off and promptly forgets what*
> *he looked like. But the one who peers into the*
> *perfect law of freedom and perseveres, and is*
> *not a hearer who forgets but a doer who acts,*
> *such a one shall be blessed in what he does.*
>
> — James 1:22-25

There are levels of intimacy with God. The moment we are baptized and become a Christian, we start to form a relationship with him. Our relationship grows richer as we understand who God is. Our faith increases as we serve him.

However, if sin enters our lives and we do not repent, Satan separates us from God. He never abandons us, but we never fully experience the depths of God's being. We have temporary glimpses of his truths and delude ourselves. We settle for snippets of God's love.

We do not have to be perfect to follow God's will. At times we have to adjust our lives to his plan. When we are truly obedient to him, our hearts overflow with gratitude and love. Seek a pure heart filled with God's teachings. Serve with constancy the author of all good. Be filled with lasting joy as he works through us. Together as we receive God's grace and persevere, we are doers who make a difference. We build God's kingdom on earth.

Psalm 24:1-6; Proverbs 8:32-36
Point to Ponder: Be a doer and serve the Lord.

Pray: God, I want to do your will. Cleanse my heart so I may serve you always.

October 21

Blessed are the clean of heart, for they will see God.
— Matthew 5:8

Christians crave a state of grace and a pure heart only God gives. Believers who return to sinful ways over and over disobey God. They have chosen a standard different than his. They repent and ask for forgiveness but fail to have pure hearts. They continue to make their own rules and return to sin. Peace eludes them.

Believe God knows us intimately. We cannot hide from him. He hears all we say and watches our actions. Develop a relationship with God that is powerful, is all-consuming, and dominates all we do. Keep our minds firmly fixed on the truths of scripture. Ask God to fill us with his holiness. He transforms us as our relationship grows. We thrive on his power and his promise to guide us.

Through baptism, God cleanses us from original sin and provides a gateway to eternal life. He purifies our hearts. His grace reaches the depths of our being. We live each day anew.

Stay close to God through prayer and praise. Keep a pure heart free from sin. Live according to God's laws for they are eternal. Dwell in God's presence every day. Enjoy peace and the hope of heaven.

1 John 3:1-3; Psalm 24:1-6
Point to Ponder: God makes your heart pure.

Pray: God, all glory and honor are yours. I praise you and love you.

october 22

*But the souls of the just are in the hand of God, and
no torment shall touch them. They seemed, in the
view of the foolish, to be dead; and their passing
away was thought an affliction and their going forth
from us, utter destruction. But they are in peace.*

— Wisdom 3:1-3

The loss of a loved one is filled with sorrow. Death causes a void in our lives. Grief settles in, and we go through stages where we feel lonely and left behind to fend for ourselves. As time passes, we eventually start to feel small glimmers of hope. The pain and sorrow slowly diminish. Grief is normal but there is no timeline. Everyone grieves differently. We learn to tuck away memories of our loved ones in our hearts and pray they have found peace.

God is with us in our brokenness. He never stops loving us. He blesses those who mourn and comforts them. Scripture tells us, "The LORD is close to the brokenhearted, saves those whose spirit is crushed" (Ps. 34:19). He is in control from birth to the time when he calls us to eternal life. He dries our tears and sends us his grace as he mends our hearts.

As we lean on Christ, words of wisdom take hold. Even when we cannot articulate our burdens and grief, he knows our hearts. We encounter the living Christ within. He gives us wisdom to understand that those who die on earth are reborn to eternal life. Death is not the end. One day, with heaven as our destiny, God will reunite us with our loved ones, and we will experience his glory face-to-face.

Psalm 23:1-6; Romans 5:5-11
Point to Ponder: Cling to God. He heals us and walks with us through sorrow.

Pray: Lord, send your peace to me. Keep me close as I travel on my journey to eternal life.

October 23

"... for everyone who exalts himself
will be humbled, and the one who
humbles himself will be exalted."

– Luke 18:14

God wants his followers to be humble and not boastful. This is difficult at times because pride and power, along with a healthy sense of self-importance, get in the way of humility. Some people take every opportunity to promote themselves to others. They brag about their accomplishments and judge others for their worthiness. These manmade tendencies do not abide by God's ways. Think about scripture. In Matthew 5:5, the Beatitudes, we hear Jesus tell the crowds, "Blessed are the meek, for they will inherit the land."

Not a natural tendency, Jesus teaches us to be humble and put others before ourselves. We have to work at giving credit to others and sharing recognition. Be wise and humble in every circumstance. Allow others to exalt us if they find us worthy but avoid being self-important and boastful. All our gifts and talents are blessings from God.

Our friends may praise us, but there is a difference in what we receive from God. When God exalts us, we are humble and return the glory to the rightful owner, our Lord and Savior. Scripture tells us he will honor those who honor him (1 Sm. 2:30). Allow Christ to crown us with the glory and honor we deserve. Give God thanks and praise for all our blessings.

Proverbs 3:33-34; Matthew 11:28-30
Point to Ponder: Be humble and meek.

Pray: God, help me place others before myself. Develop in me a humble attitude.

october 24

> *But if the wicked man turns away from all the*
> *sins he committed, if he keeps all my statutes*
> *and does what is right and just, he shall surely*
> *live, he shall not die. None of the crimes he*
> *committed shall be remembered against him; he*
> *shall live because of the virtue he has practiced.*
>
> – Ezekiel 18:21-22

God wants us to follow his will with pure hearts free of sin. Our hearts must be like God's: loving, kind, joyful, gentle, generous, forgiving and virtuous in every way. People question what virtuous behavior is today. *Webster's Dictionary* defines *virtuous* as "morally excellent, righteous."

God knows we are not perfect and sometimes overpowered by Satan's temptations. Sin separates us from the Lord. Repent and seek forgiveness from God. He releases us from sin immediately. He wants us to enjoy his blessings and live in a virtuous manner.

Christ is always ready to give us his love if our hearts are pure and not filled with emptiness and guilt. He cleanses our hearts when we seek him. Let God be a living tabernacle for our spirits. God pours his love into our hearts so we move forward and grow closer to him. Trust him to lead us to live virtuous lives.

Walk in a manner honoring the Lord. Be righteous and virtuous in all we do. Grow in spiritual strength and follow the gospel. God works mightily through us to do his will.

Proverbs 14:14; Psalm 130:5-8
Point to Ponder: You can do all things through Christ.

Pray: Lord, purify my heart so I do your will and model your love. Help me be virtuous.

october 25

Oh, the depth of the riches and wisdom and
knowledge of God! How inscrutable are his
judgments and how unsearchable his ways!
"For who has known the mind of the Lord
or who has been his counselor? Or who has
given him anything that he may be repaid?"
For from him and through him and for him are
all things. To him be glory forever. Amen.
— Romans 11:33-36

As followers of God, we pray for his mercy and love. We do not deserve his blessings, but when we choose to follow him and dedicate ourselves to service, God is pleased. We cannot pick and choose at our convenience to follow Christ. Instead, pursue holiness at all times.

There is no way to repay God for the blessings he sends each day. He wants us to build a relationship with him. Be ambassadors of his love. When we live in a righteous manner, our lives change. Every thought, word, and deed reflects the holiness of God. We feel contentment and accept how things are without losing hope. Believers express kindness and gentleness, and give with generous hearts. They approach each day with integrity.

Some may mock our righteous behaviors. Others are convinced God dwells within us and has truly touched our lives; they see the changes in our ways. Strive to be righteous. Ponder and meditate on God's word by reading the Bible. Worship him in church. Glorify God and give thanks. Rejoice!

Psalm 68:36; Psalm 107:33-43
Point to Ponder: Give glory and praise to God.

Pray: Lord, teach me to be righteous and follow your will. Let your love flow through me.

october 26

*Rejoice with those who rejoice, weep with
those who weep. Have the same regard for one
another; do not be haughty but associate with the
lowly; do not be wise in your own estimation.*
— Romans 12:15-16

Christians who live righteously are instruments in the hands of
God. He gives us blessings to share. He lives within our souls.
When we rejoice or weep, God sends us grace. The Lord has
mapped out a plan for us to live according to his will.

Believers do their best to live each day as one pleasing to God.
Some days are full of rejoicing. Others may be filled with grief. We
find strength from God to approach every situation in a righteous
manner.

The Holy Spirit warns everyone against desires of the flesh:
immorality, idolatry, hatreds, jealousy, outbursts of fury, and acts
of selfishness. In addition, occasions of envy, drinking bouts,
orgies and the like are to be avoided (Gal. 5:19-21). If we find
ourselves tempted by sin, say no to Satan and mean it. Do not turn
away from God. Recognize even righteous people stumble. When
this happens, be more on guard and realize our need for him. Ask
for forgiveness. Always stay close to God.

Pray for the Lord's mercy. We sense God in our lives as small
changes occur. They may not be exactly what we expect. Be open
to God's will. We learn many of life's lessons through our trials.
Pray for his grace.

Psalm 131:1-3; Luke 15:1-7
Point to Ponder: Be happy. God sends you grace.

Pray: Lord, draw me closer to you. Teach me to be kind and loving.

october 27

For by the grace given to me I tell everyone
among you not to think of himself more highly
than one ought to think, but to think soberly, each
according to the measure of faith that God has
apportioned. For as in one body we have many
parts, and all the parts do not have the same
function, so we, though many, are one body in
Christ and individually parts of one another.

— Romans 12:3-5

God blesses each person with unique talents and skills. No two people are alike. By the grace of God, we are who we are. His grace has never been ineffective, and neither are we.

When we seek guidance and pray for God's help, we honor him. He leads us step-by-step as we follow his will. Scripture tells us to be humble, and give God the glory. All we have comes from him. Fulfillment grows in our hearts as we serve. When we join together and serve one another, we build the kingdom of God.

Sometimes we get caught up in the heady feeling of worldly success and wealth. We may seek higher positions of authority and power. We forget about scriptures referencing our role as servants. God wants us to serve one another and bring others to him. Sometimes he gently disciplines us and brings us back to the concept of serving one another. He helps us prioritize what truly matters. Be obedient to God. We are one body in Christ.

Psalm 84:12-13; Psalm 55:23-24
Point to Ponder: Use the gifts God sends to build his kingdom.

Pray: Lord, I need you. Help me trust more fully in the love you have for me. Teach me to open myself to your guidance.

october 28

*So then each of us shall give an
account of himself to God.*

— Romans 14:12

Our lives are not, and never will be, under our control. We belong
to God and are his children. He sees all we do, hears all we say,
and knows our thoughts and needs. We have no secrets from God.
We are accountable to him on judgment day.

Scripture says, "For we must all appear before the judgment
seat of Christ, so that each one may receive recompense, according
to what he did in the body, whether good or evil" (2 Cor. 5:10). We
hope that God is merciful and that we pass the test.

As we live each day, we make decisions: how to spend our
money and time, and whom we befriend. We also decide with
whom we share our abilities, our affections, and much more. It is
not just about our financial status. It's more about our hearts. God
knows our hearts. Living to please him with a pure heart is a wise
investment.

God has commanded us to love our neighbors. It is not always
easy, but the Lord provides many opportunities for us to reach out.
If we fail to respond to the promptings of the Holy Spirit, we risk
flying blind and end up doing nothing. This is a sure way to be out
of step with God. Prepare for him to come at any time. Strive to
live a blameless life and avoid sin. Do no harm. Pray often, read
the Bible, serve one another, and give God glory and thanks. Serve
him diligently.

2 Corinthians 10:13-18; Proverbs 19:5
Point to Ponder: Prepare for judgment day.

Pray: Guide me to be your servant. Keep me living in your light,
Lord.

october 29

*Not only that, but we even boast of our
afflictions, knowing that affliction produces
endurance, and endurance, proven
character, and proven character, hope.*

— Romans 5:3-4

God rewards those who have faith and hope in him. Hope is not wishful thinking, but rather living with confident expectation. We hope for God's blessings through prayer and praise. He is sovereign over every circumstance we experience. Scripture reminds us, "But if we hope for what we do not see, we wait with endurance" (Rom. 8:25).

God is faithful to those who love and have hope. He strengthens us and guards us against the evil one. As we draw closer to him through prayer, he strengthens our hearts and helps us develop Christ-like character.

Pray every day, multiple times during the day. When we hear the voice of God as he prompts us through the Holy Spirit, we need to trust him completely. We can count on him with confident hope. Waiting on his timing is sometimes difficult but produces endurance. Learn to patiently wait, hope, and endure – as Christ did for us.

God teaches us to be optimistic. Everything is possible with God. Sometimes he places people in our lives who serve as mentors. They model how life is rich and full with God as our center. He gives us strength to do things we never felt we could do before. Rely on him to see us through. Have hope and faith in his goodness.

Proverbs 22:1; Luke 16:10-13
Point to Ponder: Put your faith and hope in Christ.

Pray: Lord, strengthen my hope. Give me wisdom so I know you.

october 30

*Boast not of tomorrow, for you know
not what any day may bring forth.*

— Proverbs 27:1

Each day, start fresh with a simple prayer of thanks. Live the day full of joy, knowing that God loves and cares for us. If troubles abound, do not lose heart. God knows the perfect timing to send us what we need to live according to his plan.

Sometimes when life seems to be on an even keel, we lose focus and turn from Christ. We get busy and find little time to pray. He continues to send us grace as we do good works. We forget to give him thanks and praise.

Then without warning, we find ourselves stressed and facing challenges that could cripple us financially, emotionally, or physically. If God never allowed us to experience need, people around us may never have the opportunity to witness God's provision in our lives. Be thankful for strong emotional reactions that require us to return to God.

He hears our prayers when trials and troubles occur. His response is not based upon our worthiness but upon his love and grace. Please God and turn from problem mode to prayer mode. Draw closer to him. He has the wisdom and knowledge to make the situation better.

Do not boast about tomorrow because we do not know what tomorrow holds. Give God the glory as he sends us what we need and rescues us. Others see him working through us as he makes his plans known. Believe!

James 4:7-8; Psalm 18:47
Point to Ponder: Place your trust and hope in God.

Pray: Lord, you are my strength and my shield. I trust you to help me live one day at a time.

October 31

Probe me, God know my heart; try me, know
my concerns. See if my way is crooked,
then lead me in the ancient path.

— Psalm 139:23-24

Every day, strive to live a righteous life following God's commandments and laws. Sometimes we find ourselves living in such a way we question if our lifestyle is pleasing to Christ. When we find our choices have shifted away from his teachings, our hearts are troubled. We have conflicting emotions, and we feel God's spiritual power has left us. We may find prayer difficult and our thoughts turn into worries. We make hurtful remarks or demonstrate negative behaviors. Everything about us has changed. Sin has found its way into our being.

When this happens, find a quiet place to pray. Draw closer to God. Ask him for help. Feel the Holy Spirit prompt us and challenge us to be all God wants us to be. Lean on him throughout the day to show us the way. Give our worries to God.

Things may not change overnight, but keep praying for his grace. God reveals himself in the most surprising places. Be aware that over time, we no longer harbor negative attitudes, continue harmful relationships, or take part in sinful activities. God's love is powerful. Strive to obey God in all things. Practice being positive and encourage others to do the right thing. Watch as we grow in spiritual strength as we are used mightily by our Savior.

Wisdom 1:7-15; Luke 17:1-6
Point to Ponder: God knows my heart.

Pray: Lord, I want to follow your commandments. Direct my life in the way of love. Cleanse and purify my heart.

November 1

*Therefore, we who are receiving the unshakable
kingdom should have gratitude, with which we
should offer worship pleasing to God in reverence
and awe. For our God is a consuming fire.*

— Hebrews 12:28-29

Take time to give thanks to God each day. Proclaim and live his word. Spiritual power is fundamental when living a life blessed by the Lord. He uses us in many ways. God gives us the gift of life and calls us his children. He blesses us with family and friends and our own unique gifts and talents. God promises us the gift of salvation and prepares a place for us in heaven.

Serve the Lord with love, honor, and praise. Let thankfulness temper our thoughts. Strive to have a humble attitude as our thoughts and behaviors become the grid through which we perceive life.

Be a messenger for God. Our service to others glorifies him and fills us with joy. We feel his presence in our hearts when we serve. When we volunteer our time and talents, God works mightily through us. He sends us the strength to be his hands and voice on earth. Only his power restores us and removes our natural self-centeredness. Be thankful for opportunities to serve. Give thanks for each event that pulls us closer to God. We read in the Bible, "Give thanks to the LORD, who is good, whose love endures forever" (Ps. 118:1). Our daily lives should be saturated with prayers of thanksgiving and praise to our Lord and Savior.

Wisdom 2:23-24; 1 Corinthians 10:12-13
Point to Ponder: Lift up prayers of thanks throughout the day
to God.

Pray: Thank you, God, for loving me. Help me to serve you and others with joy in my heart.

> *For you were once darkness, but now you are*
> *light in the Lord. Live as children of light, for*
> *light produces every kind of goodness and*
> *righteousness and truth. Try to learn what is*
> *pleasing to the Lord. Take no part in the fruitless*
> *works of darkness; rather expose them.*
> — Ephesians 5:8-11

Time stands still for no one. Wise people invest their time in things pleasing to God. In the chaos of this world, do not be tempted by Satan and his evil ways. Instead, listen for the voice of Christ calling. In our busyness, we typically choose the easiest path and seldom question whether the choice honors God. We sometimes settle for easy and good instead of challenging and best.

Take a step into the unknown and lean on God for strength. Stop to ponder and pray before major decisions. He wants us to feel his presence.

Most of us have a few dark memories which cause us anxiety and fear, but we understand we cannot let our fears control our activities. God is merciful and forgiving, and he wants to extend his love to everyone. He desires that we live in the light without fear. Our faith in his mercy is what determines our level of anxiety. Pray for increased faith. Live each day fully in communion with God.

Question what choices please God. Do not settle for good. Strive always for the best. He knows our hearts and blesses us with grace and strength to meet any challenge.

Psalm 119:89-90; Luke 17:20-21
Point to Ponder: Stay in communion with God through prayer.

Pray: Lord, help me follow your light. Teach me your ways and work through me.

November 3

*Rising very early before dawn, he left and went
off to a deserted place, where he prayed.*

— Mark 1:35

There are passages in the Bible where the disciples reported Jesus would go off by himself and pray to his Father. When the disciples needed Jesus, they would go to his quiet place to find him. Jesus prayed daily and always before important decisions. Even at the end of his time on earth, he asked his Father through prayer to spare him. Jesus understood he had to follow the will of God (Mt. 26:36-46). He remained obedient to his Father.

The way we pray and the times we pray say a lot about our relationship with God. The more we pray, the closer we feel to him. He may choose to answer our prayers differently than what we ask. Even when we consistently pray, we may not hear or feel his presence. Have faith. God hears our prayers and knows the right time to answer them.

God teaches us things we only learn through trials. Remain obedient, be patient, and pray without ceasing. Be touched by the power of God by his blessings. Enjoy sacred moments in his presence. Go to a quiet place and be alone to pray. Jesus is waiting to fill us with love and hope. Have a hunger to return to him every day in prayer. Seek to know God better and understand his will.

Hebrews 5:7-9; Matthew 26:36-46
Point to Ponder: Find time every day to pray.

Pray: Jesus, teach me to pray and hear your voice. Lead me on a righteous path.

November 4

Enter, let us bow down in worship; let us kneel
before the LORD *who made us. For this is our God,*
whose people we are, God's well-tended flock.

— Psalm 95:6-7

When we praise God through singing, rejoicing, and kneeling in prayer, we honor him. God is with us and protects us wherever we go. With God as our master, we trust he has gone before us and walks each step with us as we journey on earth. Sing to him with deepest praise now and when we gather around him in heaven.

God is worthy of our praise, and he keeps calling us back to have a personal relationship with him. He has given us life and provides for us abundantly. Encounter him daily through heartfelt prayer.

When we turn away from God and fall for Satan's temptations, which lead us into sin, God waits for us to seek him. He wants to bring us back in love, not fear. Kneel before the Lord and ask him for forgiveness and mercy.

He has boundless love for all who repent and honor him. Praise through song is real and personal and sweet music to God. He hears the melody of our voices. Sing joyfully with others in worship. As his life flows into us, be strengthened with divine might. Praising him is an expression of a grateful heart. His love propels us forward as we seek to follow our Savior.

Proverbs 16:13; Zephaniah 3:17-20
Point to Ponder: Bow down in worship to God.

Pray: Lord, I want to worship you through praise and song. All glory and honor are yours now and forever.

November 5

Your laws become my songs wherever I make
my home. Even at night I remember your name
in observance of your teaching, Lord. This is my
good fortune, for I have observed your precepts.
— Psalm 119:54-56

The Lord does not force us to follow his will, but a wise man realizes he is an all-knowing master. Our faith in the power of God is a gift.

How do we live our faith and show others what God has in store for those who believe? We serve others by living the word of God every day. What we say, how we act, and how we choose to serve the Lord matters. Others watch as we demonstrate acts of kindness, gentleness, generosity, peacefulness, and love.

When God gives us a task that seems impossible, be open and do not turn away. There is no place to hide. He watches our reactions to the challenges he places before us. Trust God. Be vigilant and train our minds to focus on him. He has perfect timing. Look for his loving hand as he sends us the strength and resources we need. Others around us observe his divine power and influence at work through our responses.

Trust in God and watch how things change. The transformation may not happen quickly, but a spirit of optimism develops, and good things come through us and into our lives. God recreates us in his image. He confirms his presence in our lives when we believe.

2 Corinthians 5:9-10; Luke 18:35-43
Point to Ponder: God never stops loving you.

Pray: Lord, give me faith to trust you in every situation. Protect and guide me.

November 6

In contrast, the fruit of the Spirit is love,
joy, peace, patience, kindness, generosity,
faithfulness, gentleness, self-control. Against
such there is no law. Now those who belong to
Christ Jesus have crucified their flesh with its
passions and desires. If we live in the Spirit,
let us follow the Spirit. Let us not be conceited,
provoking one another, envious of one another.
　　　　　　　　　　　　　　– Galatians 5:22-26

God gives each person a helper who lives within our souls. This helper is the Holy Spirit. The Spirit works as God does to form Christ's character within each of us. We strive to demonstrate these traits throughout our lifetime. This honors God.

The Holy Spirit guides us to experience love through our families, as God did with Jesus. He wants us to have a kind and gentle heart so we extend a helping hand to others. The Spirit works to instill joy and peace in our souls as we serve. He continually teaches us self-control so that we win the battle against ungodly behaviors and have the strength to avoid sin and the temptations of Satan.

The Holy Spirit protects, guides, and prompts us to follow God's plan. As we imitate Christ-like behaviors, we live differently. We constantly have things renewed in our lives through God. Rejoice!

1 Thessalonians 5:23-25; Hebrews 6:9-12
Point to Ponder: The Holy Spirit is powerful.

Pray: Holy Spirit, teach me. Guide me to be more like our Lord and Savior.

November 7

My son, to my words be attentive, to my
sayings incline your ear; Let them not slip out
of your sight, keep them within your heart;
For they are life to those who find them,
to man's whole being they are health.

                     – Proverbs 4:20-22

God reveals himself through scripture. There are lessons to be learned. Biblical scholars have studied the writings in the Bible since the beginning. Today, we study scripture to grow closer to our master. We are in awe of those who quote scripture and converse with biblical scholars. Like these scholars, we pray we experience the truths found in the Bible. Our goal is to know God and his Son, Jesus, and practice his word.

We do not have to memorize scripture, but we should be able to demonstrate little acts of love bringing light and spiritual insight to others. God sees our acts of kindness. Actions such as consciously wearing a smile, bringing a coworker coffee, speaking uplifting words to a young person, or writing a note of thanks, please him. God wants us to minister out of his love and not just our own good intentions. This is how friends get a glimpse of God in us.

Knowing God brings us more joy, satisfaction, and pleasure than any other activity. Let nothing come before our personal, vibrant relationship with him. Following his word allows us to live vibrantly and joyfully close to him. Grow closer to God every day. Read and practice the truths of the Bible.

John 5:39; Psalm 37:4
Point to Ponder: God is with you, sustaining you at every step.

Pray: Help me, Lord, to quiet my heart so I hear your voice and follow your teachings.

November 8

The L*ord* *redeems loyal servants; no one*
is condemned whose refuge is God.

– Psalm 34:23

When Jesus came into the world, the light followed him. Those who lived in darkness, Jesus redeemed. He cured the sick, healed the blind, and gave strength to the crippled so they could walk. All became followers. He wanted them to shine as a brilliant testimony to his presence and almighty power.

Christ designed our lives to be like his: summons to spread the gospel, love and serve our neighbor, and preserve righteousness. He gives us the strength we need to help those who are suffering from alcoholism and other drug dependencies, divorce, painful health issues, or dealing with a wayward child, or a grieving heart. As his servants, his saving grace and power are dispensed from us to others. We become his voice and hands as he works through us.

God wants a close relationship with us. Be still in the presence of God. Take refuge in him. God is merciful to everyone who comes to him. Allow God's light to shine into our hearts and set us free. Darkness is dispelled. He redeems those who follow his ways. Pray every day to be in his presence.

Proverbs 5:21-23; Matthew 5:13-16
Point to Ponder: Take refuge in God.

Pray: Have mercy on me, Jesus. Cleanse and purify my heart. Teach me to be merciful to others as you have been with me.

November 9

*Whatever you ask for in prayer
with faith, you will receive.*

– Matthew 21:22

When we pray, how much faith do we have that God will answer our prayers? Do we waiver when we pray and allow doubt to creep in?

Sometimes we find ourselves in situations that seem to have no earthly solution. Our faith dwindles. We are tested. Do we take the easy way, accepting the first resolution to relieve the anxiety and unrest, or do we stand firm with our belief in God's power to work through us for a solution pleasing for all? When these challenging times occur, practice patience and wait for God.

Focus on fervent prayer. Seek his presence not one time but many. This is a sign of trust. Do not rush ahead of God; he lives within us and directs our paths. As he works through us, he teaches and helps us gather wisdom, knowledge, and understanding of his ways.

Trust his hand in all we do. He may send his grace and choose to respond to our prayers differently than we expect. God addresses our needs, not just our desires. Have the type of faith in God that does not require a constant supply of miracles. Do not let our actions speak differently than our beliefs. Go to the Lord in faith. He provides for us. We never make a poor choice when Christ leads us and speaks to our hearts.

Psalm 140:2-4; Romans 8:10-13
Point to Ponder: Pray throughout the day. God listens and responds.

Pray: Lord, remove my doubt in your almighty power and increase my faith.

November 10

*Know this first of all, that there is no prophecy of
scripture that is a matter of personal interpretation,
for no prophecy ever came through human
will; but rather human beings moved by the
holy Spirit spoke under the influence of God.*

— 2 Peter 1:20-21

God has given man many gifts. Believers use these gifts to minister to others. Be alert when neighbors struggle. If we do not pause, we may miss an opportunity to serve God and our neighbor. Christ sends the resources we need to help others. He does nothing by happenstance. God wants us to grow as we model his behaviors. By reaching out to others, we develop pure hearts filled with his love. Our nature changes and we find giving to others a natural response to God's calling.

Sometimes we sense the Holy Spirit prompting us to help the poor and unloved. Our actions and words are visible signs of the condition of our hearts. When we serve the poor, God places words from the gospel in our mouths, and we take actions that do not threaten. By imitating Christ, many on the margins form a deeper understanding of his teachings.

We are moved by the Spirit, who dwells within our souls, to be kind and gentle when others need understanding and comfort. Do not miss God's activity because of reluctance to get involved. He places people and challenges in our lives for reasons we do not understand. Reach out and be courageous knowing God walks with us every step.

Mark 16:15-16; 2 Peter 3:14-16
Point to Ponder: God dwells within you.

Pray: Lord, lead me to speak uplifting words and perform kind acts.

November 11

*Therefore, since we have a great high priest who
has passed through the heavens, Jesus, the Son
of God, let us hold fast to our confession. For
we do not have a high priest who is unable to
sympathize with our weaknesses, but one who has
similarly been tested in every way, yet without sin.*

— Hebrews 4:14-15

At times, each of us has felt pressure to compromise our beliefs.
We succumb to Satan's temptations, which initially entice us. Once
sin enters our being, Satan pounds his evil ways into us. We move
farther away from God and his light, and find ourselves in darkness
and confusion.

Choosing to disobey God and partake in sinful acts impacts
us. Unsettled and fearful, our optimistic attitude is overshadowed
by negativity. Money may become our god, and we use it to better
ourselves in a materialistic world. We may fall short as a parent, a
church member, or a friend. We are too busy to include God in our
lives, and we reject the freedom we gained when Jesus died for us.

When we feel alone and far from God, be still, quiet our racing
thoughts, and pray. He wants us to repent and ask for forgiveness.
Only God heals us. He mends the brokenhearted, restores love in
a marriage, and removes bitterness in severed relationships. He
makes life whole again. Experience his healing grace and believe
he is there, ready to guide and walk each step with us along the
journey of life.

James 1:13; Proverbs 10:25
Point to Ponder: Reject Satan. Remain close to God.

Pray: Lord, show me your ways so I follow you. I trust you to
guide me now and forever.

November 12

At once [Jesus] spoke to them, "Take
courage, it is I; do not be afraid."

— Matthew 14:27

Jesus found he had to reassure his disciples often. When they saw him walking on the sea, they were terrified and thought him a ghost. He called out to them and asked why they doubted. It was only after saving Peter from death by drowning because of his lack of faith, that his disciples believed Jesus was truly the Son of God (Mt. 14:22-36).

Christ leads us to situations which challenge our intelligence, our physical capacity, and our emotional state. Do not avoid these challenges or fear the unknown. Jesus promises to guide and protect us. Answer his calling and step out in faith. Acknowledge God's work in our actions. Realize that others see him working through us. When we give God glory, we experience joy.

Only in our weakness do we learn to trust implicitly in God. When we call him in prayer, he sends blessings of grace and strength so we find calm in the midst of adversity. Whatever the circumstance, whether easy or difficult, remember to ask for God's guidance. Give him our fears and anxious worries, and then listen and wait. Be alert to his activities and the growth opportunities he provides. God controls what happens to us. Receive his blessings gratefully. Rejoice! He is always with us and for us.

Psalm 73:23-26; 2 Corinthians 12:9-10
Point to Ponder: Have no fear. God remains faithful.

Pray: Open my eyes so that I see you more clearly, Lord. Cleanse my heart so that you work through me.

November 13

*Jesus entered the temple area and drove out all
those engaged in selling and buying there. He
overturned the tables of the money changers and the
seats of those who were selling doves. And he said
to them, "It is written: 'My house shall be a house
of prayer,' but you are making it a den of thieves."*

– Matthew 21:12-13

Jesus had to teach the people how to be responsive to God,
especially in a place of worship. God desires a close walk with him
everywhere we go, especially where we go to pray. Our actions
matter because if we are genuinely seeking the Lord, he promises
we will find him (Mt. 7:7).

God is pleased when we worship and glorify his name. The
atmosphere in church may be charged with people praying
together, musical instruments sounding, singing joyful songs, and
offering loving praise.

We draw closer to God as we pray. He hears us and responds
with love, healing, and grace. We can pray anywhere – kneeling at
church, walking in a park, riding the bus, driving to work, before
eating, or doing other ordinary daily tasks. Lift up short prayers of
praise throughout the day.

God never stops giving or providing for us. Every good
attribute we have is a gift. Look for God's handiwork everywhere:
in church, in nature, and in the eyes of family, friends, or strangers.
Respect God and his church at all times.

Luke 19:45-48; Mark 11:15-17
Point to Ponder: Be humble and prayerful in every circumstance.

Pray: Help me dwell in your presence with a joyful heart, God.

November 14

The righteous will shine like the sun in the kingdom of their Father. Whoever has ears ought to hear.
— Matthew 13:43

God knows our hearts. Be obedient to him and follow his commandments and teachings. Take time daily to be in his presence. Tune out the chaos of a busy world and strive to recognize his voice among so many competing voices.

Time waits for no one so use time wisely. Go to a quiet place, remove distractions, and pray to the Lord our Savior. God knows our weaknesses and our failings so ask him to lead us away from temptation and evil. He wants to restore our faith. Be patient and wait for God. Do not be tempted to fill our schedule so full with good things; we have no time for him.

God's messages come from many different sources. Read scripture to hear his word, and encounter and talk to friends who have God as their focal point. Wait for God's guiding word to penetrate our hearts.

In order to live righteously demonstrate love, joy, peace, and kindness to everyone. Do not settle for less than what God wants to give. If we find we do not have these blessings to share, stop following the world's ways and listen to the Lord's voice. Walk in faith and truth. God is by our side every step of the way. Believe!

Psalm 9:2-7; Luke 20:34-38
Point to Ponder: Pray without pretense.

Pray: Lord, lead me on the path of righteousness. Show me your ways so I can imitate them.

November 15

I am the vine, you are the branches. Whoever
remains in me and I in him bear much fruit,
because without me you can do nothing.

— John 15:5

In the parable, The Vine and the Branches, Jesus tells us he is the source of life. We are like branches on a tree nourished by him to produce fruit.

In our zeal to follow Christ, we sometimes become exhausted from our activities; we fail to pray and build a relationship with him. We strive to be righteous and motivated by good things such as his love, compassion, and generosity, but we have no energy or time to be still and communicate with God. We are not nourished daily and as a result are spiritually poor.

Slow down. Be in God's presence and pray every day. He stands ready to build our character and teach and mold us into his image. Read the Bible. Ponder how the passages impact us. God answers our prayers and carries our burdens when they weigh us down. He protects us from temptations that lead to sin. This takes time, so learn patience and be alert to changes.

The important thing is not so much the activities we perform for God but rather our relationship with him. Remain steadfast in his love. Allow God to clothe us with grace so our hearts are in tune with his heart and burn brightly with his love. Grow the branches on the tree of life so they produce heavenly fruit.

Ezekiel 18:3-32; Proverbs 13:9
Point to Ponder: God is the answer.

Pray: God, teach me to do your will and to love more deeply. Open my heart to your love.

November 16

Give thanks to the Lord, for he is good, for his
mercy endures forever. Bless the God of gods,
all you who fear the Lord; praise him and give
him thanks, because his mercy endures forever.

— Daniel 3:89-90

God's love and mercy are everlasting. Even though we may
not praise God and thank him as we should, he is merciful and
continues to love us. Christ knows exactly when and where we
have difficulty. In times of grief and when we have lost hope, God
watches and waits. Sometimes the only way we return to him is in
our brokenness. God leads us through the darkness, reassuring us
with each step toward his light. During these times, we experience
his mercy and love deeply. Our lives change forever with such an
encounter.

Honor God by giving thanks and praise for his love. Go to
a quiet place and pray. We hear him better when we remove the
static. The quiet place makes us slow down, listen, and rest. Hear
the Lord speak in silence. When we dwell in God's presence, we
receive his grace. His love picks us up.

God is with us in good times and during times of great
challenges. Do not fear the unknown. He is there and ready to walk
with us to make all things right. Praise him both publicly at church
and privately through prayer. Be still and recount the blessings he
sends. Rejoice! God's mercy and love endures forever.

Proverbs 3:5-6; Psalm 23:1-6
Point to Ponder: Give thanks to God. He is merciful and never
abandons you.

Pray: Lord, help me praise your holy name and be joyful for your
everlasting love.

November 17

Hear my cry, O God, listen to my prayer! From the brink of Sheol I call; my heart grows faint. Raise me up, set me on a rock, for you are my refuge, a tower of strength against the foe. Then I will ever dwell in your tent, take refuge in the shelter of your wings.

— Psalm 61:2-5

Rejoice in God's presence. Give him praise. Use this weapon against temptation and sin. Praise helps to alleviate discouragement, fear, and confusion. Recall God's goodness and mercy, his kindness, and wisdom. God is always with us and for us, and he is our refuge and strength.

Whisper his name. Feel God's grace as we draw closer to him. Even though we may be walking a path through darkness and troubles, God is by our side. He reassures us. We have nothing to fear. Nothing intimidates the Lord. Nothing surpasses him, because he has defeated every form of wickedness.

Say yes to God. He has gone before us in triumph and is present with us now. In spite of our human frailty, God works through us. His love is unconditional, and he wants good for us.

We do not have to journey alone. Trust God and pray. Lean on him with all our hearts and minds. Surrender and ask for God's protection and deliverance. He dispenses grace to us. We cannot control all the events in our lives, but trust him to lead us on our journey all the way to eternal life.

Isaiah 26-4; Luke 21:25-28

Point to Ponder: God is a tower of strength. Pray for his protection.

Pray: Lord, keep me in your presence. Fill me with the desire to walk with you always, praise you, and follow your will.

November 18

*Likewise, you younger members, be subject to the
presbyters. And all of you, clothe yourselves with
humility in your dealings with one another, for: "God
opposes the proud but bestows favor on the humble."*

− 1 Peter 5:5

The greatest service we provide in our lifetime is to be a servant to
God and our fellowmen. The person who serves without complaint
and lovingly without seeking recognition is pleasing in God's eyes
(Lk. 22:27).

We like to say we serve the Lord, but we seldom experience
happiness in a servant's position. Some people feel serving others
is beneath them. These people have adopted the world's standards,
not Jesus's standard. Jesus was a servant who washed the feet of his
disciples (Jn. 13:1-20). Be more like Jesus. Follow his example. Let
our thoughts, actions, and words be controlled by the heart. Reach
out to the poor, the needy, and the marginalized. Be generous with
time and gifts, use uplifting comments to encourage others, and
exhibit a calm and gentle spirit.

Worldly wealth is fleeting and hinders our ability to give
generously. Money cannot buy a place in heaven or a pure heart.
Pride leads to isolation, where we feel we have reached a pinnacle
and are not accountable to anyone, not even God.

Humble servants of the Lord are rich in the ways that truly
matter. They have Christ as their focal point. Only he gives the gift
of eternal life. Be rich in what matters to God.

Proverbs 16:5; James 4:6
Point to Ponder: Model the example of Jesus. Be humble and serve
others.

Pray: Lord, take away sinful pride so that my life is abundant in
good works.

November 19

Blessed be the God and Father of our Lord Jesus
Christ, who in his great mercy gave us a new
birth to a living hope through the resurrection
of Jesus Christ from the dead, to an inheritance
that is imperishable, undefiled, and unfading,
kept in heaven for you who by the power of God
are safeguarded through faith, to a salvation
that is ready to be revealed in the final time.

— 1 Peter 1:3-5

We are children of God who fall short of his standard. He loves us with an unending love that surpasses our understanding. God's love cannot be overcome by anything, including our sins. The devil lurks and entices us to follow him. When we let down our guard and sin, we move away from our heavenly Father. Darkness takes hold. Evil is the norm.

But wait. God never abandons us. His mercy is a gift we do not deserve. He has paid the penalty for our sins himself. He does not punish us each time we sin, but rather extends his loving hand and forgives us when we repent. The miraculous resurrection of Jesus gives us hope for salvation.

God never tires of walking with us. He protects us, his children, and reaches out to those in need. God understands and forgives. Ask him for mercy. No one is excluded. Watch how his grace lightens our burdens as the seeds of repentance grow in our hearts. Live in faithful obedience to his will. He is compassionate, merciful, slow to anger, and filled with unending love. Have faith.

Colossians 3:13; James 2:12-13
Point to Ponder: Trust God. He is merciful and understands the human condition.

Pray: Lord, be merciful. Forgive me. Help me trust in your will.

November 20

All goes well for those gracious in lending, who
conduct their affairs with justice. They shall never
be shaken; the just shall be remembered forever.

— Psalm 112:5-6

As we journey in life, we face controversy and judgmental people. These people look at others with a critical eye. They may challenge the good we practice and criticize how we use our money, how we give of our time, our child rearing practices, or our involvement in political and social justice activities. They need to remember each person faces God for a recounting of what was accomplished on earth. God's judgment counts.

Be alert! Satan strives to steal the good from us. He tries to make us too busy to pray, study scripture, attend church, and serve others before ourselves. Satan tempts us to spend excessive amounts of money on things that do not honor God such as gambling, alcohol, and material possessions. The devil is powerful but dims in strength to the Lord.

When we abide by scripture, seek justice in all interactions, pray continually, and demonstrate acts of kindness and service, we honor God. He supplies every need we have (Phil. 4:19). Be happy. God sends grace so our character changes to be more like his. Do not fret. Only Christ is perfect. He lives in us and works through us. This increases our joy and glorifies him. Stand tall before the judgment of God knowing we have done our best.

1 Thessalonians 5:14-25; Colossians 3:23-25
Point to Ponder: The Lord upholds you.

Pray: God, build my character to be Christ-like. Help me find enduring truths in your word.

November 21

> *My son, if you receive my words and treasure my*
> *commands, Turning your ear to wisdom, inclining*
> *your heart to understanding; Yes, if you call to*
> *intelligence, and to understanding raise your voice;*
> *If you seek her like silver, and like hidden treasures*
> *search her out: Then you will understand the fear*
> *of the LORD; the knowledge of God you will find.*
> — Proverbs 2:1-5

When reading scripture, make the connection between our lives
and what God says. If we find ourselves in the verses within the
Bible, allow the word of God to wash over us and find any sin or
wrongdoing. In Ephesians 4:31-32 we read, "All bitterness, fury,
anger, shouting, and reviling must be removed from you, along
with all malice. Be kind to one another, compassionate, forgiving
one another as God has forgiven you in Christ."

When Christ purifies our hearts, others see the transformation.
There is a light and a sense of enthusiasm from the righteous
person. God is present in us as he works through us to build his
kingdom.

It takes the presence of God to open the eyes of a nonbeliever.
If we lead someone to God, he reaches out to the individual. He
invites the person to walk with him in an intimate and powerful
way. He stirs hearts. Rejoice in his presence through reading,
reflecting, and living according to scripture.

John 10:27-30; Psalm 32:8
Point to Ponder: Read the Bible and practice God's truths.

Pray: God, teach me your statutes. Help me demonstrate to others
your ways.

November 22

O Lord, our Lord, how awesome is
your name through all the earth!

– Psalm 8:10

Some of us search all our lives for the peace and joy God brings to those who love him. We feel his presence during the good times and when blessings are abundant. When sickness and sorrow come into our lives, we allow doubt to enter our being and we question God. Our faith is challenged. We let down our guard and become vulnerable to the devil's temptations. The evil one lulls us into a sense that there is nothing wrong with violating God's commands. Satan's worldly knowledge easily leads us to prideful behavior, and this impedes us from turning to God. We fail to nurture our relationship with the Lord. He seems far from us.

When life becomes troublesome, stop and seek God. Do not give in to Satan. Human reasoning does not begin to compare to God's. When things do not go according to our plans, pause, reflect, pray, and listen for God's voice. He directs our paths and transforms our minds. He sends his spiritual strength so we say no to temptation. Be patient and wait for God.

Change is difficult. If thrust into a situation that requires us to change, do not panic. Let go of worldly pride and call God's name. He responds. Be alert to his guidance. The more we fill our minds with virtuous and holy thoughts, the more strength we find from God.

Lamentations 3:25-26; Deuteronomy 4:29
Point to Ponder: Hope in the mystery of God.

Pray: Lord, show me how to persevere and put my hope in you. Help me pause and pray often throughout the day.

November 23

For everyone who does wicked things hates the
light and does not come toward the light, so that
his works might not be exposed. But whoever
lives the truth comes to the light, so that his
works may be clearly seen as done in God.
— John 3:20-21

Those who know God and experience his goodness realize we are called to be intentional about our Christianity. God provides opportunities daily to demonstrate righteous acts. When he calls us to serve others, do not hesitate. Instead, be diligent in reaching out to those in need. God sends his blessings to us according to how we respond. If we serve him with generous hearts, he responds to us in a like manner. Scripture says, "Consider this: whoever sows sparingly will reap sparingly, and whoever sows bountifully, will also reap bountifully. Each must do as already determined, without sadness or compulsion, for God loves a cheerful giver" (2 Cor. 9:6-7).

God knows our hearts. He sees if we give freely of our time, talents, and gifts. Sometimes prideful attitudes cause us to be stingy. Say no to selfishness and yes to a generous heart. God blesses us continually and sends new mercies every day.

There is no room for misers in God's kingdom. When our hearts are pure and we give abundantly, he makes every grace abundant to us. Do everything for the glory of God.

Psalm 93:1-5; Acts 4:32-37
Point to Ponder: Receive God's unexpected gifts every day.

Pray: Lord, teach me to be generous and kind and filled with your love.

November 24

The Lord will give you the bread you need and
the water for which you thirst. No longer will your
Teacher hide himself, but with your own eyes you
shall see your Teacher. While from behind, a voice
shall sound in your ears: "This is the way; walk in
it," when you would turn to the right or to the left.
— Isaiah 30:20-21

Listen for God. Believe with a sense of awe that he hears and answers every prayer. He answers in his time and not according to our schedule. God is not bound by time as we are on earth.

When we pray, we draw closer to God and build a relationship with him. Think of prayer as an intimate conversation with him. He knows our problems and thoughts before we utter any words. Do not hurry off before he has time to respond. Be persistent with prayer. God is present. He hears the softest whisper or the fervent cry for help. We may encounter him as we walk in nature, read the Bible, attend worship services, listen to spiritual music, or hear a friend's comments. He is everywhere.

When we trust in him, and walk in his presence, our lives change. Live each day to the fullest in unity with others. Do not dwell on the past. God is with us yesterday, today, and forevermore. He directs our steps. Rejoice in his mercy and love!

Matthew 15:29-31; Hebrews 13:8
Point to Ponder: Look for God's lessons in each detour and delay. Be flexible.

Pray: Lord, help me to focus and follow you. Teach me to live one day at a time.

November 25

Who among you is wise and understanding? Let him show his works by a good life in the humility that comes from wisdom. But if you have bitter jealousy and selfish ambition in your hearts, do not boast and be false to the truth. Wisdom of this kind does not come down from above but is earthly, unspiritual, demonic. For where jealousy and selfish ambition exist, there is disorder and every foul practice.

– James 3:13-16

No one is immune to jealousy, pride, or sin. When we are jealous of someone's possessions, position, status, or outward beauty, we concentrate on things we cannot change. Often we find ourselves becoming increasingly angry, resentful, or selfish.

Changing our perception of ourselves helps to lessen these negative feelings. Jesus gives us our own individual talents and character. We are wonderfully made and are his chosen ones. He wants us to be humble and thankful for the gifts he sends.

The best way to avoid jealousy and prideful behavior is to fill our minds with Christ-like thoughts and actions, surround ourselves with friends and family, and demonstrate acts of kindness, love, and generosity. Many little acts build character. Jesus desires us to keep in proper perspective the comments of praise and the gifts we have to share. The words of recognition and congratulations people speak matter, but they should not go to our head. We have special gifts from God no one else has. Use these gifts and give thanks.

Romans 13:11-14; Proverbs 14:30
Point to Ponder: Be happy with your unique self.

Pray: By the grace of God, teach me to serve gratefully, humbly, and faithfully.

November 26

The LORD is a stronghold for the oppressed,
a stronghold in times of trouble. Those who
honor your name trust in you; you never
forsake those who seek you, LORD.

— Psalm 9:10-11

The Lord is a stronghold at all times. He sends blessings when we experience times of joy, and is there to carry us through the darkness in times of sorrow. Trusting God protects us from worry. He never abandons us.

Build a relationship with God. When we whisper his name, we bring him to the forefront of our conscience. We make the Lord central in our thoughts. As we have a conversation with him in prayer and then listen for his voice, we receive grace and peace. These blessings transform us. The more we pray and trust God, the stronger our relationship. He is sovereign over every aspect of our lives.

We are stewards of his love. Everything we have comes from God. This includes our intellect, work, health, and family. Look at all circumstances as growth opportunities. Remember, be a doer in Christ. This is far better than doing everything for our own advancement. Maintain a joyful spirit and be filled with God's love.

God sends strength to us so we do his will and navigate even the most difficult situations. He is everywhere helping us accomplish things we could never do with our own strength. Honor God in prayer and praise and watch the floodgates of grace open. Trusting him is a golden pathway to eternal life.

John 3:33-36; Luke 10:25-28
Point to Ponder: Be grateful for the blessings of daily life.

Pray: Lord, fill me with your love. Be with me every moment of every day.

November 27

Those who err in spirit shall acquire understanding,
and those who find fault shall receive instruction.
— Isaiah 29:24

How many times have we failed to understand a person or situation and jump to the wrong impression, only to find out later we regret the action? When this happens, slow down and be less judgmental. Guard impulsive thoughts. Work on reframing situations and being more open to others. Do not be oppositional or satisfied with seeing everything as questionable. Search for deeper meaning.

Christians must work to keep our thoughts pure. We meet people who go through life without knowing God. They do not own a Bible or attend church. Since they do not read scripture and seldom pray, they choose to adopt human reasoning. Ungodliness and negativity may become common in their daily routines. Their thoughts and actions do not imitate Christ. They do not realize we need to be fed each day with spiritual food from God.

Help unbelievers acquire behaviors which please God. As they observe our lives, they become aware of the victorious power of the Lord. Our lives ought to be convincing proof that God continues to work powerfully in the lives of all his children. Bring others to him. Share his love and goodness with everyone. Let the joy of God become our strength.

Proverbs 2:9-11; Psalm 119:130
Point to Ponder: God is great. He teaches us how to love.

Pray: Lord, thank you for my daily blessings. Teach me to focus on you and understand your ways.

November 28

My son, forget not my teaching, keep in mind
my commands; For many days, and years
of life, and peace, will they bring you.

— Proverbs 3:1-2

Be persistent and practice God's truths, and follow his commandments every day. Go about each day sharing his blessings and serving others. Be happy and have an optimistic attitude.

Be on guard and do not drift away or become apathetic to what God asks. Do not turn a cold shoulder when thoughts are jumbled with uncertainties. In our rush to complete daily tasks, we often fail to pray and read scripture. We are too tired. Return to God and pray fervently. He knows our hearts before we come to him. He never changes, but we do. He waits to comfort us and send his strength.

Follow God's will. Take time away from the busyness of life and find a quiet place to be with Christ. Converse and grow closer to him. Seek guidance. Reflect on his commandments. Are we following them or have we been swept away by worldly attractions?

For our children, model obedience by saying grace before meals, praying as a family, attending church, and discussing blessings each day. Read the Bible together.

We approach life differently with God as our best friend. We see good in situations instead of malice. Be assured, all things are possible with God as our anchor and strength.

Deuteronomy 31:6; Isaiah 30:6
Point to Ponder: Keep the Ten Commandments.

Pray: Lord, lead me along a path to holiness so I dwell in your presence.

November 29

And now, Lᴏʀᴅ, what future do I have? You
are my only hope. From all my sins deliver
me; let me not be the taunt of fools.

— Psalm 39:8-9

Sometimes we are impatient and lose hope. We forget all things happen according to God's timing and not ours. Especially when we want something to change that suits us, we want him to intervene quickly. God knows our needs, and if we wait with confident expectation instead of sinking into the throes of despair, his promises come to pass. God has given his word on things he will do.

Always trust God. He is faithful and does not deceive those who love him. When doubt enters, know Satan places thoughts in our minds to tempt us. He makes situations seem intolerable. Take steps to avoid the evil one. Pray continuously and seek the hand of God to address the situation. Do not rush ahead without clear direction. Wait for God before pressing on, even though it is difficult. We live in a world of instant answers from the Internet or our cell phones. When answers do not come quickly, practice patience.

Be optimistic. Stand firm and refuse to give up on God. Focus on positive outcomes that give us hope. Always choose what pleases God, finding his hand in all good things. He guides us to make correct choices. He graces us with wisdom so that we better understand his ways.

Deuteronomy 31:6; Romans 5:1-5
Point to Ponder: Hope in God. Be patient and wait for him.

Pray: Come Lord; teach me to wait with confident expectation. Give me hope in your promises.

November 30

But the Lord is faithful; he will strengthen
you and guard you from the evil one. We are
confident of you in the Lord that what we instruct
you, you [both] are doing and will continue
to do. May the Lord direct your hearts to the
love of God and to the endurance of Christ.
                          – 2 Thessalonians 3:3-5

Through faith God releases his promises. When we doubt his word or his faithfulness, we do not know him as we should. Our prayer lives may be affected by our limited trust. If so, we have denied ourselves the most powerful avenue that God has made available to us to be in his presence.

The Lord waits for us. Stop and focus on him. Seek his presence to resolve our lack of faith. When we ask God with pure hearts to rid us of doubt, he acts on this. Be patient and wait for him. Say yes as he leads us to see his merciful acts and glorious blessings.

Sometimes we are so preoccupied with our own needs that we miss God working in our lives. We fail to see signs and do not pick up on the opportunities he provides. Do not worry. God is forgiving and merciful. He provides other opportunities. Be alert and respond to his promptings. Pray and be obedient to the quiet voices within our souls. His will for us is perfect and leads us all the way to eternity.

Psalm 89:14-19; Luke 1:67-79
Point to Ponder: Be faithful to God as he is to you.

Pray: Strengthen my faithfulness. Remove my unbelief. I trust you to be there for me, God.

December 1

*Put on then, as God's chosen ones, holy and
beloved, heartfelt compassion, kindness,
humility, gentleness, and patience, bearing
with one another and forgiving one another,
if one has a grievance against another; as the
Lord has forgiven you, so must you also do.*
— Colossians 3:12-13

Seek to live a righteous life filled with gifts from God. He gives us
gifts to share, but sometimes we stumble and turn away from him.
In our busyness we fail to keep God central in our thoughts. We
forget to be still and listen for his voice. We lose focus. Far from
the normal acts of kindness, gentleness, patience, and compassion,
we wrong or hurt others.

God calls us back when we inevitably fall short of his standard.
Our inner voices guide us to right the errors and shortcomings.
God understands how difficult it is to ask for forgiveness and
mercy when our emotions get in the way and we feel justified
giving back the hurt. First, admit to ourselves and to God that our
actions are not Christ-like. God then sends the courage to right the
wrongs and hurt we have caused.

He forgives sin immediately through repentance. He makes
us work hard to rebuild our character. What God does next in our
lives depends on how much effort we put into building a character
that is pleasing to him. Demonstrate kind acts and use uplifting
comments to others. Apologize, and be humble and compassionate.
God develops our character as we open our hearts to his love.

Romans 14:1-8; Psalm 94:16-19
Point to Ponder: Pray for God's forgiveness and mercy.

Pray: Lord, help me forgive others as you have forgiven me. Let me
hold no grudge.

December 2

Blessed is he who comes in the name of the Lord. We bless you from the Lord's house. The Lord is God and has given us light ... You are my God, I give you thanks; my God, I offer you praise. Give thanks to the Lord, who is good, whose love endures forever.
— Psalm 118:26-29

God is the light of the world. We seek him and avoid the darkness of sin. Even when we succumb to sin, God does not abandon us. He wants us to repent and seek forgiveness so his light shines upon us again. No matter how horrific our sins, we live in the hope of God.

When someone lives in his light, his spirit shines as a brilliant testimony to God's love. We enjoy being around people who love the Lord. They are optimistic and caring. They believe, remember, and practice God's teachings.

How does someone grow closer to God, receive his love, and live in the light of his presence when there are many detours, disasters, and unexpected challenges in life? Build a relationship with God. He works through us and prepares the way. He desires that we read scripture and practice his ways. Look for the good in others and be an encourager. Turn to the Holy Spirit for guidance and protection. Pray without ceasing. Seek God in every circumstance.

He is sympathetic to our endeavors to live in a righteous manner. Rejoice and give thanks. Blessed are those who come as children of God.

1 John 2:1-6; Micah 7:8-9
Point to Ponder: Give thanks to God. His love is everlasting.

Pray: Lord, let me shine as a brilliant testimony of your love. I want to be a sign of your presence.

December 3

Then Jesus approached and said to them, "All
power in heaven and on earth has been given to
me. Go, therefore, and make disciples of all nations,
baptizing them in the name of the Father, and of the
Son, and of the holy Spirit, teaching them to observe
all that I have commanded you. And behold, I
am with you always, until the end of the age."
— Matthew 28:18-20

Christ is with us every minute. He lives within our souls. He knows everything about us – our hopes, actions, doubts, and most importantly our hearts.

In his death and resurrection, Jesus triumphed over sin. He suffered so that our sins would be forgiven. He followed his Father's will and died a painful death. The prophet Isaiah tells us the Lord's thoughts are not like our thoughts, nor are his ways like our ways (Is. 55:8). He thinks and acts on a level different than man. We are his children now and forever. Even when times are less than perfect, he never leaves us.

Never underestimate how much God uses us to bring others to him. Persevere and view each encounter with God as an opportunity to demonstrate love and service. He sends all the resources we need. We do not fully understand how his grace works, but the faithful know the peace that comes when in his presence and doing his will.

Turn to God in every circumstance. The more he lives in us, the more he works through us. Live in peace knowing God is in control. Rejoice in the Lord!

Matthew 5:6-7; Psalm 121:2-8
Point to Ponder: Walk in holiness hand in hand with God.

Pray: Lord, bless me with your grace. Give me courage to tell others about you.

December 4

A clean heart create for me, God;
renew in me a steadfast spirit.

— Psalm 51:12

Our hearts must be pure and receptive to God's will. If not, we ignore or respond to his word in ways not pleasing to him. Some days are better than others. If our hearts were receptive to a word from God yesterday, this does not guarantee a receptive soul today. Prepare our hearts for God daily. Begin each day anew with prayer and thoughts of thankfulness.

Whether God speaks to us through scripture, at worship services, or through prayer, the way we respond to him rests on how we have cultivated our hearts. If we are worried about worldly matters, and they rise to the forefront, we have trouble hearing God's voice in all the confusion and static. Take a step away and find a quiet place to pray. Open the Bible and read several verses. Meditate on God's word until the truths enter deep into our hearts. Focus on today and give worries to God. Make requests known to him.

Protect our lifestyle but always have Christ as the central focus. When situations evolve and there seems to be no simple solutions, heed God's commandments. This requires discipline and self-control. Trust God. He sends his grace to those who seek him with a pure heart.

Every chance we have to model and respond is an opportunity to affirm we are followers of Christ. He transforms us to be Christ-like in our behaviors. God is pleased when we have steadfast love in our hearts for him. We shine with the love and grace of the Lord.

2 Corinthians 4:16-18; Ephesians 4:17-24
Point to Ponder: Enjoy the life God has given you.

Pray: Lord, cleanse my heart. Work through me for your glory.

December 5

*Behold, the hour is coming and has arrived
when each of you will be scattered to his own
home and you will leave me alone. But I am
not alone, because the Father is with me. I
have told you this so that you might have peace
in me. In the world you will have trouble, but
take courage, I have conquered the world.*

— John 16:32-33

When we face trials and struggles, we should not turn away from God. During these times, we need his wisdom, comfort, and refuge the most. Pray immediately and reach out to him. He whispers to our hearts. God does not set anything before us we cannot conquer with his guidance and protection.

Timing our obedience to God matters. If he places a situation in our path, but we linger and do not respond, the opportunity to serve him may pass. We may be busy and ignore the promptings, or we pretend his signs are not there. For example, if a neighbor calls upon us to help with an elderly adult, and we cannot find the time, we have missed an opportunity to serve. The peace we could have received from this measure eludes us.

Be persistent and do the right thing. Say yes to God. Let service to others become a part of our moral being. Immerse ourselves in God's love. Allow him to work through us. By serving the Lord and following his will, he sends peace and grace. Praise and worship God for his steadfast love.

2 Thessalonians 3:16; Psalm 73:23-24
Point to Ponder: Let your peace shine upon me.

Pray: Lord, thank you for always being with me. You fill me with opportunities and courage to serve others.

December 6

Shout joyfully to God, all you on earth; sing of
his glorious name; give him glorious praise.
Say to God: "How awesome your deeds!
Before your great strength your enemies
cringe. All on earth fall in worship before
you; they sing of you, sing of your name!"

— Psalm 66:2-4

Christians want to glorify God. We have choices as to how we approach each day. We can be filled with the light of Christ and impart joy to others through our acts of kindness and generosity, or we can be pessimistic, downcast, and have little hope. Positive thinkers allow God to work through them and grow their spiritual wealth. Negative people watch others from the sidelines and cry, "Poor me!"

God gives those who walk close to him big assignments. He works through strong believers to get things done. Followers have a relationship with him built on love and optimism. Spiritually rich people have an inner conviction that God works all things together for good. He does not allow any of his followers to fail from his eternal perspective. If God leads the way, his plans are always right.

Trust him to build unique character. This takes a while, and many get impatient for earthly results but remain faithful. God's timing is always perfect. Look for signs. God takes ordinary experiences and makes them extraordinary. He transforms trials into blessings. God is so much more capable of handling our tomorrows than we are. Persevere in faith.

1 John 4:12; Philippians 2:12-15
Point to Ponder: Praise God!

Pray: Lord, build my character so my words and actions please you.

December 7

*Hear my voice, Lord, when I call; have mercy on
me and answer me. "Come," says my heart, "seek
God's face"; your face, Lord, do I seek! Do not
hide your face from me; do not repel your servant
in anger. You are my help; do not cast off, do not
forsake me, God my savior! Even if my father and
mother forsake me, the Lord will take me in.*
– Psalm 27:7-10

We pray and hope to hear God's voice and be in his presence while worshiping, reading scripture, walking in the beauty of nature, or at any other time when God sends us a message. Our relationship with God is one of closeness. We feel his presence and know his voice.

Sometimes we may experience a dry spell, where we have difficulty connecting to God. Pause and reflect. Have we stopped attending church or lessened our praying? Have we focused on material riches? Do we depend on friends and family for our happiness? If we find ourselves in any of these circumstances, turn back to God for renewal. Find a quiet place and call out to him to provide what we need. Be still and listen.

God hears every prayer no matter the length or the place where we pray. He is always with us and waits for us to return to him (Prv. 4:20-22). As we build our relationship with Christ, feel faith grow. By demonstrating righteous behaviors through our actions and words, we feel his grace working through us. Our overall attitude reflects contentment and love. Hold onto Christ and be grateful for his precious blessings.

Colossians 1:9-10; Romans 10:17
Point to Ponder: Be faithful to God. Pray often.

Pray: Lord, open my ears and heart to know your presence. Teach me to hear you more clearly.

December 8

It is the LORD who marches before you; he
will be with you and never fail you or forsake
you. So do not fear or be dismayed.

— Deuteronomy 31:8

When we doubt and find ourselves living with fear and anxiety, seek God. He wants to heal and restore us, and take our fears away. God knows our hearts. Everything is exposed to him. When we seek God and pray, he answers us, all the time.

God waits for us to call on him to show us the way. Believing this with profound faith is the difference between coping and giving up. Never rely on our own strength. Instead, have faith because God never fails us. Depend on him and be patient. Never give up on God.

Some people talk about their spiritual knowledge and try to convince us of their opinions about Christ. If a person speaks forcefully about scripture but continually sins, his words are discounted by his actions. This wishy-washy behavior is confusing.

Those who have strong faith and demonstrate steadfastness to God, live in a state of grace. He sends strength through his powerful presence within us. Others see the difference he makes in our lives. This transformation is often so significant others are drawn to us. Be change agents and bring others to know God. He takes nonbelievers and teaches and guides them. His love has the ability to penetrate the soul of a completely unresponsive person.

Be faithful to God. Bask in his love. Give thanks for he never forsakes us.

Isaiah 61:10-11; 1 Peter 2:9-10
Point to Ponder: God marches with you. Call on him daily.

Pray: Teach me to turn to you in all circumstances. Strengthen my faithfulness, Lord.

December 9

*He made from one the whole human race to dwell
on the entire surface of the earth, and he fixed
the ordered seasons and the boundaries of their
regions, so that people might seek God, even
perhaps grope for him and find him, though indeed
he is not far from any one of us. For 'In him we live
and move and have our being,' as even some of your
poets have said, 'For we too are his offspring.'*
— Acts 17:26-28

We serve a merciful and loving God. He calls us his children. God lives within each of us and knows everything about us. Reach out to him daily and be in his presence. Read scripture and meditate on his word. Demonstrate the teachings of God as we live our days on earth. Give thanks for his healing and love. Even when tempted by sin, God does not abandon us. He waits for us to repent and turn back to him.

We do not understand God's divine mercy, which is beyond human reasoning. If he was not so merciful, we would feel the full wrath of his judgment. Rejoice in his mercy and love.

Anticipate God's magnificent power. Be alert to him working through us. The more we are aware of him, the more alive we feel. Imitate Christ by being merciful, gracious, loving, slow to anger, rich in kindness, generous, and patient. Demonstrate to others his saving grace. Be thankful we live and move and have our being in him. Give God thanks and praise!

Revelations 5:11-12; 2 Corinthians 13:5-9
Point to Ponder: Believe in God. Seek him throughout the day.

Pray: Lord, hear me calling you. Watch over me and guide me in your ways. You are my Savior.

December 10

For I am already being poured out like a libation,
and the time of my departure is at hand. I have
competed well; I have finished the race; I have kept
the faith. From now on the crown of righteousness
awaits me, which the Lord, the just judge, will
award me on that day, and not only to me, but
to all who have longed for his appearance.

— 2 Timothy 4:6-8

We have no power over death. When death draws near, hopefully we look back and know we have lived a life pleasing to God. We can say we ran a good race.

Life is a series of peaks and valleys, highs and lows. Many experience indescribable joy and love. At other times, pain is so sharp it punctures the heart. Life is not an easy journey. Days are filled with blessings and struggles. In whatever state we find ourselves, God is with us. He guides us so we press onward.

Scripture tells us, "In all circumstances, hold faith as a shield, to quench all the flaming arrows of the evil one" (Eph. 6:16). Satan may have stolen moments of our lives. We all have succumbed and been sidetracked from running the race. It is never too late to repent and ask God for forgiveness. He rejoices over all who return to him.

Do not fear death, for death is not the end. God has gone before us to prepare a place for us in heaven (Jn. 14:2-3). He welcomes us with outstretched arms to eternal life with him and our loved ones who have gone before us. He never abandons us and runs the race with us so we live with him for eternity.

Proverbs 16:9; 2 Corinthians 5:17-21
Point to Ponder: Have no fear, God is with us.

Pray: Help me walk in faith trusting your mercy, Lord.

December 11

*But I say to you, love your enemies, and pray
for those who persecute you, that you may be
children of your heavenly Father, for he makes
his sun rise on the bad and the good, and causes
rain to fall on the just and the unjust ... So be
perfect, just as your heavenly Father is perfect.*

– Matthew 5:44-48

God has asked us to love our enemies. We may feel uncomfortable and difficulties may evolve when we try to love those who have hurt us, are negative and have a defeatist attitude, practice strange customs, or look different. But God wants us to assume the best about others.

How do we assume the best about someone when his presence is irritating, provoking, and unwelcomed? Ask the Holy Spirit to help us find Christ in the person. If someone inadvertently says something offensive, consider the source as having a lack of knowledge and weak character. Pray for the person. If someone tries to harm us, fight the impulse to strike back with equal vengeance. Instead, forgive him. Strive for the same unconditional love toward others like God has for us.

When we find ourselves in uncomfortable situations, move away, hold our tongues, and pray for God's intervention. Seek his guidance. Avoid striking back with hurtful words and actions. God sends us grace so that we follow his example. Demonstrate God's incredible love to all people.

Proverbs 17:14; Psalm 51:7-10
Point to Ponder: Listen more. Look for Jesus in every person.

Pray: Lord, teach me to stay focused on my call in life.

December 12

How great is your goodness LORD, stored up
for those who fear you. You display it for those
who trust you, in the sight of all the people.
You hide them in the shelter of your presence,
safe from scheming enemies. You keep them in
your abode, safe from plotting tongues. Blessed
be the LORD, who has shown me wondrous
love, and been for me a city most secure.
                                        – Psalm 31:20-22

God's works are wondrous and good. Christ, through the Holy Spirit, guides and teaches us to pray, read the Bible, and worship our Savior. This is part of Christ's inheritance we share.

God knows all our thoughts and prayers. He pours out his grace with perfect love. He takes the little we give of ourselves and multiplies it immensely. God wants us to give without sadness or compulsion for he loves a cheerful giver. He makes every grace abundant so we are assured of having all we need for every good work (2 Cor. 9:6-9).

As we demonstrate our love for God through our works, he continues to reward us with new opportunities. He has plans for our lives, and fills us with joy and peace. Being close to God through prayer strengthens our faith. We grow in wisdom and knowledge.

Strive to work diligently for God. Serve others joyfully. We are called to help one another by being the hands of God and reaching out to those hurting. Nothing robs us of our inheritance of unimaginable riches and well-being. God promises salvation to those who live in his love and trust him.

Ephesians 1:13-14; Philippians 2:12-13
Point to Ponder: Give thanks to God for great blessings.

Pray: Lord, send me love and peace. I want to share these blessings.

December 13

Above all, be firm and steadfast, taking care to
observe the entire law which my servant Moses
enjoined on you. Do not swerve from it either
to the right or to the left, that you may succeed
wherever you go. Keep this book of the law on
your lips. Recite it by day and by night, that you
may observe carefully all that is written in it;
then you will successfully attain your goal.

— Joshua 1:7-8

God has given us the Ten Commandments through Moses. Be obedient to God's laws. He sends us his grace and strength to meet any challenge. Rely on him for guidance. Be flexible and open to make adjustments in our lives to respond positively to God. We have no power of our own. He is our strength.

When we follow God's commandments, read the Bible, pray, and reflect, we increase our spiritual wealth. Our calling as believers in Christ is to bring glory to his name. The way we act and honor God is a direct reflection of our relationship with him. Always have a pure heart and be receptive to his will. Christ works through us and with us every day to start fresh.

Following God's word is a pathway to salvation. Do not fear tackling things out of our comfort zone. God never gives us too much to handle. He builds our character as we walk with him. As we persevere, we develop a greater love for him and his ways. Give thanks to God.

Matthew 6:9-13; Jude 17-25
Point to Ponder: Be firm and steadfast. Follow God.

Pray: God, guide and protect me as I follow your laws. Help me persevere and have hope.

December 14

No one who lights a lamp hides it away or places
it under a bushel basket, but on a lampstand so
that those who enter might see the light. The lamp
of the body is your eye. When your eye is sound,
then your whole body is filled with light, but
when it is bad, then your body is in darkness.

— Luke 11:33-34

Happy people smile, and their eyes sparkle. Our faces, and particularly our eyes, tell much about our temperament and physical state. Christians believe Christ resides within us (Col. 1:27). His light is reflected through our eyes. Look closely at others who follow Christ; watch how the light from within radiates through. Some people actually brighten a room by being in it. They dispel darkness from the lives of many. People gravitate to happy people. The light is not hidden from their eyes.

We demonstrate to others the love we have for God. Never discount what we say and do as meaningless. Others watch and wonder. We do not have all the answers, but if our relationship with God is based on trust and love, he sends us what we need to bring others to him. Sometimes the right words or a small act of kindness make a huge difference. We do not have to carry the burdens of others, but we can lead them to the Lord.

Our happiness is from God. People are quick to judge us on worldly things and material riches. They do not connect our love for God and how he chooses us to express himself through us. Give him glory and praise. Let his light shine through.

Matthew 6:22-23; Proverbs 21:4
Point to Ponder: Be happy. Let God's light shine.

Pray: Let your light shine through me. All glory and honor is yours, Lord.

December 15

But I shall sing of your strength, extol your love
at dawn, For you are my fortress, my refuge in
time of trouble. My strength, your praise I will
sing; you, God, are my fortress, my loving God.
— Psalm 59:17-18

Praise God, who is our strength and refuge. He provides for us every day. He sends strength and grace so we accomplish great things in his name.

He has created us to be uniquely his. Often we get so busy running from one activity to the next and constantly giving of our time and talents, that we feel worn out and at our wits end. We live in a workaholic society; we forget to focus on God. At these times, God watches over us and helps us find rest. He calls us back. Remember God saying, "Come to me, all you who labor and are burdened, and I will give you rest" (Mt. 11:28). He places things in our lives that require us to pause and evaluate all our activities. He reminds us of our dependence on him, and the importance of rest and letting go of our frantic work schedule.

When we sit in his presence and pray, we hear his voice more clearly. Be still and listen. God shows us the resources he has provided to help us follow his plan. Our relationship is strengthened. We find a peacefulness that has been missing in the chaos of trying to do too much. Allow God to guide us. Today, devote time to thanking and praising him. Press on for his glory. Rejoice in God.

Isaiah 41:13; Deuteronomy 7:1-11
Point to Ponder: God is my safety net.

Pray: God, you are my strength and my fortress. Thank you for loving me.

December 16

*"And I tell you, ask and you will receive; seek
and you will find; knock and the door will
be opened to you. For everyone who asks,
receives; and the one who seeks, finds; and the
one who knocks, the door will be opened."*

– Luke 11:9-10

As we go about our day, lift prayers up to God. No matter where we are or the time of day, he is with us. The Lord continually works in our lives.

Reading scripture brings knowledge and understanding of his ways. He speaks to us through scripture. The words often touch on something we have experienced. For example, if we have a job interview or a meeting scheduled with our boss and want to make a good impression, we might pray, "our soul waits for the LORD, who is our help and our shield" (Ps. 33:20). If we know someone with an addiction or we ourselves are fighting temptations, we may whisper, "Show me the path I should walk, for to you I entrust my life. Rescue me, LORD, from my foes, for in you I hope" (Ps. 143:8-9). We learn what God expects from us.

By praying throughout the day, we reframe our thoughts. Prayer changes us. Live in the presence of God. He answers our prayers when we seek him. He knows our needs before we ask.

John 15:7; Jeremiah 33:3
Point to Ponder: God answers every prayer.

Pray: Lord, I seek your presence and guiding hands. Hear my prayers.

December 17

Endure your trials as "discipline"; God treats you as
sons. For what "son" is there whom his father does not
discipline? If you are without discipline, in which all
have shared, you are not sons but bastards. Besides this,
we have had our earthly fathers to discipline us, and
we respected them. Should we not [then] submit all the
more to the Father of spirits and live? They disciplined
us for a short time as seemed right to them, but he
does so for our benefit, in order that we may share
his holiness. At the time, all discipline seems a cause
not for joy but for pain, yet later it brings the peaceful
fruit of righteousness to those who are trained by it.
– Hebrews 12:7-11

God disciplines us to bring necessary change to our lives. When
we focus on material wealth and find our primary happiness
coming from man-made riches, God teaches us humility by
removing something we cherish that has no spiritual value. Not
every hardship we face is the chastisement of God, but scripture
tells us he disciplines those whom he loves (Rev. 3:19). He does this
so we are keenly aware of our dependence on him.

As a just Father, God corrects and disciplines us when we stray.
He always looks for the good in people and uses that goodness to
draw them closer to him. If we never experienced correction, we
may feel we do not need God in our daily lives. This is far from the
truth. God never stops loving us. He sets us on a righteous path.

Psalm 50:16-23; Proverbs 30:5-6
Point to Ponder: God disciplines his children because he loves them.

Pray: Lord, thank you for loving me enough to gently discipline
me. Teach me.

December 18

Be eager to present yourself as acceptable
to God, a workman who causes no disgrace,
imparting the word of truth without deviation.

— 2 Timothy 2:15

God guides us as we plan our day. He knows our needs and what we face, today, tomorrow, a week from now, and all the way to eternity. Be eager to show others his goodness and mercy as he works through us. Strive to present ourselves every day as honorable followers of Christ.

Concentrate on staying close to God. Remain in constant communication with him. Whisper his name in reverence. His plan for us is filled with good not evil. Our future is blessed with hope (Jer. 29:11).

With God as the focal point of our lives, everything changes. Our lives become richer and fuller as we please him through our simple acts of kindness, our gentle ways, and our persuasive words. He sends strength and courage to us to attempt things we have never done in the past. We are less fearful. Our optimistic attitudes allow us to grow in knowledge and understanding.

Start now. Turn to God. Believe he blesses us with remarkable gifts and talents. He sees something beautiful and valuable in us. Christ sees a person made in his image. Ask God to help us grow closer by praying, reading the Bible, and applying his truths every day. Allow him to fill us with his presence. He teaches us each day to live the lives he created for us. Remain forever faithful to God. Proclaim his greatness.

Psalm 32:8, 10; Psalm 5:8-9
Point to Ponder: Honor God every day. Praise him.

Pray: God, teach me your ways. Guide me with your loving gentleness. My spirit rejoices in you.

December 19

The Lord does not delay his promise, as some regard "delay," but he is patient with you, not wishing that any should perish but that all should come to repentance.

— 2 Peter 3:9

The Lord has a wonderful way of restoring us and filling us with his love. He does not humiliate us before others. God takes us aside and gently disciplines us. He works through us so we learn to lean on him and follow his will.

When we try to handle life without the Lord's guidance, we fail miserably. We may have good intentions and make promises to ourselves, but this is not enough. God expects us to be obedient, courageous, and faithful. He asks for our love. Do not forsake God. He sends saving grace and guidance to those who love him.

God is patient. He knows our hearts and loyalty, our thoughts and desires, and our weaknesses. Remember Judas and his betrayal as the disciples ate with Jesus in the upper room the night before his crucifixion (Mk. 14:17-21). The prophets predicted the betrayal of Jesus. Judas would betray him even though he had been by his side for three years. Likewise, his beloved disciple Peter denied he knew Jesus three times before the cock crowed twice (Mk. 14:27-31) just as Jesus had said.

Only God knows the full extent of the temptations we face. Depend on him when we make choices. Focus on things that provide unique opportunities to serve him. He brings good out of all our choices. His will for us is perfect!

Lamentations 3:25-26; Psalm 62:2-3
Point to Ponder: God is patient. Follow his ways.

Pray: Lord, lead me, guide me, and fill my heart with love.

December 20

Moreover, God is able to make every grace
abundant for you, so that in all things,
always having all you need, you may have
abundance for every good work.

— 2 Corinthians 9:8

Why do we visit the homeless or spend time helping the less
fortunate? We help the marginal because God is pleased when we
serve others. He works through us. The labor is difficult. People do
not understand why we continue to give of ourselves in this way. It
is because the Lord provides grace to us, his servants, and watches
over the way of the just (Ps.1:6). Our hearts are filled with his love.
We have peace in our souls from God.

God spills his strength into our souls when we tire and feel
like giving up. Courage and grace are renewed. Even when others
do not understand why we work so hard to help the forgotten, we
know God blesses us according to how we respond to his invitation
to serve. There may be little thanks for what we do, but God sees
everything. He promises us a heavenly reward for our service.

Trust God to always be faithful to his word. We never face a
shortfall of his grace when we complete tasks he has set before
us. Be a cheerful worker and serve the Lord with a pure heart and
positive mindset. Experience the fullness of God in every aspect of
life. Give generously to reap all God gives to those who love and
serve him.

Psalm 146:2-10; Romans 12:1-2
Point to Ponder: Serve others with a glad heart.

Pray: God, make me more generous and able to freely give.

December 21

"Those who love me I also love, and those who
seek me find me. With me are riches and honor,
enduring wealth and prosperity. My fruit is better
than gold, yes, than pure gold, and my revenue
than choice silver. On the way of duty I walk,
along the paths of justice, granting wealth to
those who love me, and filling their treasuries."

— Proverbs 8:17-21

Christians believe Christ is with us always and everywhere.
When we dwell in his presence, or when he sends his angels to
our assistance, we feel an unbreakable bond. His blessings include
riches, honor, and prosperity. He is our salvation.

Reach out to others who may be depressed, floundering,
homeless, jobless, or in poor health. Be like Jesus, who constantly
reached out to mingle and help Jew and Gentile, rich and poor,
important religious leaders and people of low repute. Share the Holy
Spirit with them, offering them a taste of God's healing power.

Tell friends and family when we have a personal, life-changing
walk with Christ. Seek courage from him to tell others how God
changed our lives. Demonstrate our wholeness and joy as we give
testimony of our relationship with him. He does not expect us to
convince others of his reality, but simply to bear witness to what he
has done and how our lives have been transformed.

Today let God guide us and warm our hearts. Remain close to
him. If we bring people to Christ, he will do the rest to open their
hearts and minds to his teachings.

1 John 1:5-9; Psalm 115:15-18
Point to Ponder: God is worthy of all praise and honor!

Pray: Lord, pour your love out to me. Help me share this love with
others today.

December 22

*The LORD is a stronghold to him who walks
honestly, but to evildoers, their downfall.*
— Proverbs 10:29

When we build a relationship with God, we also construct lives different than the world produces. God is the focal point. Our hearts soften. We do not seek the limelight but instead feel more comfortable with a humble nature. Worshiping God transforms us into the person he wants us to be.

No matter the environment we live in, God finds us and walks with us. As we come to know him, our relationship strengthens. We follow his teachings, strive for honesty in all transactions, and acquire the ability to make the right choices pleasing to God. We grow spiritually and demonstrate more Christ-like character.

Even though we may be tempted by Satan, we stay close to God. We pray, read scripture, and demonstrate to others what God expects. The key is not to simply read words from the Bible and understand scripture based on our experiences, but to understand our experiences in light of the Bible. God sees all we do, hears what we say to others, and knows our hearts. Our persistence in following his will matters. God continues to be our stronghold and sends his grace.

Our lives should convince those around us that the right choice is always for God. When we turn to him and seek love, he teaches us and helps us understand the riches of eternal life. We are his children and heirs. He has reserved a place for us in heaven. Rejoice in the glory of God.

Psalm 80:4; Isaiah 6:3
Point to Ponder: Build a strong relationship with God.

Pray: Lord, I love you now and forever. Be my strength.

December 23

*God is present as my helper; the LORD sustains
my life. Turn back the evil upon my foes; in your
faithfulness, destroy them. Then I will offer you
generous sacrifice and praise your gracious
name, LORD, Because it has rescued me from every
trouble, and my eyes look down on my foes.*
— Psalm 54:6-9

Trust God to be with us in every circumstance. Live in his presence
and experience his love and protection. When we busy ourselves
with the chaos of life, we sometimes forget to have God as our
focal point. We may not pray as often as we should and do not take
time to read the Bible. God knows each of us, our strengths and our
weaknesses. He sees our busyness and waits for our return. God
sends his grace and transforms us. These changes may not happen
instantly but they come. He sustains our lives with spiritual riches.
Call out to him for guidance.

Build a solid relationship with the Lord and communicate
with him every day. The relationship we have with God should be
personal, vibrant, and always growing. He embraces each of us,
imperfect though we are.

Ask God to cleanse our hearts and refresh our souls. Trust
him and be faithful to his word. When we remain steadfast in our
worship and fellowship with Christ, he produces much good in our
lives. He provides all we need to prosper. Rejoice in his love.

Proverbs 11:20; Exodus 20:2-6
Point to Ponder: Proclaim the greatness of God.

Pray: Lord, make me a joyful follower. Come into my life and
create a heart filled with love.

December 24

What will separate us from the love of Christ?
Will anguish, or distress, or persecution,
or famine, or nakedness, or peril, or the
sword? ... No, in all these things we conquer
overwhelmingly through him who loved us.

— Romans 8:35-37

There is nothing in this world that separates us from the love of Christ. The crucifixion of Jesus should settle any questions we may ponder about God's love. This ultimate sacrifice allows us to approach difficult situations with confidence and face fear head-on knowing that God stands ready to help. He never abandons us.

God never promised us a life without adversity, persecution, grief, or danger. He promised we would never be separated from his love. When a loved one dies, naturally we feel grief and pain. When we experience troubles, tribulations, and distress, God's love brings us comfort. Cling to him for support.

At times we may feel as if we are sitting on top of a mountain and nothing can harm us. No evil or wrong-doing exists and all is right. We feel God's presence and want to stay close to him. These times are a foretaste of heaven. But if God allowed us to stay on the mountaintop forever, we would never experience trials or achieve any victories. He refreshes our souls so when we leave the mountaintop, we are ready to face any challenge.

Ask God to send us comfort, strength, and his never-ending love. With these come hope and peace.

Deuteronomy 31:8; John 14:1-4
Point to Ponder: Thank you for loving me, God.

Pray: Lord, I trust you. Never permit me from being separated from your love.

December 25

Mortals are a mere breath, the powerful but an
illusion; on a balance they rise; together they
are lighter than air. Do not trust in extortion;
in plunder put no empty hope. Though wealth
increases, do not set your heart upon it. One thing
*God has said; two things * I have heard: Power*
belongs to God; so too, Lord, does kindness, And
you render to each of us according to our deeds.
— Psalm 62:10-13

Draw close to Jesus by whispering his name. Pray often. Anchor our lives in his teachings. The Lord has the power to make all things work for good for those who love him.

Even though life is full of challenges and stressful at times, do not put hope and faith in earthly riches. Money cannot buy happiness or a place in heaven. True pleasure comes from the heart and from God. Remember to live in the moment. Give thanks to God each morning for another day to serve him. Ask God to direct our steps.

Scripture tells us to be anxious for nothing (Phil. 4:6). When we meditate on this passage, we know we should turn our anxieties and worries over to God. This is difficult. Keeping our focus on his presence is a protective shield against worry and depression. God guides, protects, and leads us. There is nothing too difficult for him. His light shines unhindered through our lives. Darkness is dispelled. Trust God to live out his divine life through us. Build his kingdom and rejoice in his love.

Psalm 49:17-21; Proverbs 16:7
Point to Ponder: Power belongs to God. Follow him.

Pray: Lord, direct my steps so I follow your divine plan.

December 26

*I waited, waited for the Lᴏʀᴅ; who bent down
and heard my cry, Drew me out of the pit of
destruction, out of the mud of the swamp. Set my
feet upon rock, steadied my steps, And put a new
song in my mouth, a hymn to our God. Many shall
look on in awe and they shall trust in the Lᴏʀᴅ.*
— Psalm 40:2-4

Everything in life hinges on the revelation of the glory of God.
He keeps every promise he makes. We know through scripture all
things work for good for those who love God (Rom. 8:28). This
truth should motivate us to meditate on God's word and find ways
to implement his promises in our lives.

These revelations are gifts to us. Do not be discouraged or
impatient if spiritual insights seem few in number. God knows
the exact time when we are ready to experience the fullness of his
promises. Walk closely with him. Praise and worship God.

When we open our hearts to the Lord and say yes to him, our
lives change. Peace enters our spirits, and the light shines through.
Ask God to direct our steps. Never be satisfied with our own
dreams because they are finite, at best. Count on the Lord to send
his grace, strength, and revelations at the perfect time. Hold tight
to the hand of God as he walks with us step-by-step, all the way to
heaven.

Psalm 43:1-5; Proverbs 21:2-3
Point to Ponder: Wait for God. Pause, pray, and listen.

Pray: Lord, reveal your goodness and mercy to me. Change me to
be more Christ-like.

361

December 27

Jesus said to him, "I am the way and the
truth and the life. No one comes to the Father
except through me. If you know me, then
you will also know my Father. From now
on you do know him and have seen him.

      – John 14:6-7

When Jesus traveled from place to place, the disciples never questioned where they would go next. They followed and stayed close to Jesus. After his crucifixion, the disciples became disoriented and hid from the authorities in fear. Jesus returned and assured them he was alive. He reminded them his way was the only way to eternal life, and they should not be afraid.

Many Christians have developed a strong relationship with Christ and have placed their trust in him. They pray, read the Bible, worship, and praise God. He is the central focus of their lives. Whatever they face, God is by their side to guide them every step along the way. He has placed them with people and in places exactly where he wants them to be.

We still need reassurance that God leads us each day. There is a deep yearning in our hearts for a protector. Be alert. Talk to God about fears and concerns. Seek to understand when he is giving us a new revelation. He provides opportunities for us to serve others. Trust him to show us the way to eternal life with the Father. Walk with him each step as he protects and guides us on our journey to heaven.

Isaiah 26:7-9; John 8:23-32
Point to Ponder: God, thank you for setting me free to love and serve you.

Pray: Lord, lead me, show me, and direct me. There is nothing that can separate me from your love.

December 28

> *All who call upon me I will answer; I will be*
> *with them in distress; I will deliver them and*
> *give them honor. With length of days I will*
> *satisfy them and show them my saving power.*
>   — Psalm 91:15-16

Human emotions are powerful. They sometimes overpower reason, and we find ourselves being impulsive and irrational. We forget about God. We fail to ask ourselves what he would want us to do. God remains with us in good times as well as in times of distress.

Worry is a strong emotion. We know God guides and protects us but sometimes we are still paralyzed with worry. When worry consumes our minds, make a choice to either tremble in fear and hide or trust God.

To control worry, persevere and exercise faith and trust in God. Pray fervently. The Lord hears our cries. Open the Bible to the center and begin reading in Psalms about the power of God. Focus on his promises. Lift worries up to him. Concentrate on living in the moment and walking side-by-side with our Savior. He carries us when the burden is great.

Remember that God is our refuge and strength. His power is made perfect in our weaknesses. He never abandons us, and he has a reservoir of grace, compassion, and love waiting for us. Seek and ask for his guidance and help.

Psalm 91:10-12; Galatians 5:15-26
Point to Ponder: God is our saving grace.

Pray: Lord, take away my worries so I see your light and your presence. You are my Savior.

December 29

For in hope we were saved. Now hope that
sees for itself is not hope. For who hopes
for what one sees? But if we hope for what
we do not see, we wait with endurance.
– Romans 8:24-25

Wait in confident expectation of what God has promised. When he speaks through scripture, he stands by his word. We have hope because God is faithful. Trust him and know his plans for us will come to pass. He has plans for us to prosper and to have hope and a future (Jer. 29:11).

Be patient because God does not work in our time frame. Waiting is hard in this fast paced world where we experience instant gratification. While we wait, we come to know how to endure frustrations and hardships. We learn the true meaning of faithfulness and understand optimism. We live in hope of his promises and his plan.

Grow in wisdom and knowledge that things come to pass when God is ready. He does not get in a hurry. Following God is a matter of ongoing change and transformation filled with joy, fear, struggles, and successes.

Practice hoping for things we do not see. Approach each day with a pure heart. Follow God's teachings in the Bible. Allow him to work through us to do things in his service we have never done before. Be patient and then rejoice in his presence. He leads us to walk with him to eternal life.

Jeremiah 29:11; Romans 5:2-5
Point to Ponder: Have hope in things you cannot see; hope in the Lord.

Pray: Lord, fill me with hope. I give you my heart. Use me for great things.

December 30

Happy those whose way is blameless,
who walk by the teaching of the LORD.

— Psalm 119:1

We do not understand God's love for us. When we reject, ignore, and fail to give him thanks, he never turns away from us. God's love follows us to the depths of sinfulness until he reclaims us. We are never without his love. He never abandons us.

God wants us to have faith, hope, and love in our lives. He has told us the greatest of these is love (1 Cor. 13:13). But some of us do not know how to love. God in his grace has made provision for our human weaknesses. He teaches us by placing people in our lives: loving parents, an optimistic colleague, a stranger, and loyal friends and acquaintances to act as angels to demonstrate acts of love. As we watch others, we see God working through them. He is masterful in showing us situations filled with love. As he blesses us, we learn to share these gifts with others. God proclaims happiness and love to those who follow his teachings.

Believe God loves us. The Bible says, "We have come to know and to believe in the love God has for us. God is love, and whoever remains in love remains in God and God in him" (1 Jn. 4:16). Assurance of his love sets us free. God propels us forward, and spurs us to treat people with patience, kindness, and compassion. Walk in the love of Christ. Do everything to glorify him.

Luke 6:46-49; Isaiah 30:15, 20-22
Point to Ponder: God is perfect and blesses you with unconditional love.

Pray: Lord, may your love fill me to overflowing. Help me recognize love in many different forms. May love flow through me to everyone I meet today.

December 31

If we acknowledge our sins, he is faithful
and just and will forgive our sins and
cleanse us from every wrongdoing.

— 1 John 1:9

Build a relationship with God. Feel free to go to him in prayer at any time. Open our hearts to the Lord. Strive to be blameless. This does not mean we never sin. Being blameless means if we sin against someone, we confess our sin and ask for forgiveness. No one is perfect. If we break a commandment or try to conceal sins, we do not prosper. But when we repent and begin immediately to obey God, we obtain mercy (Prv. 28:13).

When we face a crisis or situation that causes us fear, anxiety, or hurt, we are quick to harden our hearts. We try to protect ourselves. Instead of remaining calm and kind, we sometimes display weariness and hatefulness. We fail to seek God's will or pray for guidance.

Pause and reflect. Try aligning with Christ. Think and pray before reacting. This does not come naturally; we tend to think about ourselves first. Ask God to open our eyes to understand what he intends to do through the situation. Think about God's hand at work.

Humbly ask for mercy. Pray for pure hearts so that God's blessings flow through us. No one should be outside the mercy of God. Cling to him. Trust that his ways, though mysterious, are perfect.

Hebrews 4:14-16; Lamentations 3:22-23
Point to Ponder: Accept God's ways. Follow the will of God.

Pray: Lord, forgive me when I sin. Have mercy on me.

About the Author

In 2007, Marsha Glynn experienced what every parent fears, the tragic death of her seventeen-year-old son. Her life was never the same. Living in darkness and grief and with limited hope, she wrote a memoir about the weeks surrounding his death. Writing provided a lifeline and a means to express her feelings of grief.

After writing, *Shattered Pieces of My Heart,* Marsha reached for the Bible, read scripture every day and prayed. Thoughts began to take hold and she saw glimpses of hope. Not wanting to forget the messages God placed on her heart, she began to write *Encountering God.*

Before the death of her son, Marsha worked as an elementary school principal. She earned a doctorate degree in Educational Leadership from Nova Southeastern University in FL and masters' degrees from The Citadel in SC. She is married to the love of her life, Ray, and has one other son, Rob, working as a musician in Austin, TX. They make their home in Texas.